# Oxford American Children's Encyclopedia

# 6 OXFORD American Children's Encyclopedia

**Porcupines ▶ Stock market**

**Oxford University Press**
**New York**
**1998**

Oxford University Press

*Oxford  New York*
*Athens  Auckland  Bangkok  Bogota  Bombay*
*Buenos Aires  Calcutta  Cape Town  Dar es Salaam*
*Delhi  Florence  Hong Kong  Istanbul  Karachi*
*Kuala Lumpur  Madras  Madrid  Melbourne*
*Mexico City  Nairobi  Paris  Singapore*
*Taipei  Tokyo  Toronto  Warsaw*
and associated companies in
*Berlin  Ibadan*

Copyright © 1998 by Oxford University Press, Inc.
Published by Oxford University Press, Inc.,
198 Madison Avenue, New York, New York 10016

*Oxford* is a registered trademark of Oxford University Press.

Library of Congress Cataloguing-in-Publication Data
The Oxford American children's encyclopedia
      p.   cm
      Summary: Presents alphabetically arranged articles in nine
      volumes covering a wide range of human knowledge.
      ISBN 0-19-512242-9
      1. Children's encyclopedias and dictionaries. [1. Encyclopedias
      and dictionaries.]
      AG5.084  1998
      031'.083—dc21                97-40343
                                    CIP

ISBN 0-19-51108-1 (complete set)
Volume 6: ISBN 0-19-512245-3 (not for sale separately)

**Editor:**
Ann T. Keene

**Designers:**
Cheryl Rodemeyer
Gecko Ltd.
Oxprint Ltd.
Jo Bowers

A complete list of contributors and consultants
is printed in Volume 9.

Printed in Hong Kong on acid-free paper.

# How to Use the
# Oxford American Children's Encyclopedia

Here are several ways to find information in this encyclopedia:

## 1. Using the headings and the Table of Contents

The encyclopedia has individual articles on most important topics, and they are arranged by title in alphabetical order. If you want to find an article on a topic, you can look at the inclusive title headings on the spine or cover of each volume to find the article you are looking for:

To locate the article, find the volume with a title heading that includes the first letter of the article title. When you have found the correct volume, look in the alphabetical Table of Contents, located at the beginning of the volume, until you find the article title you want.

For example, suppose you want to read about the **Declaration of Independence**. After looking over the title headings of all nine volumes, you will discover that the D's are in Volume 2: Canary Islands–Elections. Then look in the Table of Contents for that volume. You will find the **Declaration of Independence** listed for pages 138–139.

To find a biography of a famous person, choose **Volume 8: Biography** and look for that person's name—last name first—in the Table of Contents. Let's say you want to read about the second U.S. President, John Adams. In the Table of Contents, you will find that an article on **Adams, John** is on page 7.

## 2. Using the Index

What if you cannot find an article on a topic in the Table of Contents? Then the next thing to do is go to the Index, which is an alphabetical listing of every reference to every topic mentioned in the encyclopedia. The Index is located in **Volume 9: Index, Gazetteer and Timeline of World History**. First, read "How to Use the Index" on page 18 of Volume 9. Then look up your subject in the Index.

For example, let's say you want to know something about the Statue of Liberty. You discover that there is no separate article on it in the encyclopedia, so you turn to the Index and look under S. There you find the listing "Statue of Liberty," followed by a series of page numbers. On each of those pages you will find a reference to the Statue of Liberty.

The Index is useful in another way, too. In it you will be able to find additional page numbers for every other mention of a topic that is also covered in its own article. For example, when you look up **Declaration of Independence** and **Adams, John** in the Index, you will see not just the article page numbers listed but also other page numbers that indicate references in other parts of the encyclopedia to these topics. Page numbers that are listed in *italic* type indicate that an illustration of the topic is on that page.

## 3. Cross-references

Another useful feature of the encyclopedia is the listing of cross-references—references to other articles that are related to that particular topic. These cross-references are included in nearly every article under the heading

For example, on page 22 in Volume 1, at the end of the article on **African myths and legends**, four related articles are listed under **See also**: Africa, Folk tales, Myths and legends, and Voodoo. Many **See also** listings also have a subhead, **BIOGRAPHY**, which includes the names of people who are somehow connected to the article topic and are written about in **Volume 8: Biography**.

## 4. Measurements

Measurements in the encyclopedia are given in both *metric* and *Imperial* form. You probably use the Imperial form of measurement—feet, miles, pounds, quarts, etc.—most of the time because it is the common system of measurement in the United States. The metric system of measurement—meters, kilometers, kilograms, liters, etc.—may be less familiar to you, but it is commonly used throughout much of the world.

In this encyclopedia, we list the metric measurement first, followed by the Imperial equivalent. Common abbreviations for the words of each measurement have been used, as in the following sentence:

The average weight of a newborn baby is 3 kg (6.6 lbs).

For a list of measurement abbreviations, see below.

## Standard Abbreviations Used in This Encyclopedia

B.C. = before Christ—that is, before the year 1.

A.D. = anno Domini (Latin for "in the year of our Lord")—that is, including and following the year 1.

For example: 560 B.C.; 900 A.D.

Generally, only ancient dates are given with the abbreviations B.C. or A.D., to avoid confusion. If a date is given without an abbreviation, you can assume that it is A.D.—that is, it occurred after the year 1.

## Measurement Abbreviations and What They Stand For

| | |
|---|---|
| sq = square | qt(s) = quart(s) |
| cu = cubic | gal(s) = gallon(s) |
| in = inch(es) | mph = miles per hour |
| ft = foot, feet | cm = centimeter(s) |
| yd = yard(s) | m = meter(s) |
| mi = mile(s) | km = kilometer(s) |
| oz = ounce(s) | g = gram(s) |
| lb(s) = pound(s) | kg = kilogram(s) |
| pt(s) = pint(s) | l = liter(s) |
| | kmph = kilometers per hour |

# Contents

# Porcupines

The African and some other crested porcupines have especially long shoulder and neck quills, which they can stand on end to form a "crest."

▼ African porcupine family at the entrance to their burrow, in the Kalahari Desert.

Porcupines are large rodents armored with sharp spines or quills, which cover most of their bodies. Some of the forest-living species of Africa and Asia, such as the brush-tailed porcupines, have long, but spineless tails that break easily. If they are attacked, the predator is left holding the end of the tail, while the porcupine escapes with its life. The larger African and Asian porcupines have short tails, usually with very long quills, which they can rattle as a warning to predators. If this warning is ignored, the porcupine will quickly back into its enemy. Its spines are very loosely attached, so will easily come off to be left in the predator's skin. The spines are not poisonous, but the wounds can become infected and kill predators like lions and leopards.

Porcupines are mostly nocturnal animals. They have poor eyesight but good senses of hearing and smell. They feed on many kinds of plants, and in some parts of the world damage crops and trees. The tree-living North American porcupines are excellent climbers, with large feet and long tails with which they cling tightly to branches. They like to eat the tender layer beneath the tree bark, which can kill the tree. ◆

**Distribution**
Africa and the warm parts of Asia, North and South America
**Largest**
African crested porcupine: head-and-body length 60–90 cm (23–35 in); tail up to 17 cm (6.6 in); weight up to 30 kg (66 lbs)
**Smallest**
Upper Amazon porcupine: overall length about 50 cm (20 in)
**Number of young**
1 or 2, well developed at birth and suckled briefly
**Lifespan**
Over 10 years
**Subphylum**
Vertebrata
**Class** Mammalia
**Order** Rodentia
**Number of species**
22 (11 in Africa and Asia, 11 in America)

▼ **See also**
Rodents

# Porpoises

▼ Porpoises differ from dolphins in a number of ways. They are generally smaller, with rounded, rather than beaky, faces. Dolphins have pointed teeth, while porpoises have squarer teeth.

Porpoises are mammals and are considered small whales. The word "porpoise" is sometimes used to refer to small, rather plump dolphins with short faces.

Porpoises do not always have back fins, but if a fin is present it is usually small and triangular, rather than backwardly curved. They have up to 80 teeth in their mouths, but these are flat or spade-shaped, not pointed the way dolphin's teeth are.

The common or harbor porpoise gets its name because it often swims near land, although in the western Atlantic it migrates to deeper water during the winter months. At sea, it is usually seen in small groups, called schools, cartwheeling through the surface water to breathe about four times a minute. It can dive to over 50 m (164 ft), though its average time below the surface of the water is only about four minutes.

Dall's porpoise is more playful than the other porpoises and is said to be the fastest swimmer of all of the small whales, reaching speeds of 50 kmph (31 mph) over short distances. Both species feed on small, non-spiny fish, such as herring. Large numbers of both species are killed each year, caught in fishing nets or hunted as food. ◆

**Distribution**
Northern Hemisphere coastal water and waters near the far south of South America
**Largest**
Dall's porpoise: about 1.8–2.1 m (6–7 ft) long; weight 100–160 kg (220–352 lbs). Females slightly smaller than males
**Smallest**
Gulf of California porpoise: 1.2–1.5 m (4–5 ft) long; weight as little as 30 kg (66 lbs)
**Number of young**
1, suckled for 8 months (common porpoise) or 2 years (Dall's porpoise)
**Lifespan**
10–20 years (varies with species)
**Subphylum** Vertebrata
**Class** Mammalia
**Order** Cetacea
**Family** Phocaenidae
**Number of species** 6

▼ **See also**
Dolphins
Mammals
Whales

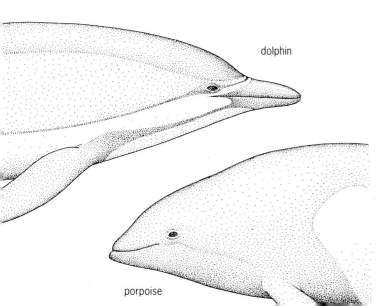

dolphin

porpoise

# Portraits

A portrait is an image of a particular person. A good portrait is not simply an accurate record of the shapes that make a face; rather it tells us something about the person behind the face, catching the person's personality as well as looks. When we use the word "portrait" we usually think of a painting, but portraits can also be sculptures, drawings, prints or photographs.

## Historical records

In addition to being fascinating as works of art, portraits are of great interest as historical records. Several countries have a national portrait gallery that collects and displays images of its famous men and women. The Greeks and Romans were the first great portraitists. Very few paintings from ancient times have survived, but fortunately there are vivid portrait sculptures of such famous personalities as Alexander the Great and Julius Caesar.

▶ This portrait of Gabriele Fonseca is by Gian Lorenzo Bernini (1598–1680), and was commissioned to mark his death. It is framed like a picture, but it is a sculpture in marble, and bursts out of its frame. Bernini was the greatest Italian sculptor of the 17th-century, the Baroque era. Here he uses the deep folds in clothing, the texture of skin, bones and hair, and above all the sunken eyes to create a portrait of great feeling and expression.

During the Middle Ages, when almost all art was religious, hardly any portraits were produced, but portraiture became popular again during the Renaissance, which began in the 15th century. At first only high-ranking people had their portraits painted or sculpted and the sitter (the person portrayed) was often mainly interested in conveying the right kind of image. A king would want the artist to make him look powerful and perhaps rather frightening—someone who was a fit and proper person to govern. He would usually dress very splendidly to stress his wealth and position. Gradually, however, portraiture spread to other ranks of society and became much more varied.

## The sitter's self-image

Most portraits are commissioned by the sitter rather than done for the artist's own satisfaction. The artist, therefore, has to bear in mind how the sitter wants to appear to the world. Some of the most successful portraitists have been good at subtle flattery. They make their sitters look more handsome or elegant than they are in real life. Few people are as unconcerned with their looks as the 17th-century British ruler Oliver Cromwell, who told a portraitist not to flatter him at all, but to include his "pimples and warts." ◆

▼ **See also**
Drawing
Painting
Photography
Sculpture

◀ *Old Man and his Grandson*, by Domenico Ghirlandaio (1449–1494). Portrait painters are not only concerned with beautiful subjects. They try to show us the uniqueness of all sorts of people. This picture, painted in the late 15th-century, shows the contrasting portraits of youth and age. The artist has not spared us the truth of the old man's face, which is distorted by a disease commonly known as "potato nose." Yet he gazes so lovingly at the grandson, who is affectionately staring at his strange features.

# Ports and harbors

People have traveled the seas for thousands of years. Places on the coast where there is shelter from the open sea have always been good spots to start a port. All over the world, natural harbors have grown up to be important ports used by trading ships. The Middle Eastern port of Muscat, in Oman, has a fine natural harbor. It is a deep-water bay protected by rocky headlands, and it has been a trading port for over 500 years. In other places, the natural landscape has been changed to make a better port. Rotterdam, in the Netherlands, was founded in the 13th century as a small fishing harbor 25 k (15.5 mi) up a river from the North Sea. Today, Rotterdam is the world's busiest port. Ships dock all the way to the sea along a channel dug at the end of the 19th century.

## Trading ports

Many countries need to buy and sell goods from other countries. They need to have ports that are able to deal with the very large ships that carry goods across the oceans. In the 1950s few oil tankers were larger than 50,000 tons, but now there are very large crude carriers (VLCCs) of between 200,000 and 400,000 tons, and ultra-large crude carriers (ULCCs) of more than 400,000 tons. These require much larger ports, where the water may need to be up to 30 m (98 ft) deep. There are also bulk carriers for grain, metal and manufactured goods. Container ships need special cranes and loading equipment on the dockside to load the containers from trains and trucks onto the container ships. Road and rail links are also needed to deliver the containers overland to

▶ Containers are loaded onto ships in Rotterdam in the Netherlands.

◄ Ferries and a hydrofoil leaving the natural harbor of Skiathos, a small Greek island in the Aegean Sea.

the port. Many industries grow up around a port, such as shipbuilding and engineering, refineries and food-processing plants.

## Fishing ports

Some ports just handle fish. There are small fishing ports along coasts around the world. From the fishing ports along the coast of Portugal, for example, the trawlers catch sardines, squid, cod and sole in the Atlantic Ocean. Every day men and women can be seen sitting on the harborside surrounded by piles of nets and floats. There is always a lot of work to do mending holes in the nets and packing fish in boxes to be sold.

Aberdeen is a fishing port on the eastern coast of Scotland. One of the most important fish landed in Aberdeen is herring. While most fish are sold fresh, herring are usually preserved and then sold. A big industry has grown up over the past 200 years in Aberdeen to preserve herring.

Many fishing ports in Europe and North America are suffering from unemployment now because too many fish have been taken from the world's oceans. The European Union and other authorities are trying to limit the number of fish caught so that stocks can be conserved.

## Passenger ports

Some ports are mainly for people traveling on ships and ferries. Dover is a passenger port in the southeast of England. It has been a port

since Roman times, for it is just 34 km (21 mi) from the French port of Calais. Dover is an important port for ferries carrying people across the English Channel to the European mainland.

Ferries from Dover carry cars, trucks and pedestrians. Drivers wait in large parking lots to drive their vehicles on to "roll-on–roll-off" ferries. Foot passengers show their tickets and passports in a terminal building and walk onto the ship. Cargo carried in trucks can be moved quickly, because it is very easy to move the trucks on and off without unloading them. When the port is very busy, a ferry comes and goes every half an hour to and from the ports on the other side of the Channel. However, the ferries have lost business to the Channel Tunnel since it opened in 1994. ◆

▲ Dover, England, is the main cross-Channel ferry port, with a boat arriving or leaving every half hour at the busiest times.

▼ **See also**

Docks
Fishing industry
Merchant marine
Ships

# Portugal

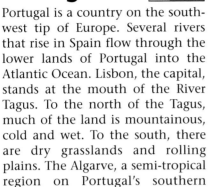

Portugal is a country on the south-west tip of Europe. Several rivers that rise in Spain flow through the lower lands of Portugal into the Atlantic Ocean. Lisbon, the capital, stands at the mouth of the River Tagus. To the north of the Tagus, much of the land is mountainous, cold and wet. To the south, there are dry grasslands and rolling plains. The Algarve, a semi-tropical region on Portugal's southern coast, is a popular tourist resort.

Portugal is famous for its port wine, which comes from Oporto. Other important exports include textiles, cork, wood and sardines. The islands of Madeira and the Azores, in the North Atlantic, also form part of Portugal.

**Area**
92,390 sq km
(35,670 sq mi)
**Capital** Lisbon
**Population**
9,830,000
**Language**
Portuguese
**Religion** Christian
**Government**
Parliamentary republic
**Currency**
1 escudo = 100 centavos
**Major exports**
Textiles, cork, food
products, machinery

▲ Bridge over the Tagus River in the center of Lisbon, the capital of Portugal.

## LOOKING BACK

Portugal has a great seafaring tradition. In the 15th and 16th centuries bold Portuguese sailors traveled far to discover and explore unknown parts of the Earth. Bartolomeu Dias sailed round the Cape of Good Hope; Pedro Cabral landed in Brazil; and Vasco da Gama discovered the sea route to India by way of Africa. The Portuguese empire included Brazil, Angola and Mozambique. Portuguese is still widely spoken in those countries, although all were independent by 1975. ◆

▼ **See also**
Angola
Brazil
Explorers
Mozambique

**BIOGRAPHY**
Dias, Bartolomeu
Gama, Vasco da

# Postal services

All countries have an official postal service. The systems used to collect, transport and deliver mail vary. In some countries letters are delivered to people's homes. In others, people collect them from the nearest post office. However, the basic system is the same. As long as an item is properly addressed and paid for, it can be taken to a destination in any

▼ **See also**
Fax machines
Stamps
ZIP codes

▼ **HOW THE U.S. MAIL SYSTEM WORKS**

A stamped letter is mailed at a mailbox.

A postal service employee gathers the mail and takes it to the local post office.

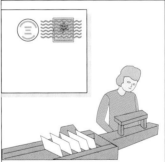
At the post office, mail is *canceled* (marked so stamps cannot be used again) and sorted by ZIP code.

Trucks take sorted mail to the airport, where it is loaded onto planes and flown to destination cities.

Large trucks bring the mail from the airport to the local post office, where it is sorted for delivery.

A postal employee ("mailman") delivers the mail.

Mail service was established in the American colonies in the late 17th century. The Post Office Department was created in 1775, and Benjamin Franklin became its first head with the title of postmaster general. The department was renamed the U.S. Postal Service in 1971.

country in the world. The country from which the item is sent keeps the money paid, and handles mail from other countries free of extra charge.

The official postal service is in competition with private courier services, which promise special benefits such as extra security or more rapid delivery.

Modern technology is providing an electronic way to send letters and documents. Electronic mail (e-mail) systems send information from one computer to another either by cable or by telephone link. Fax (facsimile) machines code information so that it can be sent along telephone lines and decoded at the receiving fax. Individuals and companies may have this equipment for their own use. In some countries, post offices and courier companies offer e-mail and fax services to help the public send messages more quickly. ◆

# Posters

Hasten the Homecoming

BUY VICTORY BONDS

Posters are large printed sheets that use words and pictures to send a clear, specific message.

Posters of the sort we know today were not made until about 1860, when lithography (a printmaking technique) became widely used, allowing colorful advertising posters to be made easily and cheaply.

With the outbreak of World War I in 1914 the poster became a political tool. For example, posters were used to promote patriotism, and to encourage men to do their duty and enlist. In a changing political world, posters began to be used as propaganda.

With the great industrial growth of the 20th century came a huge increase in the number of posters advertising all sorts of products and services, and for announcing events such as concerts or films for the growing leisure services industry. Today photography is used much more than artwork to illustrate posters, but posters are still a common feature in many public places. ◆

◄ This poster by U.S. illustrator Norman Rockwell was created to sell so-called victory bonds during World War II (1939–1945). The bonds raised money to help the government pay for the war. Rockwell (1894–1978) was one of America's most famous illustrators and created many posters for patriotic causes.

▼ See also
Advertising
Design
Printmaking

# Pottery

Another term for pottery is *ceramics*, which comes from the Greek word *keramos*, meaning "potter's clay."

Containers and other objects made from baked clay are known as pottery. Pottery is our oldest known technology involving the use of fire.

Clay looks and feels like mud, but it has special qualities. When it is wet, it can be shaped. When it is baked until it becomes red hot (at least 700 °C/1,300°F), it changes into a permanent material.

Many different kinds of clay can be used to make pottery. Those which are fired at the lowest temperatures (below 1,100 °C/2,000°F) are used for making *earthenware* (for example, flowerpots). When dug, these clays may be gray, brown, cream or blue-black. They are often found near rivers and lakes, where they have been deposited by water. Unglazed earthenware is not waterproof.

*Stoneware* is fired at a higher temperature than earthenware (above 1,200 °C/2,200°F). It is strong and waterproof because the clay particles fuse together during firing to form a kind of glassy stone. Stoneware clays contain some impurities, so they are rarely white.

China clay (kaolin) is white and can be fired at a very high temperature of up to 1,400 °C (2,550°F). It is one of the ingredients used to make *porcelain* and *bone china*. This kind of pottery is very fragile and translucent, which means that light can be seen through it.

## The potter's wheel

Before the potter's wheel came into use, all pots were made using hand-building techniques like those shown in the activity box.

To make a pot on a wheel, the potter "throws" a ball of clay onto the middle of the wheel. The wheel is made to spin, using hand or foot power, or electricity. The potter works the clay into a wet mound, hollows it out with the fingers into a cup shape, and then draws up the sides of the pot. The centrifugal force of the spinning wheel helps to raise the clay.

Archaeologists have dug up pottery made over 9,000 years ago. Fine, decorative pottery was first made in China and Japan. Some Japanese pottery has been found that is possibly the earliest in the world. These first pots were made by modeling slabs of clay, which were then fired, using the same method as that described in the activity box.

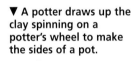

▼ A potter draws up the clay spinning on a potter's wheel to make the sides of a pot.

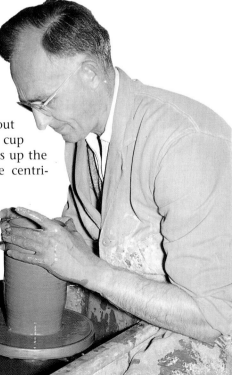

## Hand-Made Pottery

### Pinch pot

1 Push your thumb in a ball of soft clay.
2 Turn the clay, pinching it between thumb and fingers, until the walls of the pot are formed.

### Coiled pot

1 Roll out a flat base of clay and place it on a wooden board.
2 Press the first roll of soft clay onto the base, and smooth the joint with liquid clay called "slip."
3 Build up coils to make the sides of the pot, continuing to smooth joints.

### Slab pot

1 Roll out a ball of clay and cut four square tiles from it.
2 Score the edges lightly and join the four sides with slip.
3 Cut a larger tile for a base. Use slip to attach the four sides, and trim the edges of the base.

## Firing pottery

For centuries potters fired their pots in bonfires. These pots were fragile and were often discolored by the ashes. Potters gradually learned to fire pots in a kiln. This increased the temperature and produced much stronger pots.

A kiln is a kind of oven in which pots are placed to separate them from the fuel. The oven holds the heat, but allows smoke from the fuel to escape. Pots are heated and then allowed to cool before being taken out of the kiln. Traditionally, potters used wood as fuel, and they still do in many parts of the world. In 18th-century England, Josiah Wedgwood and other potters used coal. Modern potters use gas, electricity or oil to fire their kilns.

## Glazing pottery

A glaze is a thin layer of melted glass that covers the clay pot. This makes it smooth, waterproof and often very colorful. There are many types of glazes. All contain a substance called silica, which is found in sand and many rocks. Lead, common salt, wood ash or other ingredients are added to the glaze to make it melt on the pot when it is fired. Colored glazes are made by adding coloring agents. Cobalt makes a beautiful blue. Copper makes blue, green or red. Iron makes yellow, pale blue, green, brown or black.

## Molding pottery in factories

Mugs made in a factory are cast in a mold. The mold is made in two parts out of plaster of Paris, which is porous. Clay is diluted with water until it can be poured like cream into the mold. The plaster absorbs some of the water, and a coating of clay forms inside the mold. The rest of the clay is poured out again. When the clay left in the mold is firm, the mold is opened and the mug is taken out. The handle is then added.

## Decorating pottery

The simplest way to make a pattern on a piece of pottery is to make marks in the clay while it is still soft. Shells, seed pods, twigs and buttons can all be used.

Pots can be colored in several ways. Low-fired unglazed pieces can be painted with colored clays mixed with water. They can then be polished using a smooth pebble. ♦

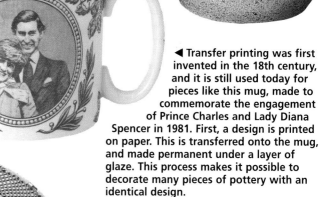

◄ Transfer printing was first invented in the 18th century, and it is still used today for pieces like this mug, made to commemorate the engagement of Prince Charles and Lady Diana Spencer in 1981. First, a design is printed on paper. This is transferred onto the mug, and made permanent under a layer of glaze. This process makes it possible to decorate many pieces of pottery with an identical design.

◄ Potters can paint their pieces with glaze colors. In the 17th century, European potters developed a method of porcelain decoration that had long been used by the Chinese. Earthenware was covered with white glaze. It was then hand-painted before being fired.

◄ Stacking pitchers in a kiln ready for firing.

▼ One method of decorating is to use liquid clay (slip). The slip is piped onto the pot through a nozzle. This is called *slip trailing*. Patterns can be made by cutting into layers of colored slip. This is called *sgraffito*. This modern pot is decorated in sgraffito.

▼ **See also**
China
Japan

# Poverty

▼ **See also**
Developing countries
Drought
Famine
Malnutrition
Population
Third World

What is it like to be poor? How many people in the world are living in poverty? People who do not have enough to eat, or a proper place to live, or other basic essentials for life, are clearly poor. But even if most people in a country have enough to eat and comfortable, well-equipped homes, there are still likely to be people who are poorer than others. Even the richest countries in the world have people who are unemployed or homeless. One way of looking at poverty is to say that anyone who has a standard of living far below the average for the whole country is poor.

## Reasons for poverty

Many millions of people in the world live in absolute poverty, and some estimates put the number at almost a billion. There are many reasons for this. Some countries have too few resources to support the number of people living there. They may also be affected by natural disasters, such as the floods in Bangladesh, which can ruin harvests. In the mid-1980s drought caused famine in Africa, which killed millions of people. Sometimes such cases of famine are caused or worsened by poor people not being able to buy what food there is available. To make matters worse, 10 of the 13 worst-affected countries have suffered from war, fighting and refugee problems. Some of the poorest countries in the world spend a large part of their national income on their armed forces, even though some of their people are starving.

## Financial problems

Such countries are also likely to have high birth rates and high infant mortality rates. Over-population puts even more strain on resources.

► Russian children pick through a rubbish dump, searching for anything they can use, or sell to others. Millions of people around the world make their living this way.

Many governments cannot afford to provide health care and education to help people break out of poverty. Instead they are forced to borrow money from richer countries and foreign banks. But then they have to pay interest on these loans, and the more they borrow, the more interest they have to pay back. Countries such as Mexico and Brazil have found themselves owing more than half of their yearly income in foreign debts.

## Rich and poor

In many countries there is a sharp contrast between the lives of the rich and the poor. Wealthier people live in comfortable houses and apartments in the suburbs, while poor people live in squatters' huts on the edge of town. São Paulo in Brazil is such a city, and Johannesburg in South Africa is surrounded by poor townships and shanty towns. There poor people often have to make a living by picking through the rubbish discarded by their richer neighbors. ◆

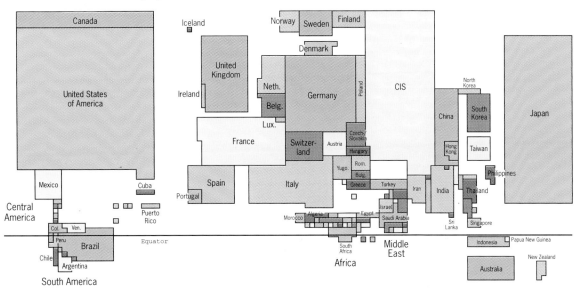

◄ In this map each area's size is proportionate to the wealth it produces. Our world is clearly divided into a generally wealthy North and a poorer South. The nations of the North, with a quarter of the world's population, earn 80 percent of the world's income. The South, with three-quarters of the population, earns only 20 percent of the world's income.

# Power stations

The power output of a large power station is 2,000 megawatts (2 billion watts).

When you plug a toaster, radio or other appliance into an electrical outlet, the electricity comes from a power station that may be hundreds of miles away. A large power station can supply enough electricity for over a million homes.

In a power station, the electricity comes from huge generators. To deliver power, the generators must be turned. Usually, they are driven by turbines (fan wheels), which are blown around by jets of steam from a boiler. However, turbines can also be turned by running water, wind or the gases pushed out from a jet engine. There are three main types of power station: coal- or oil-fired, nuclear-powered, or CCGT (combined-cycle gas turbine) stations. Of the three types, coal- or oil-fired power stations are most common.

## How Power Stations Work

### Oil- or coal-burning power station

### Nuclear power station

### Combined-cycle gas turbine (CCGT) power station

### Oil- or coal-burning power station

Most power stations burn fuel, such as coal, oil or natural gas. For example, a coal-fired power station burns powdered coal. In the boiler, the heat turns water into steam for the turbines. Once the steam has passed through the turbines, it has to be cooled and condensed (changed back into a liquid) so that the water can be reused in the boiler. For this, a supply of cooling water is needed. Some power stations take cold water from a nearby river or estuary and put it back in again a little warmer. Others recycle their cooling water. It passes through huge cooling towers where the heat is removed by an upward draft of air.

### Nuclear power station

Nuclear power stations also have boilers, steam turbines and generators. However, instead of a furnace for burning fuel, they have a nuclear reactor. Here, heat is released by the fission (splitting) of atoms of uranium-235.

### Combined-cycle gas turbine (CCGT) power station

Combined-cycle gas turbine (CCGT) power stations have a jet engine that uses gas as its fuel. The shaft of the engine turns one generator. The heat from the jet exhaust is used to make steam to drive another generator. CCGT stations have a smaller power output than other types. However, they can start up more rapidly when the demand for power rises. Also, they are more efficient so they can extract more energy from fuel.

## Waste heat

Fuel-burning and nuclear power stations use heat energy to drive their generators. Unfortunately, they deliver less than one-half of their energy as electricity. The rest is wasted as heat. This is not due to poor design. Once heat has been removed by the cooling water, it becomes so spread out that it is no longer useful for the generating process. To make steam, concentrated heat is needed at a high temperature.

## Pollution problems

Fuel-burning power stations pollute the atmosphere with unwanted exhaust gases from their chimneys. All give out carbon dioxide, which adds to global warming. Coal-fired stations also give out sulphur dioxide, which causes acid rain. Amounts can be reduced either by burning only low-sulphur coal, or by fitting flue-gas desulphurization units to the chimneys. However, these units are expensive.

Nuclear power stations do not burn their fuel, so they do not produce large amounts of polluting gases. However, they produce highly radioactive waste that will need safe storage for thousands of years. Also, very high safety standards are needed to make sure that nuclear power stations do not leak radioactive materials into the atmosphere.

## Alternative power schemes

The world's supplies of oil, natural gas and coal are limited, so, where possible, it makes sense to use power stations that do not need these fuels and produce no polluting gases.

Hydroelectric power stations use the flow of water from a lake behind a dam to drive their turbines. The dam is usually built across a river, which keeps the lake full. Tidal power schemes also rely on a dam, but the lake behind it is filled by the rising tide. Wind farms are collections of aerogenerators. These are generators turned by giant windmills.

Geothermal power stations use the heat from underground rocks to make steam for their turbines. The heat comes partly from the Earth's core and partly from radioactive materials in the rocks. Cold water is pumped down to the rocks through a borehole, a kilometer (0.62 mi) or so deep. It comes up a second borehole as hot steam. In some areas, hot water occurs naturally deep in the ground, and there are geysers (hot springs) at the surface. With steam coming out of cracks in the

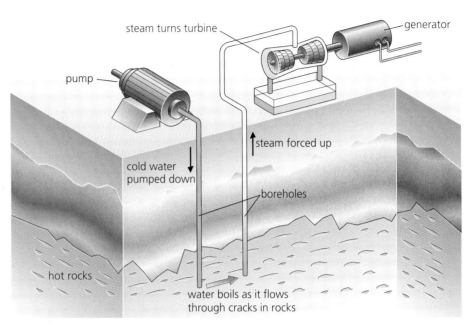

▲ In a geothermal power station, cold water pumped down one borehole is heated by underground rocks. Steam coming up the other borehole is used to turn a generator.

ground, water does not have to be pumped down in the first place.

Waste materials can be a useful additional source of power. Some power stations burn waste paper. Others burn the gas given off by the rotting materials in trash dumps. In the U.S., there is even one power station that burns drugs captured by the police.

### LOOKING BACK

The world's first power station was built in Godalming, England, in 1881. The generator was turned by a water wheel, and mainly provided power for the new electric street lighting. However, some local homes were also connected to the system through cables in the gutters. The first power station in the U.S. opened in 1882. Its generator was driven by a steam engine.

In the 1890s, there was a battle between two rival generating systems. One used alternating current (AC); the other used "one way" direct current (DC). AC eventually became more common because its voltage could be increased or decreased using transformers, and it was more suitable for long-distance transmission.

Power stations with steam turbines appeared about 1900. The first power station to use a nuclear reactor was opened in 1954 in Obninsk, Russia. ◆

To cut down on energy wastage, some power stations use their cooling systems to supply the houses in their area with hot water. Strategies like this are ways of using fuel more efficiently.

Sometime in the 21st century, nuclear fusion power stations may be developed. Like the Sun, they will use hydrogen as their nuclear fuel. Unlike today's nuclear power stations they will produce almost no radioactive waste.

Wave-driven power stations may be developed in the future. One idea is to use the motion of waves to pump air through a turbine, which is connected to a generator.

# Pregnancy

A female animal is pregnant when she is carrying developing young inside her body that will be born as babies rather than as eggs. The pregnancy may last from 12 days in some small marsupials to over a year in large whales. Pregnancy occurs in almost all mammals, and a few fish and other non-mammals can also bear live young.

In humans (as in other mammals), pregnancy begins when a sperm from the father fertilizes an egg inside the mother and the fertilized egg begins to grow. This is called *conception*.

The growing fertilized egg is called an *embryo*. It soon becomes attached to the wall of the mother's uterus (womb) through a spongy structure that develops called the placenta. The placenta contains many blood vessels, through which food and oxygen are passed, via the umbilical cord, to the growing embryo from the mother's blood.

After eight weeks of development the embryo is called a *fetus*. By 12 weeks of growth the fetus, although only 8 cm (3 in) long, looks like a tiny human being. It has hands, feet, eyes, nose, mouth and ears, and is moving. It will be another 12 weeks or so before it has grown enough to have any chance of surviving if born early. Normally births take place about 40 weeks after conception.

During those 40 weeks the womb has to grow enormously to provide room for the growing baby. It is this that gives a pregnant mother a "tummy bulge." The mother's breasts also become bigger. At the end of pregnancy they start to produce milk to feed the newborn baby. ♦

Sometimes if the baby is not developing normally, or the mother is ill or cannot cope, she may enter a hospital to have the fetus removed. This is an abortion, and is usually done in the early stages of pregnancy.

Sometimes a developing baby dies during pregnancy. The womb usually expels the fetus and placenta. This is called a miscarriage.

▶ This photograph was taken using a special lens at the end of a very fine fiber-optic cable. The baby is in its fifth month of development. It is surrounded by a protective liquid, called *amniotic* fluid.

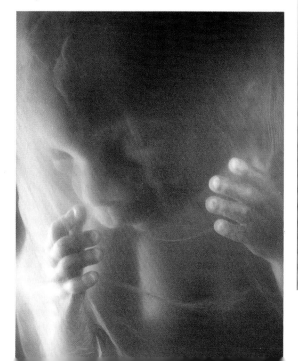

# Prehistoric animals

The term "prehistoric animals" means all the animals that lived before humans began to write about their history and the things that they knew. Most of the creatures that have ever existed lived before human beings evolved, so "prehistoric animals" could be taken to mean those that we know only from their fossils, such as the great armored fish, the ammonites and the dinosaurs. But although human beings are among the last species to have evolved, our ancestors shared their world with many animals that are now extinct.

So how do we know about prehistoric animals? Before people could write they sometimes drew pictures or made engravings of the animals that they knew. Besides these, archaeologists find the bones of creatures that were used for food, or sometimes perhaps for magic purposes, in the places where the first people lived.

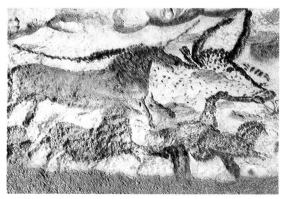

▲ This painting of a bull and some horses, from the Lascaux cave in France, was painted between 15,000 and 14,000 B.C.

## Painted caves

At the end of the last ice age in Europe, hunters in France and northern Spain painted pictures of animals on the walls of caves. Most of them were of wild horses, deer and bison, which were their main food. Animals like these, which still exist today, make a link with the past, because knowing what they are like helps us to understand the bones and drawings of other, less familiar animals left by prehistoric people. This is more important when we find the remains of animals that are now totally extinct. The mammoth, the woolly rhinoceros, the cave lion and the cave bear were all well known to our ancestors. They probably feared these large and powerful creatures because their best weapons were lightweight spears, which were no match for the strength of big animals.

## Frozen and pickled fossils

Most prehistoric animals are known only by the fossils of their hard parts—their bones, teeth and shells. But a few creatures have been more completely preserved, and we can see their muscles and skin. In parts of Siberia and North America, wooly mammoths fell into crevices in the frozen ground of their tundra habitat and were unable to get out. These animals were in a natural deep freeze, in which they have been preserved for over 10,000 years. The most famous was discovered in 1903 and is now in a museum in St. Petersburg, Russia. More recently a baby mammoth that had been separated from her mother was found. Her long coat of reddish hair was not enough to save her. The people who dug her up nicknamed her Dima, which means "little girl."

In a place called Starunia in Eastern Europe there was once a bog where the waters contained a waxy material, and also salt. This probably did not freeze, even in the cold of the ice age, so animals went there to drink. One of them was a wooly rhino. It got stuck and eventually became pickled in the minerals in the water. When it was dug out, it was found to have a fatty hump over its shoulders. The cave artists always showed woolly rhinos looking like this. The archaeologists had thought that they were drawn like that to make the rhino look extra frightening—though the ancient artists were, we now know, showing exactly what they saw.

It is not always clear which species a cave painting represents. One is thought to show a kind of giraffe with big antlers called *Sivatherium*. Another, about 10,000 years old, from northern Australia, is thought to

◄ A mammoth fossil, found in Siberia in 1903, It had been deep-frozen in the soil for thousands of years.

show a rhinoceros-sized marsupial (pouched mammal) called *Diprotodon*, which has been extinct for at least 6,000 years.

In North America the remains of a kind of extinct elephant called a mastodon tell us that these creatures were sometimes hunted successfully by humans, because one fossil skeleton has been found with a small stone implement stuck into one of the bones. At another place in North America, in Los Angeles, asphalt made small pools on the surface of the ground in an area now called the La Brea Tar Pits. Big animals, such as mastodons, must have tried to drink there and become trapped. They attracted flesh-eaters, which were caught in their turn. Thousands of bones of now extinct wolves and saber-toothed cats have been found there. Though there were human hunters in the area, they must have been clever enough not to get caught. ◆

It is likely that early human beings were wasteful hunters, so they may have contributed to the extinction of some of the animals that we now know only as fossils or cave art.

◄ These saber-toothed cats ranged over North and South America, and probably fed on mastodons and ground sloths. It is now thought that they attacked the softer underbellies of their prey, using their teeth *(see fossil, above)* to remove its innards.

# Prehistoric people

"Prehistory" is the name archaeologists give to the enormous period of time in the past before written records. The word was invented in the 19th century. The period of prehistory varies from place to place. It all depends on the time when someone invents writing or introduces it from another country. In Great Britain prehistory means before the Romans (before the invasion of 43 A.D.), while in China prehistory ends with the invention of writing in the Shang period (from about 1600 B.C.). In most of America prehistory lasted until the Europeans arrived in the 16th century.

## The surviving evidence

Archaeologists must try to understand the past from what survives to be studied. In the prehistoric period there were no records. The further back you go in time the more chance there is that things people used or built will have rotted away. For example, in the

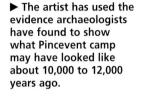

▶ The artist has used the evidence archaeologists have found to show what Pincevent camp may have looked like about 10,000 to 12,000 years ago.

▼ The timeline below shows the development of prehistoric peoples around the world, from the time when the first human-like "hominids" evolved, about 5 million years ago, until 700 B.C.

| 5,000,000– 2,000,000 B.C. | 2,000,000– 250,000 B.C. | 250,000– 120,000 B.C. | 80,000– 30,000 B.C. | 50,000– 25,000 B.C. | 25,000– 10,000 B.C. | 10,000– 9000 B.C. | 9000– 7000 B.C. |
|---|---|---|---|---|---|---|---|
| Early tree-dwelling "hominids" evolve in Africa. | Upright human *Homo erectus*, evolves, spreading to Asia and Europe. | Modern human, *Homo sapiens*, evolving in Africa and moving north. | Cave-dwelling *Neanderthals* living in Europe. | Modern human, with brain capacity of today (*Homo sapiens sapiens*), spreading through Europe, Asia, Australia, America. A wide variety of tools (knifes, axes, adzes, scrapers, awls, harpoons, needles) made in a variety of materials (wood, bone, stone, antler, reed, leather, flint). | Early round houses; cave painting and carving. | Climate change as ice age ends. | Beginning of farming in several parts of the world. Village settlements in Syria, Palestine, Cyprus. Beans and wild grains (wheat and barley) cultivated. Maize (corn) and root crops grown in South America. Dogs domesticated. |

earliest periods of the past, people were hunters and made tools and weapons out of a variety of material they found. However, it is usually only the stone tools or stone parts of things which have survived; wooden handles, wooden bowls and clothes from animal skins will usually have perished long ago.

## Hunters and gatherers

At first, people all over the world hunted and fished to eat and gathered food from natural sources. They had to learn to understand the landscape around them and to live off it. Few peoples in the world do this today, but some of the Aborigines of Australia still know how to survive by hunting and food gathering.

The earliest peoples anywhere in the world developed in East Africa. These early peoples hunted and gathered food and left behind them tools made of flint and other types of stone. Many prehistoric peoples developed their own special art, from cave paintings to carving.

## Life in a camp

The drawing on the left shows what archaeologists think a hunters' camp looked like in a place called Pincevent, on the banks of the River Seine in France, about 10,000 to 12,000 years ago. This picture has been put together as a result of carefully excavating the site and collecting the evidence.

Evidence shows that this was a site occupied, though not permanently, by nomadic groups of men, women and children. These wandering people would set up camp there for a few weeks at the end of summer. Their main activities centered on hunting reindeer, which they ate, gathering plant food and cooking meals. They also processed the deer, so they could use their skins as well.

## America and Africa

Prehistoric hunting tribes probably crossed the Bering Strait to North America between 30,000 and 23,000 B.C. They moved south, hunting mammoths and bison. Flint spear-heads were in use by about 9000 B.C. By then South America was populated. In Peru there is evidence of early cultivation of maize (corn) and llamas were domesticated. Around the Gulf of Mexico a series of prehistoric cultures grew up: the Olmec, the Maya, the Toltec and the Aztec. They cultivated a wide variety of crops and built great cities. Although skilled astronomers, they seem not to have developed writing systems. In Africa south of the Sahara, a number of prehistoric empires also flourished such as Ghana, Zimbabwe, Songhay and Benin, but these, too, relied solely on memory and oral traditions, rather than writing systems.

The first farming period is often called the *neolithic period*, meaning "new Stone Age." *Paleolithic* means the oldest Stone Age period. *Mesolithic* means "middle Stone Age."

| 7000–6000 B.C. | 5000–4000 B.C. | 4000–3000 B.C. | 3000–2000 B.C. | 2000–1000 B.C. | 1000–700 B.C. |
|---|---|---|---|---|---|
| Goats, sheep, pigs and cattle domesticated in eastern Mediterranean. Linen, textiles and pottery first made. Copper used in Anatolia, Turkey. Earliest cities built. | Copper and lead made in Anatolia. Domestication of horse and donkey in eastern Mediterranean. Maize (corn) cultivated near Gulf of Mexico; cotton grown in Peru. Rice grown in China and India. | Sumerian civilization. First writing. Metalwork in copper, tin, bronze, lead, silver, gold. Ox carts. Irrigation. Sails on Nile and Euphrates. Llama domesticated as pack animal in Peru. Stone temples and tombs in Malta and Europe (Avebury). | First pharaohs in Egypt; hieroglyphic writing system. Chariot invented in Mesopotamia. Indus civilizations with cotton textiles. "Beaker culture" spreads copper and textile technology through Western Europe. | Bronze technology throughout Europe. Stonehene completed. | Olmec culture in Mexico. Celts spread into Central Europe and Britain. Iron technology in Europe by 700 B.C. Prehistoric culture develops in America and Africa. |

▲ The cattle used here are a type called *Bos longifrons*, which have been found from the earliest farming periods in Europe. These strong, horned cattle were specially bred to pull a simple wooden plough called an *ard*. The ard cuts a furrow across the field by stirring up the soil. Modern ploughs turn the soil over.

## Farmers

Hunting peoples in various parts of the world gradually discovered how to become farmers. At first this probably meant trying to control the herds they were hunting, and collecting wild crops such as wheat to grind into flour. By 9000 B.C. the first farmers were planting and cultivating crops in the Middle East. Evidence has been found for two types of wheat, barley and various vegetables, such as peas, at one of the world's oldest prehistoric towns, Çatal Hüyük (Turkey). These farmers were breeding sheep and cattle but were also hunting.

## Prehistoric technology

When the prehistoric period was studied in the 19th century, archaeologists found stone and metal tools. These materials were used to give names to the various periods they identified. They talked about the Stone Age, the Bronze Age and the Iron Age. Although you will come across these terms today, archaeologists now usually talk about the hunting or farming periods.

The first hunters, in many parts of the world, used flint and other stones, such as obsidian, to make their tools and weapons. Gradually people discovered how to make a whole variety of tools, and skilled specialists were needed. Hunters needed different types of weapons for different animals, such as fine arrows for birds, or large cutting tools for cleaning animal skins. The first farmers needed many more stone tools. They had to have axes for cutting the forests to make way for farming land. In Europe, flint was the favorite material and it was actually mined in Britain, France, Denmark, Belgium and Poland. Prehistoric peoples also invented the wheel, pottery, spinning and weaving.

▶ A cross-section of a flint mine at Grimes Graves in Norfolk, England. Farming peoples dug hundreds of great open pits to get at the black flint, and then followed seams of it deep underground. Its main use was for making axes and it was exported to other areas. These mines were worked from about 2100 to 1600 B.C.

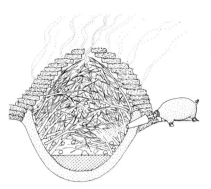

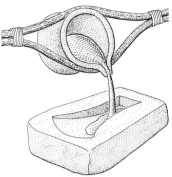

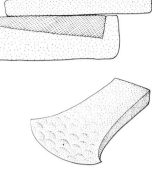

◀ Making bronze tools.

Copper and tin ore were heated in a clay-lined pit filled with charcoal. Molten metal collected at the bottom.

Copper and tin, mixed in the right proportions, made bronze. The bronze was melted and poured into a stone mold.

The bronze was covered with another stone. When cool, the flat axe-head was removed and sharpened by hammering.

## Discovering metals

Prehistoric peoples discovered how to use metal to make tools at different times and in different parts of the world. Copper was first used before 6000 B.C. in West Asia. A copper knife made about 3000 B.C. was found in the Gansu region of China. Specialists discovered that mixing copper and tin produced a harder and more useful metal, bronze. In Britain the farming peoples first started to use metal for their tools about 2300 B.C.

Iron occurs naturally in many parts of the world. Prehistoric peoples discovered that they could make iron by "smelting": melting iron ore and charcoal together. While hot, it was beaten into shapes with stones to make knives and other tools and weapons. In about 2000 B.C. the first people to use iron lived in Anatolia (part of Turkey today). In China it was being smelted in the 6th century B.C. In West Africa iron was being worked before 500 B.C. Ironworkers dug out the ore in mines and transported it to furnaces for smelting. In Great Britain people began using iron about 700 B.C. Some of it was made into bars and used for currency.

## Iron Age Britain

From about 700 B.C. until the Roman invasion in 43 A.D. the people in Britain were Celtic. This period is often called the Iron Age because iron was used; but they used many other materials as well. The people were mainly farmers living on small farms, in settlements or in hillforts. Their houses were usually built of wood with daub (a mixture of clay and straw) on the walls and a reed or thatch roof. In some parts of Britain they used local stone for the walls. In north and west Scotland they built tall, strong circular houses, called "brochs," to withstand attacks.

These Celtic farmers ploughed fields and planted crops such as wheat (for bread), barley (for beer), various vegetables, such as beans, and flax (for making linen cloth). The Celtic peoples liked brightly colored clothes, ornaments and jewelry. There were many specialists living in the settlement, such as gold, bronze and iron workers.

Many of their goods were traded throughout Britain. They took the idea of using coins from Greek traders. Toward the end of this period they were also trading with the Romans.

## Celtic tribes

The Celtic peoples were very warlike. One ancient writer said they were "mad keen on war, full of spirit and quick to begin a fight." They guarded their territories and raided other people's lands. They were divided into a number of tribes, each with its own name. We know some of them: the *Parisi*, who give us the name for the capital of modern France, moved to eastern Yorkshire. The *Helvetii* used to live in what is now Switzerland, the *Iberians* in Spain, the *Caledones* in northwest Scotland and the *Belgae* on the northeast coast of France.

## Prehistory to history

We know a lot about the prehistoric Celtic peoples in Britain and Northern Europe from archaeological evidence. We know the names of their tribes and some of their customs because we do have some written evidence. It comes from their contact with the Roman world. Julius Caesar conquered the Celtic tribes in Gaul (now mainly France) in the 1st century B.C. The Celts in Britain, although still in "prehistory," traded with the Romans in Gaul, an area that was now part of "history." ◆

# Presidents

A chart of all the U.S. presidents is in the article United States of America in Volume 7.

The title of president is usually given to the head of state in a republic. Some presidents, such as those of the United States, France, Italy and Russia, are elected. Others seize control and become dictators, and depend on force to keep their political power.

The extent of a president's power varies. In some countries, such as India, the president is a ceremonial head of state and the prime minister has the real power. In others, such as Zimbabwe, the president runs the government.

In France, a president is elected for seven years. The president chooses the prime minister and both of them are powerful.

The president of the United States is elected for four years, and no president may be elected for more than two four-year terms. The president is head of state, prime minister and commander-in-chief of the armed forces in times of peace as well as war. Although Congress makes the laws, the president has the right to veto (forbid) a new law. He also has the duty to make sure that laws are carried out. ◆

**See also**
Dictators
Government
Republics
United States of America

# Pressure

Pressure tells you how concentrated a force is. If the same amount of force is spread across two areas, one large and one small, the *pressure* acting on the smaller area will be greater than that on the larger area.

Pressure from gases like air pushes out in all directions. In liquids like water (and in gases), the pressure gets greater as you go deeper down in the liquid. If divers go too deep under the sea, the water pressure will crush them. ◆

**See also**
Air
Atmosphere
Forces

Scientists measure force in newtons (N). They measure pressure in newtons per square meter (N/m²), also called pascals (Pa).

▼ When the force being applied to the pencil is spread out by the coin, the pressure on the plasticine is less and it does not get pushed in so far.

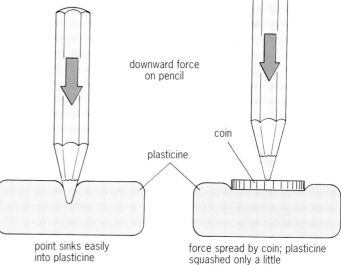

downward force on pencil

coin

plasticine

point sinks easily into plasticine

force spread by coin; plasticine squashed only a little

# Priests

The ancient Greeks and Romans had priests who conducted worship in their temples.

In some religions there are specially trained men, and sometimes women, who are appointed by their church to carry out certain rites during worship. They either belong to a family that inherits priestly duties (hereditary priests), or are trained as priests because they believe this is what God wants them to do. Eastern Orthodox, Roman Catholic and some Anglican (Church of England) Christians generally use the word "priest," but most Protestants prefer the title "minister" or "pastor."

Most Hindu priests come from Brahmin families. They perform many temple rites, but Hindus worship mostly at home, and a Brahmin priest is invited only to conduct special religious ceremonies.

In many other religions there is no equivalent of a priest. Hereditary Jewish priests made sacrifices in the Temple at Jerusalem before it was destroyed in 70 A.D. But today, worship in the Jewish synagogue can be led by anybody; rabbis are basically teachers, not priests.

For Muslims, the *imams* are prayer leaders in the mosques. In Buddhism, there are monks, *bhikkus*, and nuns, *bhikkunis*, who teach and give advice, but they are not priests. In Sikhism, all men and women are equal, and they are allowed to perform any of the religious ceremonies. ◆

**See also**
Catholicism, Roman
Christianity
Hinduism
Rites and rituals
Temples

# Primates

"Primates" is the name given to the order (group) of mammals that includes the lemurs of Madagascar, the pottos of Africa, the lorises of Asia, the monkeys of South America, the monkeys and true apes of Africa and Asia and, most widespread of all, human beings. Most primates live in tropical forests. As they climb, they hold the branches with fingers and a thumb that folds across the palm of the hand. This is called an "opposable thumb," and it enables the primates to grip things very strongly with hands and feet, as their big toes are also opposable.

Eyesight is a primate's most important sense. Its eyes are at the front of its face, so it looks at things using both eyes together. This is called *binocular vision*, and it enables primates to judge distances accurately. This is very important as they leap among the branches. Most primates do not have a good sense of smell. Long snouts, like those of animals that rely on smell, would interfere with their vision.

Most primates are social creatures living in family groups. They have large brains, and are more

intelligent than most other animals. In general, primate mothers have only one baby at a time. It is cared for by its mother and learns both from her and by playing with other members of the group.

Many primates have long tails. In most cases these are used only for balancing, though some South American monkeys have prehensile (gripping) tails that they can use like an extra hand. Humans, like their closest relatives the apes, have no tails. ♦

▲ A spectral tarsier eating an insect in northern Sulawesi, Indonesia. Tarsiers live in dense forests on tropical islands to the southeast of Asia. They are much smaller than most primates, rarely weighing more than 150 g (5 oz). They feed almost entirely on insects, which they locate with their huge eyes and ears. Unlike almost all other primates, they are active only at night.

# Prime ministers

The head of government in the United Kingdom and in many other countries is known as the prime minister, or premier, a title which means "chief minister." As a rule, prime ministers are the leaders of their country's strongest political party. They govern with the aid of a group of ministers known as a cabinet.

In the United Kingdom the prime minister is in theory appointed by the sovereign (king or queen), who must accept the prime minister's advice on all political and constitutional matters. In fact, the prime minster is democratically elected.

The first British prime minister was Sir Robert Walpole, who served from 1721 to 1742 under kings George I and George II. He did not use the title "prime minister," which he regarded as a term of abuse. His official title was First Lord of the Treasury, a title still given to British premiers. The name "prime minister" was not made official until 1905.

The world's first woman prime minister was Sirimavo Bandaranaike, who became premier of Sri Lanka in 1960. Britain's first woman prime minister, Margaret Thatcher, took office in 1979. Other female prime ministers have included Pakistan's Benazir Bhutto and Turkey's Tansu Ciller. ♦

# Printing

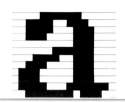

▲ Modern typesetting machines use lasers to set type. This is a letter "a," which has been enlarged to show how it has been made from a series of lines.

▲▼ A small section of the photograph above is enlarged below to show the dots of the halftone.

Printing is a way of making many identical copies from one original. For every page in a magazine, for every stamp, poster, book, cereal box or bus ticket, there is one original. From the original (called camera-ready artwork) a printing plate is made. Hundreds, thousands and in some cases millions of copies can be printed from a printing plate.

## Camera-ready artwork

Nearly all the printed material we see is made up of one or more of the following: type (which may be words or numbers), photographs and artists' illustrations. This page has all three. A bus ticket may have only type, while a stamp usually has type and a photograph or illustration.

Type is mostly set on a computer very similar to a word processor, and all the typefaces and sizes are stored electronically in its memory. Sometimes artists' illustrations and photographs are stored in this way as well. Designers can also use the computer to arrange the type and illustrations on the page. A finished page can be stored electronically and used to produce film from which the printers can make printing plates. Alternatively, the computer can print out just the type on a special paper, and use it together with the illustrations and photographs to make camera-ready artwork.

## Making the printing surface

Before any printing can be done, the words and pictures on the camera-ready artwork have to be transferred to the *plate* (printing surface), which is usually metal. This is done by putting a negative photograph of the original on a printing plate that has been coated with a light-sensitive material, and then exposing it to a bright light. When the coating is removed from the plate, the image of the original remains in those areas where the light has shone through the negative.

Type is solid black, but photographs and illustrations need a range of different tones from black to very light grays. The tones are produced by breaking the picture up into a series of very small dots called a *halftone*. Each dot prints solid black, but little dots with big white spaces between them appear light gray, and big black dots with very little white spaces between them appear almost black.

## Printing

There are two main printing processes used today: lithography and gravure. A third process, letterpress, using a printing surface with a raised image, was for many years the main printing technique, but is now little used.

*Lithography* is the most widely used printing process today. A lithography printing plate does not have a raised image. The image is the whole "picture" of type, illustrations and photographs that is to be printed. The printing image on the plate is greasy and so ink sticks to it, while the non-printing parts are not greasy but wet, and therefore do not get inked. Litho plates are usually made of aluminum, which can be easily wrapped around the plate cylinder. On the printing press, one roller wets the plate and another one inks it. The plate then comes into contact with the blanket cylinder, which is made of rubber. The inked image is offset (transferred) to a blanket cylinder and then onto the paper. Because the printing plate does not come into contact with the paper, the process is frequently called *litho offset*. The offset litho printing press can print on a giant reel of paper (a *web*) at speeds of more than 500 meters (1,640 ft) per minute.

In *gravure* the printing plate has cells (like tiny wells) sunk into its surface. The whole plate is inked and then a metal blade scrapes all the ink off the surface leaving it only in the printing cells. Paper is fed between the printing plate roller and another roller. Making gravure plates is very expensive, so this process is usually used for very long print runs such as magazines, packaging and wallpaper.

## Color Printing

Color pictures are made up of tiny dots of magenta (a bluish red), yellow, cyan (a greenish blue) and black. All other colors can be produced from a combination of these. Four printing plates are needed, each making its impression separately. Black is always the last color printed.

yellow plate

magenta plate

cyan plate

black plate

complete plate

## The Main Printing Processes

### Letterpress

The printing plate has raised letters. (The letter on the plate is a mirror image of the printed letter.)

A roller inks the raised letter.

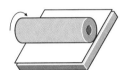

Paper is pressed against the plate.

The ink transfers to the paper to give an image of the letter.

### Gravure

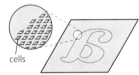

cells

The letter is made up of hundreds of tiny cells, recessed into the plate.

The plate is inked as for letterpress, but the ink covers the whole surface.

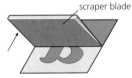

scraper blade

A metal blade scrapes ink off the plate surface, leaving it only in the cells.

The inked letter is transferred to the paper.

### Lithography

The letter image is a thin layer of a greasy material that repels water but attracts printing ink.

A roller spreads a thin layer of water over all the plate except the greasy letters.

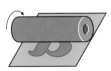

The plate is inked. The ink sticks to the greasy letters, but is repelled by the water on the rest of the plate.

The inked letter is transferred to the paper.

## LOOKING BACK

Printing was known in China, Japan and other parts of Asia many years before it came to be used in Western countries. The first books were made in China by hand-carving characters and designs (back-to-front) onto a flat block of wood, then inking the block and pressing paper or cloth against it. By the 15th century block books and block prints were well known in Europe.

All printing in Europe was done from wooden blocks until about 1450, when Johann Gutenberg of Mainz, Germany, developed movable metal type that could be used again and again. He designed a type mold that would hold any number of individual letters. These letters could be put together to form words and pages, and then reassembled to print different pages. He also adapted a wine press so that he could make many copies of a page quickly by squeezing the inked type and paper together in the press. This is the letterpress form of printing, and it remained the principle used by all printing presses for the next 350 years. Around 1800 the process of lithography was introduced. ◆

The word "lithography" comes from two Greek words: *lithos,* meaning "stone," and *graphia,* meaning "writing."

The earliest printed text that has survived is a Buddhist scroll printed in China and kept in South Korea. The scroll was printed between 704 and 751 A.D.

The earliest surviving printed book is a Buddhist collection of discourses (sermons) called the Diamond Sutra. This was printed in China in 868 A.D.

A "printer's devil" was the name given to a young boy who helped out in a letterpress printing office.

Paper, which proved to be the ideal material for printing, was also invented in China.

▲ Movable type invented by Pi Sheng in China between 1041 and 1048, and a page printed from it.

◄ A modern web offset printing machine.

# Printmaking

The printing press was first used to produce books in Europe about 1450. About 20 years earlier artists had begun to experiment with ways of printing pictures, using the same basic principle. They cut a design into a smooth, flat block of wood, applied ink to it, and then pressed it very hard against a sheet of paper. A picture produced in this way is called a print or engraving, and these earliest prints are known as *woodcuts*. They were often used as illustrations in books.

In the middle of the 15th century another method of printmaking was invented, called line engraving, or *engraving* for short. In this method the print was made from a metal (usually copper) plate. It was much harder to cut a design in metal than in wood, but artists could use finer lines and create more detailed effects in metal.

Since these early days many other techniques of printmaking have been invented. One of the most popular is *etching*. In etching, the copper plate is first covered with a thin layer of wax. The artist draws in the wax with an etching "needle," which is much easier than pushing a gouge through metal. When the design is finished, the artist places the copper plate in a "bath" of acid. The acid has no effect on the wax, but in the places where the needle has scratched it away it eats into the metal. This transfers the artist's design to the plate, which can then be inked and printed in the normal way. The great attraction of etching is that the artist can draw fluently on the wax, so it can produce more subtle and personal effects than earlier techniques. The Dutch artist Rembrandt was a great etcher.

Color prints are made by using several blocks or plates—one for each color. Color woodcuts

▶ Japanese artists were masters of color wood-block printmaking. This print—*Watanabe Meets the Beautiful No Tsuna on the Bridge*—is by Ando Hiroshige (1797–1858).

have played a particularly important part in the art of Japan, where they were immensely popular from the 17th century until the 19th century.

One of the most recent printmaking techniques is silkscreen printing. In this method the artist cuts a design in a stencil and places this on top of a fine silk mesh. The artist then squeezes color through the parts of the screen that are not covered by the stencil onto a sheet of paper below. A simpler modern technique is linocut, which uses a sheet of thick linoleum. This is much easier to cut than wood or metal and it is popular for teaching art in schools. You can even make a very simple type of print using a potato sliced in half as the printing "block." ◆

▶ Making a silk screen print. In the first photograph, the printmaker is using a wooden bar with a rubber edge to press ink through the stencil and the silk screen onto the paper below. The second photograph shows the results. Prints with a second color added can be seen drying in the background.

# Prisons

If a person commits a crime, he or she may be locked up in prison. The length of a prison sentence depends on how serious the crime was. Prisons have four purposes: to punish people for wrongdoing; to reform criminals; to protect the public from people who are a danger; and to deter other people from committing crimes.

## Types of prisons

In the U.S. and Western Europe, separate prisons are usually provided for male and female prisoners. Closed prisons are surrounded by high walls, and are for dangerous criminals or those convicted of serious offenses. In closed prisons most prisoners must share a cell with one or two other people. Certain prisons are for prisoners who are also certified as insane.

Prisoners who can be trusted may be allowed to serve all or part of their sentences in an open prison, where they do not live in cells. Detention centers are for young people sentenced to a period of youth custody.

## Life in prison

Convicted prisoners must wear special prison clothes. They are allowed only a few personal possessions. They have very few rights, but are allowed to leave their cells for exercise each day. In practice they may spend about eight hours a day in the prison workshops, gardens, kitchens and laundries. The number of visitors they can have and letters they can send are restricted by prison regulations.

Well-behaved prisoners are generally allowed a number of privileges, such as using the prison library or receiving books from friends outside.

In open prisons the prisoners do farming and other outdoor work. Sometimes they are allowed to work outside the prison and are known as "trusties."

Prison is considered to be a place where wrongdoers are reformed as well as punished, so some prisoners have the chance to receive training in various trades.

## Length of sentences

In practice most prisoners do not serve the full term for which they are sentenced. If they are well behaved, they may be allowed out on parole after serving only one-third of the sentence. About half of all prisoners get parole. If they misbehave while out on parole, they may be called back to serve the rest of their sentence.

Some countries are now using other forms of punishment to keep people out of prison, especially those convicted of minor offenses. Often a prison sentence may be suspended, and if the convicted person behaves during a certain period he or she will not have to "go inside." Many people have to perform a set number of hours of community service as a punishment, which will take up their spare time but allow them to keep their jobs. ◆

In the U.S. ordinary prisons can be called prisons, penal institutions or penitentiaries. The term "jail," which is used in the U.K. as just another word for any prison, means a prison for lesser offenses in the U.S.

Until the 1830s minor offenses in the U.S. and England were punished by setting people in a pillory, or stocks, where any passers-by could laugh at them and even throw things at them.

Political prisoners are people who are held in custody because of their political beliefs, not because they have committed any crimes. Such prisoners are often held in prison camps, with armed guards. Prison camps are used, too, for prisoners of war (servicemen or women captured during fighting).

◀ Alcatraz, an island in San Francisco Bay, off the California coast, was the site of a U.S. military prison from 1863 until 1933, when it became a federal penitentiary, shown here. For 30 years, some of the country's most dangerous prisoners were sent to Alcatraz because it was nearly impossible for them to escape. The prison closed in 1963, and today the island is part of the Golden Gate National Recreation Area.

▼ See also
Law and legal systems

# Probability

If there are 23 people in a class, the probability that they all have different birthdays is only 0.4927, so it is more likely than not that two of them have the same birthday.

The chance of throwing 10 heads in a row is 1 in 1,024. The chance of throwing 20 in a row is less than 1 in a million.

**▼ See also**
Averages
Decimals
Fractions
Gambling
Percentages

A probability is a number that gives a more precise estimate of how certain you are about something. Probabilities are given numbers between 0 and 1, where 0 means impossible and 1 means certain. So the nearer the number is to 1, the more likely you think something is to happen.

If you toss a coin, there are two ways it can come down, so the probability of its being a head is one-half (written as $\frac{1}{2}$ or 0.5). People say that the chances of throwing a head are "one in two" or "fifty-fifty." Even if you throw 10 heads in a row, the probability of the next throw being a head is still $\frac{1}{2}$. If you throw a single dice (a die), there are six ways it can land, so the probability of throwing the number you want is $\frac{1}{6}$.

Probabilities can also be given as percentages. If the weather forecast says there is a 25 percent chance of rain, this is the same as saying that the probability of rain is $\frac{1}{4}$.

Probability is also used to tell us the likelihood of several things happening one after the other. ◆

The probability of getting two heads when you toss two coins is $\frac{1}{4}$. The reason for this is that there are four different ways that the coins can land: two heads; a head on the first and a tail on the second; a tail on the first and a head on the second; two tails. These four ways are often written as {HH, HT, TH, TT}. Each of these is equally likely, so the chance of two heads is one in four or $\frac{1}{4}$.

# Prohibition

One of the leading anti-drinking organizations in the U.S. was the Women's Christian Temperance Union, founded in 1874.

Opposition to Prohibition increased markedly after the Great Depression began in 1929; this was because taxes on legal sales of alcohol were potentially a major source of income for the government.

**▼ See also**
Alcohol
Constitution, U.S.
Depression, Great
United States of America

The name "Prohibition" was given to the period in the U.S. between 1920 and 1933, when the manufacture and sale of alcoholic beverages were prohibited (banned) by an amendment to the Constitution. This was the result of a movement that dated back to the early 19th century, when Americans had begun consuming huge quantities of wine, beer and whiskey. This was believed to be responsible not only for many health disorders but also for an increase in poverty and crime.

After the Civil War, religious leaders and women's groups began forming so-called temperance organizations, which got local laws passed to regulate alcoholic beverages. Some worked successfully for the passage of a constitutional amendment to ban all such beverages. This "Prohibition" amendment—the 18th—went into effect in 1920.

During Prohibition, alcoholic consumption did decrease, but other problems were created. Smugglers called "bootleggers," who were usually associated with criminal gangs, secretly brought alcoholic beverages into the U.S. and sold them, and they fought violently for control of this illegal business. Many people also made alcohol secretly at home, creating beverages that were often unsafe.

Opposition to Prohibition grew. Finally, in February 1933, a new amendment—the 21st—to the Constitution was proposed to repeal (end) the 18th. After its approval by the required majority of states, the 21st Amendment went into effect on December 5, 1933, ending Prohibition. ◆

One of the most notorious bootleggers was gangster Al Capone (1899–1947), whose headquarters were in Chicago. Capone and his gang were responsible for the infamous St. Valentine's Day Massacre in February 1929, during which seven members of a rival gang were gunned down. For his many crimes Capone was hunted down by legendary federal agent Eliot Ness, but he was convicted only for not paying income taxes and served just a few years in prison. However, Ness's fight against criminal gangs during the 1920s and 1930s made him a legendary hero, and inspired both a famous TV series and a prize-winning movie, The Untouchables.

# Prophets

Many people believe that God has chosen certain men and women to proclaim a message. These people are called prophets.

Some of the most famous prophets are those whose stories are told in the Old Testament of the Bible.

Christians believe that all the Old Testament prophets as well as John the Baptist prepared the way for Jesus. Jesus is like a prophet, but to Christians he is more than that: he is the son of God. Muslims accept all the biblical prophets and Jesus. They believe that Muhammad is the greatest of God's prophets. ◆

**▼ See also**
Bahaism
Bible
Christianity
Islam
Judaism
Koran

**BIOGRAPHY**
John the Baptist
Moses
Muhammad

# Proteins

Protein structure is determined by genes. Each gene controls the manufacture of a separate protein.

Animal proteins, such as meat and fish, have all the essential amino acids, but individual vegetables do not. Vegetarians need to eat a mixture of vegetable proteins, such as grain and beans, to get all the essential amino acids.

A single protein molecule of average size contains about 500 amino acids linked together in a long chain.

Proteins are among the most important substances that make up living things. Proteins can carry out almost any task that a living cell requires. Structural proteins are the "building blocks" that cells use to make their different parts.

Enzymes are proteins that enable all the chemical reactions of the body to occur quickly and efficiently. Digestive enzymes, for instance, break down food into smaller parts so that it can be absorbed quickly from the gut. Other enzymes in plant cells enable photosynthesis to occur. Some proteins are hormones. These are chemical messengers that are passed around the body, usually in the blood, to help control the body's functions.

Proteins are large complicated molecules built out of smaller units called amino acids. Plants make their own amino acids. Animals cannot do this. For health the human body needs 20 amino acids. Twelve of these can be made by the body. The other eight must be present in the diet and these are called the "essential" amino acids. Animal or plant proteins in food are broken down to their amino acids in the digestive tract. Once absorbed, these amino acids can be built into new proteins.

The different functions of proteins depend on their shapes and the types of amino acids they are made of. With about 20 different types of amino acids, the number of different combinations that can make up a protein is enormous. The amino acids are strung together in long chains that are folded into complex shapes. ◆

**Good Sources of Protein**
Soybean flour 40%
Peanuts 28%
Cheddar cheese 25%
Raw meat 23%
Raw fish 15%
Eggs 12%
Bread 8%
Rice 6%

▼ **See also**
Cells
Diets
DNA
Enzymes
Genetics
Hormones
Molecules

# Protestant Christianity

**Major Protestant Denominations in the U.S.**
Baptist Church
Christian Science
Church of Christ (Disciples)
Church of Jesus Christ of Latter-day Saints (Mormons)
Episcopal Church
Jehovah's Witnesses
Lutheran Church
Methodist Church
Pentecostal Church
Presbyterian Church
Society of Friends (Quakers)
United Church of Christ

At the time of the Reformation in the 16th century, some Christians began to protest against the authority and teaching of the Catholic Church.

These Christians objected to the power of the pope, the wealth of bishops and monasteries, and the custom of selling indulgences (pieces of paper saying that your sins were forgiven). Because of these protests, Luther, Calvin, Zwingli and their followers were called "Protestants."

The Protestants said that each individual Christian should try to read the Bible for him or herself. This was possible only when the Bible was translated from Latin into the ordinary language of the people, and when plenty of copies were printed. Reading the Bible for themselves meant that Protestants could rely on their own conscience to interpret it, rather than on what the priests told them.

Protestants also changed the way in which Jesus' last supper with his disciples was remembered. Instead of a priest saying the mass in Latin, the service was spoken in the language of the people. Christians now gathered for a memorial meal around a table in a plain church where they were treated as equal members of a family served by a minister.

In time the Reformed and Non-conformist churches developed from these movements. They include the Lutherans, especially in Germany, Calvinists in Switzerland and Scotland, and Anglicans (Church of England) and the Anglican Communion Overseas which includes the Episcopal Church in the U.S.

Some Protestants are named after their ideas. For example, those served by presbyters (ministers) are Presbyterians; those organized as separate congregations are Congregationalists. Baptists believe that they should wait until they are adults to be baptized. The Methodist Church developed in the 18th century on the basis of John Wesley's teachings. ◆

There were Christians who criticized the Catholic Church long before the Reformation. In England in the 14th century, John Wyclif wanted people to read the Bible and so he arranged for it to be translated from Latin into English.

▼ **See also**
Amish
Bible
Catholicism, Roman
Christianity
Christian Science
Church of England
Mormonism
Quakers
Reformation
Shakers

**BIOGRAPHY**
Calvin, John
Luther, Martin
Wesley, John and Charles
Wyclif, John

**See also**
Bible
Literature

**BIOGRAPHY**
Confucius
Franklin, Benjamin
Solomon

## Collecting and Creating Proverbs and Sayings

In the novel *Don Quixote*, by 17th-century Spanish writer Miguel de Cervantes, the character Sancho Panza utters many proverbs. One of the best-known is "He went for wool and came back shorn." What do you think this means? Can you think up a new proverb that says the same thing?

Choose a saying quoted in this article. Try to write a new proverb that expresses the same meaning.

Try to remember sayings you have heard from older relatives, including your parents, aunts and uncles, and grandparents. Write them down, and then try to re-create them in your own words.

# Proverbs and sayings

Proverbs and sayings offer wisdom and advice in short sentences that are easy to remember. Both words are usually used interchangeably to mean the same thing; they are also called *maxims* or *adages*. They often use rhyme, as in "Haste makes waste." Sometimes they use contrast, as in "Waste not, want not."

## Ancient proverbs

Some of the earliest proverbs come from ancient Mesopotamia, where highly developed societies existed as early as 4000 B.C. Here is an example of a Mesopotamian proverb: "Do not strike the face of a walking ox with a strap." Many modern versions of this proverb exist, such as "Leave well enough alone" and "If it ain't broke, don't fix it."

One of the oldest collections of proverbs in the Western world is the Book of Proverbs in the Bible. It contains hundreds of sayings that are believed to have come from King Solomon, who ruled over Israel about 1000 B.C. The Book of Proverbs offers rules for the conduct of government and advice on personal conduct; it also offers observations on human behavior, such as "A fool's mouth is his own destruction."

Solomon's counterpart in the Far East was Confucius, a Chinese philosopher who lived about 500 B.C. His sayings are as famous as those of Solomon, and they have been studied for thousands of years. One of the best-known

Confucian proverbs is "The cautious seldom err."

Many proverbs and sayings originated in Africa. Nearly every African culture has a large number of proverbs that have been passed orally from generation to generation. A knowledge of these proverbs was often essential. In the Asante kingdom, for example, anyone who wished to occupy a high government post had to be familiar with such Asante proverbs as "One who follows the track of the elephant never gets wet from the dew on the bushes"—which means that by gaining the protection of an important person, one can be shielded from harm. Many Asante citizens could recite hundreds of such proverbs.

## Proverbs in literature

In Europe and North America, proverbs are a part of every nation's literature, from ancient Greece to the present day. Chaucer's *Canterbury Tales*, written in the 14th century, includes such sayings as "The greatest scholar is not the wisest man." A number of famous sayings—including "All the world's a stage" and "All's well that ends well"—are from the plays of William Shakespeare.

In American literature, the best-known source of proverbs is Benjamin Franklin's *Poor Richard's Almanack*, published in the 18th century. Franklin is the source of many familiar sayings, such as "God helps those who help themselves" and "Early to bed and early to rise makes a man healthy, wealthy and wise." ◆

## Some Familiar Proverbs and Sayings

Here are some common proverbs and sayings that are familiar to Americans. A translation of their meaning is given in parentheses. Most of these are so old that no one knows who wrote or spoke them first.

• Actions speak louder than words. (*What someone does is often more important than what he or she says.*)
• Don't cry over spilt milk. (*Don't waste time being unhappy over something that has already happened.*)
• A friend in need is a friend indeed. (*People find out who their real friends are when they most need help.*)
• Two heads are better than one. (*It's easier to solve a problem if you have help.*)
• Don't look a gift horse in the mouth. (*If you get something for nothing, don't complain about it.* [This proverb is based on the custom of determining a horse's worth by looking at its teeth to discover its age.])
• Don't count your chickens before they hatch. (*Don't plan on something that hasn't happened yet.*)
• Make hay while the sun shines. (*Do something when you have the chance—don't put it off until later.*)
• Don't lock the barn door after the horse has been stolen. (*It's silly to try to prevent something from happening after the damage has been done.*)
• *Quien mal anda, mal acaba.* (*Spanish proverb meaning "A person who does bad things will come to a bad end."*)

# Psychologists

**See also**
Mental illness

Psychologists are people who study other human beings in order to understand them better. They work in a wide variety of settings, where people's needs are different.

Educational psychologists help children in school who are having trouble with their work or their behavior. Occupational psychologists help people find the right job for their type of personality. Clinical

psychologists help people with personal problems such as shyness or lack of confidence and with mental illnesses. In every case, the psychologist is concerned to help people understand themselves better. Psychologists use different types of treatment. They usually talk with patients until they have the confidence to say what is really on their minds. People who consult a psychologist may discover how they sometimes go wrong and how to make their lives better. ◆

# Puberty

**See also**
Adolescence
Hormones
Human body
Menstruation
Pregnancy
Reproduction
Sex and sexuality

Puberty is the time, usually occurring in the early teens, when the bodies of girls and boys change so that they are capable of producing a baby. Along with the physical changes at this time, mental and emotional alterations are happening, too. Adolescence includes all these changes.

During puberty, first girls, then about a year later boys, go through a growth "spurt." For a few years they grow very rapidly. At the end of puberty, which usually occurs between the ages of 16 and 20, they will have grown as tall as they ever will.

With the increase in height go other body changes that turn young teenagers into young adults. In girls, the breasts develop, periods (menstruation) begin and pubic hair grows.

A girl's body becomes more curved and her waist usually narrows. Her voice also becomes less childlike. In boys, puberty causes the voice to deepen ("break") and hair to grow on the face, above the penis and elsewhere on the body. The penis and testicles enlarge.

All these complicated changes, involving so many parts of the body, are started and controlled by hormones, the chemical messengers of the body. Changing amounts of sex hormones start the alterations of puberty. In girls a changing monthly pattern of these hormones controls the cycle of changes that bring about periods. Periods are necessary to make sure that for a few days in each month there is a fertilizable egg inside the girl's body and that, if it is fertilized and she becomes pregnant, the womb is ready for the embryo to attach to it. ◆

# Puerto Rico

**Area** 9,085 sq km (3,508 sq mi)
**Capital** San Juan
**Population** 3,819,000
**Acquired by U.S.** 1898

**See also**
Caribbean
Spanish-American War
United States of America

**BIOGRAPHY**
Muñoz Marin, Luis

▼ The historic fortress of El Morro, in San Juan, built by the Spanish in 1584.

The island of Puerto Rico, located in the Caribbean, is a self-governing commonwealth in association with the United States. It has belonged to the U.S. since 1898, when it became a possession under the terms of the treaty ending the Spanish-American War.

Prior to that time, the island had been claimed by Spain for nearly 400 years. The first European to visit Puerto Rico was Christopher Columbus, in 1493. In the early 1500s, the Spanish explorer Ponce de Leon claimed the island and its native Arawaks for his nation and named it Puerto Rico, which means "rich port" in Spanish. San Juan, the first Spanish settlement, was founded in 1521.

The Spanish established sugar plantations on the island and brought in African slaves to work on them. Coffee was introduced as an agricultural crop in the 18th century and also used slave labor. Slavery was not abolished on the island until 1873.

In the years following the U.S. acquisition of Puerto Rico in 1898, Puerto Ricans began to campaign for self-rule. In 1917 the U.S. granted Puerto Rico the status of a U.S. Territory and made all of its residents U.S. citizens. After World War II ended in 1945, island residents demanded an even greater voice in their own affairs, and in 1948 they elected their first governor, Luis Muñoz Marin. Four years later, the Commonwealth of Puerto Rico was established.

Puerto Rico's status as a commonwealth gives

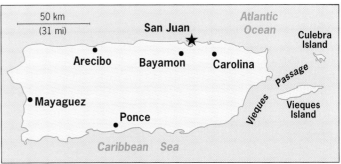

the island no representation in the U.S. Congress, but it does exempt its residents from paying federal income tax. Many Puerto Ricans continue to demand total independence from the U.S., while others call for the admission of Puerto Rico to the Union as the 51st state.

Puerto Rico's climate is tropical, and hurricanes often occur. The island's topography consists of coastal plains and several mountain ranges, including the Cordillera Central. Puerto Rico has fertile farmland and rain forests.

Puerto Ricans work mainly in commerce, finance, communications, manufacturing and the tourist industry. Textiles, electronic equipment and plastics are major industries. There are also oil refineries and chemical plants on the island. Farmers continue to grow sugarcane and coffee as well as tobacco. ◆

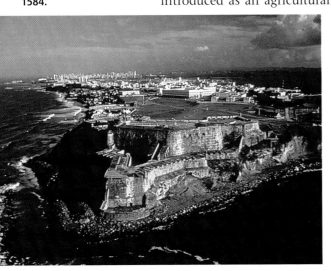

# Pulitzer Prize

**▼ See also**
Nobel Prize

Winning a Pulitzer Prize is one of the greatest honors that an American can receive, and many of the nation's best-known journalists, writers and composers have been recipients of the prize.

Pulitzer Prizes are awards given each year for achievements in American journalism, literature, drama and music. Joseph Pulitzer (1847–1911), a newspaper publisher who founded the *St. Louis Post-Dispatch*, established the prizes in his will.

As part of Pulitzer's $2 million gift to Columbia University in New York City for the creation of a school of journalism, he provided a fund for the prizes. He stipulated that the awards would be made annually by the school, three years after its founding.

Pulitzer Prizes have been awarded each May since 1917 on the recommendation of an advisory board consisting of journalists, the president of the university, and a faculty member of the Columbia School of Journalism who serves as board secretary. Prizes of $3,000 are awarded in various categories of journalism, as well as fiction, drama, American history, biography, poetry, and music composition. ◆

Several noted American writers have won both the Pulitzer Prize for fiction and the Nobel Prize in Literature. They include Sinclair Lewis (Pulitzer 1926, Nobel 1930); Pearl Buck (Pulitzer 1932, Nobel 1938); John Steinbeck (Pulitzer 1940, Nobel 1962); Ernest Hemingway (Pulitzer 1953, Nobel 1954); William Faulkner (Pulitzer 1955 and 1963, Nobel 1949); Saul Bellow (Pulitzer 1976, Nobel 1976); and Toni Morrison (Pulitzer 1988, Nobel 1993).

# Pulleys

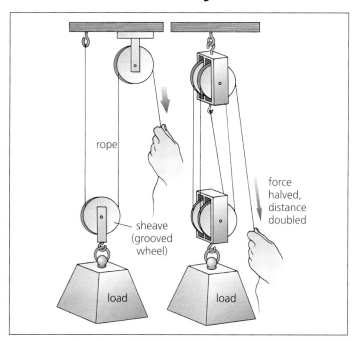

rope

sheave (grooved wheel)

load

force halved, distance doubled

load

▲ **Adding more wheels to a pulley system makes it easier to lift the load. In the system on the right the distance that the rope is pulled is doubled, but the force required to lift the load is halved.**

It is much easier to pull down than it is to lift up. So if you have a heavy load to lift, you can make the job easier by attaching a strong rope to it and passing it over a fixed point. When you pull down on the end of the rope, the load goes up. This is a simple pulley. Putting the rope over a sheave (a grooved wheel) reduces the friction in the pulley, and the job becomes even easier as the sheave turns smoothly on its axle.

You can make the load even easier to lift by putting more sheaves into the pulley system. Putting a greater length of rope in the system means the load moves a shorter distance, the distance pulled increases, but the force raising the load is greater.

Double, or even triple, sheaves are put into a pulley system called a block and tackle. A lock keeps the load from slipping back. Pulleys can be used wherever we need to lift heavy loads—farms, factories, mills and garages. Elevators are also worked by pulleys; an elevator works like a bucket in a well. ◆

Using a block-and-tackle system, one person can lift a car engine.

Disabled people find pulleys very valuable; with very little effort, they can sit up in bed, get out of chairs, or sit down in the bath.

**▼ See also**
Elevators
Levers
Machines

## Making Your Own Pulley

Try making a pulley system like the one in the picture. You will need some wire from an old coat hanger, two empty thread spools, two pencils and an empty soap-powder box. Make sure you put something heavy in the box to keep it from falling over.

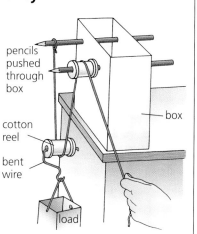

pencils pushed through box

box

cotton reel

bent wire

load

# Pulsars

The fastest pulsars spin several hundred times a second, making one flash each turn.

Pulsars are stars that send out radio signals as a series of quick, short bleeps. They are the remains of ordinary stars that reach the ends of their lives and explode. Pulsars were discovered in 1967 by radio astronomers at Cambridge University in England.

The time between the bleeps is different from one pulsar to another; it ranges from a few seconds to a small fraction of a second. A pulsar acts something like a lighthouse. It is a spinning star sending out two beams into space in opposite directions. Radio astronomers can catch the beams as they sweep past their telescopes.

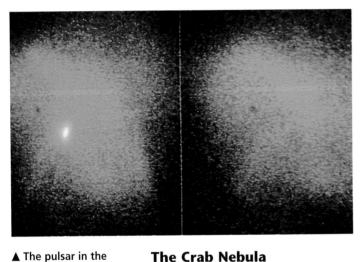

▲ The pulsar in the middle of the Crab Nebula. It is flashing in the left-hand picture and "off" in the right-hand picture.

## The Crab Nebula

The most famous pulsar is in the middle of the Crab Nebula, a patch of glowing gas in the constellation Taurus. Chinese observers saw a star explode at this point in the sky in the year 1054. Exploding stars of this sort are called *supernovas*. (A *nova* is a star that suddenly increases its output of light briefly and then fades.)

The Crab pulsar sends out 30 bleeps every second. Light and X-rays are also emitted by the star at the same speed. ◆

▼ **See also**
Astronomers
Constellations
Nebulas
Stars
Telescopes

# Pulse

When the heart beats, it pumps blood round the blood vessels of the body. The strongest part of the beat is the contraction of the portion of the heart called the left ventricle. It is the largest and most muscular part of the heart. When it contracts, it pushes blood out through all of the arteries of the body except those to the lungs. If you feel an artery where it comes close to the skin surface, you can feel the repeated surges of blood caused by these contractions. This is your pulse.

It is most easily felt on the underside of the wrist or at the sides of your neck. If a nurse or a doctor measures your pulse rate (the number of beats per minute), they can tell how fast your heart is beating and how strongly. A normal rate in an adult would be somewhere around 70–80 beats per minute. Women's pulse rates are usually slightly higher than men's. In a child the rate is faster. A newborn baby's pulse rate can be as high as 140 beats per minute. Measuring the pulse rate can help check someone's health. In many infections the rate goes up, in other conditions it may go down. ◆

Exercise increases the pulse rate, as the body needs more oxygen, so the heart beats faster.

▼ **See also**
Blood
Hearts
Human body

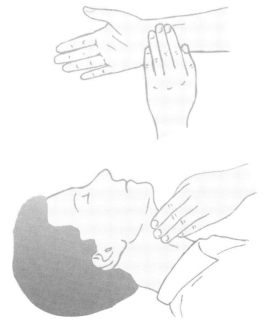

◄ **Two ways to measure a pulse: on the inside of the wrist (top), or at the side of the neck.**

# Pumas

▲ The puma is the biggest member of the cat family found in North America. It feeds on anything from mice to adult deer.

The puma is sometimes called the cougar or the mountain lion. Although it may be as big as a leopard or jaguar, it is more closely related to the small cats.

Pumas live alone. They do not have fixed dens, but travel through their territories, which are usually over 30 square kilometers (11.6 sq mi). They have very good eyesight and hearing, but their sense of smell is poor. They have very powerful hind legs, and it is said that they can leap upward more than 5 meters (16 ft).

Pumas catch beavers, porcupines or hares, but their main prey is deer, usually sick or old animals. They make about one kill a week, and drag the carcass to a safe place to be eaten over several days.

At one time pumas lived in more habitats in North and South America than any other animal. So long as there was cover and prey, they were found in forests and swamps, deserts, mountains and plains. But, as with many flesh-eating creatures, they have been hunted to extinction in many of these places, and now live mainly in remote areas where there are few humans. ◆

**Distribution**
South and Central America, and in North America mostly in the mountains of the west.
**Size**
Head and body length up to 195 cm (76 in); tail length 78 cm (30 in)
**Weight**
Up to 100 kg (220 lbs)
**Number of young**
Usually 3 or 4, generally born late winter or early spring. Suckled for 3 months, but remain with their mother for at least a year.
**Lifespan**
In captivity, over 19 years
**Subphylum** Vertebrata
**Class** Mammalia
**Order** Carnivora
**Family** Felidae (cat family)
**Number of species** 1

▼ **See also**
Cats
Cheetahs
Jaguars
Leopards
Lions
Tigers

# Pumps

In the 3rd century B.C., Ctesibius, a Greek inventor, made the first known reciprocating pump for pumping water.

▼ **See also**
Hearts
Heating systems
Irrigation
Refrigerators
Valves

Pumps are devices for moving liquids and gases. They can put air in your bicycle tires, squirt water on car windshields and pump up inflatable boats. They push water around central heating systems and refrigerant around the pipes in a refrigerator. Your heart is a pump, pushing blood around your body and through your lungs.

Some pumps work with a back-and-forth movement. They are called reciprocating pumps. A bicycle pump works like this. When you pull the handle out, the inlet valve opens and allows air to be drawn into the barrel. When you push the handle in, air pressure closes the inlet valve and air is forced into the tire. A valve in the tire lets the air in but keeps it from getting out again. All reciprocating pumps need two valves, an inlet valve and an outlet valve. In a bicycle pump, the outlet valve stays in the tire.

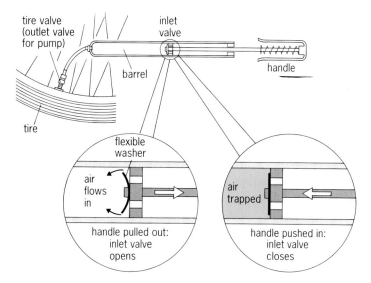

Some pumps have a paddle wheel in them, called an impeller, which spins around. They are rotary pumps. Often, they are driven by electric motors. A central heating pump is like this. An impeller draws in water near the middle and flings it outward so that it is forced out of the pump. ◆

▲ In a bicycle pump, the barrel fills with air when the handle is pulled out. Air is pushed into the tire when the handle is pushed in.

# Pupae

A pupa is an insect in the process of changing from a larva to an adult, as a caterpillar changes

▶ Honeybee pupae shown at various stages of development.

▼ **See also**

Insects
Larvae
Metamorphosis

to a butterfly or a grub turns into a beetle. The word comes from the Latin word for a doll, for the pupae of some moths look a bit like crude wooden dolls. Pupae are helpless and can hardly move to escape from enemies; they are usually protected by a tough skin. Many insect larvae, when they are full-grown, look for a place to hide in order to pupate. Some burrow underground, or creep beneath the bark of a tree. Some moth caterpillars spin a silk cocoon to keep the pupa warm and safe.

Because the pupa does not move much, it used to be thought that it was resting, but this is far from true. Inside the pupa case, great changes occur. To begin with, almost all of the cells of the body of the larva separate, so it is no longer possible to see its legs or its breathing tubes. There is a small group of cells that are not affected by this general breakdown of the body. These act as the center for rebuilding the cells into the body of the adult insect. The changes that go on inside the pupa can be compared to knocking down one building and reusing all of the bricks and other parts to make a new and different building.

When the changes are complete, the adult insect pushes its way out of the pupa. Its wings take a little time to expand, but once this has happened the adult insect is ready to start on the last part of its life. This involves finding a mate and breeding before dying. ◆

# Puppets

▶ A Javanese puppeteer holds a shadow puppet on a wooden stick. Shadow puppets are often intricately cut out, in order to make interesting shadows.

Puppets are a kind of doll made to represent humans or animals in drama. They need someone to manipulate them either with the fingers or by using strings or rods. They can then mime the actions of a play and express emotions. Today puppets are used for advertising and education as well as for entertainment.

Puppets can range in size from tiny finger puppets to huge figures larger than people. There are many different types of puppet, but the four most common are glove puppets, rod puppets, shadow puppets and marionettes. Glove puppets fit on the hand, and are worked by the fingers. Rod puppets are moved by rods attached to the limbs. Shadow puppets are also often worked by rods, but they are flat, and a light behind the puppets casts their shadows onto a screen. Marionettes, or string puppets, are operated from above by strings fastened to different parts of the puppet.

▼ **See also**

Mime
Sewing

For centuries puppets have been used to enact folk stories and scenes from religious books. In medieval Europe puppets enacted stories from the Bible and from famous battles and scenes from history. There are puppet theaters today in the countries of Eastern Europe, all with elaborate costumes, staging and music.

In India there is a long and living tradition of puppet plays dramatizing scenes from the *Ramayana*, a great epic story. Puppeteers travel around the towns and villages and set up their stage. The show might last for several nights in a row as one episode leads on to another. In Japan a revolving stage was developed for the puppet theater in the 17th century and puppets became very elaborate.

### Punch and Judy

*Punch and Judy* is the best-known puppet play in Britain. The story is simple. Punch strangles his baby, Judy beats him with a club, and then he takes the club and beats her to death. A policeman puts Punch in prison, and then the hangman tries to hang him. Punch pretends not to know how to put his head in the noose and gets the hangman to show him. As soon as he does that, Punch hangs him. Sometimes there is a crocodile in the story, which eats Punch, and sometimes Punch steals a string of sausages as well.

The puppets are hand (also called glove) puppets, and they are operated by one person, who stands hidden in the booth. Punch has an odd strangulated voice. The operator produces this with the help of a "swozzle," a little instrument held in the mouth.

The story of Punch is so old that no one can be sure when it first appeared. Probably Punch started in Italian *commedia dell'arte*, a kind of acting using masks and mime. A puppet called Pulcinella copied the character of the living actor. When the puppet came to England, the name changed to Punch. ◆

▼ Jim Henson and his team of puppeteers hold the Muppets high above their heads and manipulate the movements with their hands.

---

### Making a Glove Puppet

A glove puppet is one of the easiest types of puppet to make. You can make this one from a small piece of felt or other material, plus some odds and ends for decoration.

**What you need**
*a piece of felt 40 cm by 25 cm (15 in x 10 in), a needle and thread, and sequins, embroidery thread or other items for decoration*

**1.** Fold the material across so that it is double. Draw a mitten shape with two arms. To do this keep your fingers closed and draw around your hand, but not too close to it.

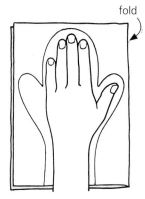

**2.** Pin the material together around the shape you have drawn. Tack along the line with big stitches, then sew with small running stitches. Cut out the shape as shown above.

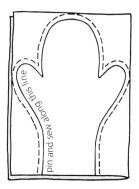

**3.** Turn the puppet inside out, so that the stitches do not show. Now you can decorate it, either by sewing or gluing decorations on, or with a felt pen.

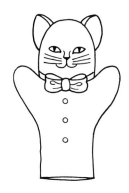

# Puritans

Puritans were English Protestants who wanted to "purify" the Church of England, and make it less like the Catholic Church. They did not want the English Church to have powerful bishops; some did not want it to have bishops at all. They wanted church services to be simple and plain. They believed everyone should rely on the Bible, so they wanted more sermons to teach the Scriptures. They wanted churches to look plainer, too, without crosses, candles, pictures and statues.

Some Puritans believed that they should practice their religion by living very simply. They wore plain, dark clothes, worked hard, and disapproved of pleasures like dancing and theater-going. Puritans got their nickname in Elizabeth I's reign (1558–1603). The queen refused to listen to them because she did not want any changes in the Church of England, of which she was head.

Under James I and Charles I, important Puritans in Parliament feared (wrongly) that Catholics were a real threat to the whole country as well as to the Church. They became known as "Roundheads" during the English Civil War because of their short, plain hairstyles. Others left England and settled elsewhere. The Pilgrims were Puritans who came to America by way of the Netherlands. ◆

**See also**
Catholicism, Roman Christianity
Church of England
England
Pilgrims
Protestant Christianity
Reformation
United States of America

**BIOGRAPHY**
Bunyan, John
Charles I
Cromwell, Oliver
Elizabeth I
Milton, John

# Pygmies

The Twa people of Rwanda and Burundi grow to about 1.2 m (3.9 ft) tall.

The pygmies who live in the hot forests of central Africa are small people, less than 1.5 m (4.9 ft) in height. They are found in parts of Burundi, Cameroon, Congo, Gabon, and Rwanda. There are about 150,000 pygmies.

Pygmies live in bands of up to 100 people. They get their food by hunting animals with bows and arrows and nets, and gathering plant foods, such as berries and nuts. They regard honey as a delicacy. When they find some, they often have a celebration.

Pygmies live in camps, which they occupy for only a few weeks before moving to a new site. Their homes are made of frames of branches covered by leaves. In the camps, adults make arrows, baskets and cloth from tree bark, boys learn hunting skills, and girls work with their mothers. Many of them are skilled potters. Pygmies enjoy singing, dancing and telling stories that show their love for the forest, which they call "mother and father." The forest supplies nearly all of their needs, and they try not to harm it.

Long ago, pygmies probably lived throughout central Africa, but farmers have taken most of their land. Their life is changing. Some pygmies have left the forests and some children are now attending school. ◆

◀ Pygmy families often live together sharing their responsibilities. Behind the woman preparing a meal, the man holding a spear is not much taller than his children.

**See also**
Hunter-gatherers

▼ See also
Aztecs
Egypt
Egyptian mythology
Maya
Mummies
Seven Wonders of the
   World
BIOGRAPHY
Tutankhamen

**Egyptian Tombs**

Later on, instead of pyramids, the Egyptians decided to use tombs cut into the rock as royal burial places. The Valley of the Kings at Thebes has many royal tombs. Although many of these were attacked by robbers, some remained hidden until modern times. The most famous was that of Tutankhamen, a boy king who died in 1352 B.C. His tomb, with many precious objects, was discovered by the English archaeologist Howard Carter in 1922.

# Pyramids

The pharaohs (kings) and other important people of ancient Egypt were buried in fine tombs from the earliest times. At first, mud-brick (later stone) tombs called *mastabas* were built for the dead person to be buried in. About 2686 B.C. a new type of tomb was built for the Pharaoh Zoser at Saqqara. His pyramid-shaped tomb is called a "step pyramid" because it was built as a series of steps or platforms.

Later, the Egyptian builders and engineers worked out how to construct a smooth-sided pyramid of enormous height. The pyramid had to contain a place for the actual burial. This was reached by a long passage carefully blocked and hidden from tomb robbers.

Gangs of workers were sent to build the pyramids. Each gang had about 20 people in it, and hundreds of gangs worked on each pyramid.

Pyramids were built close to the River Nile. The stone blocks could

then be brought to the site by boat and moved on sledges. Later the body of the pharaoh also arrived by boat. The pyramid was surrounded by a wall that had a temple and storage places inside. A causeway led to the river, where an elaborate temple-shaped landing stage was built to receive the dead pharaoh. ◆

▲ The Great Pyramid at Giza near Cairo was built for the pharaoh Khufu, who is also known as Cheops. He reigned about 2570 BC. It was constructed of 2,300,000 blocks of limestone by a workforce of as many as 100,000.

▼ Although we normally think that pyramids are Egyptian, other peoples built these huge pointed monuments, too. The most famous outside Egypt are the ones built to honor the Sun and the Moon in the prehistoric city of Teotihuacán, in Mexico. This is the Pyramid of the Sun.

# Qatar

Qatar is a small country in the Persian Gulf, consisting of a low-lying peninsula and some nearby islands. It is hot and humid. There are not enough natural sources of water, so people use sea water that has been through a desalination process. This means that the salt has been taken out and the water made fit for general use. The land has too much sand and gravel to grow many crops or herd animals. In the 1940s oil was discovered. Qatar is also rich in natural gas. These resources have made Qatar one of the world's richest countries and have paid for free health, education and social services for its citizens. Only one-quarter of the population are native Qataris. The rest came mostly from Egypt and southern Asia to work in the oil, chemicals and construction industries. ◆

**Area**
11,000 sq km
(4,247 sq mi)
**Capital**
Doha
**Population**
540,000
**Language**
Arabic
**Religion**
Muslim
**Government**
Monarchy
**Currency**
1 Qatar riyal = 100 dirhams

▼ See also
Arabs
Middle East

# Quakers

Quakers have founded a number of colleges in the U.S., including Bryn Mawr, Haverford and Swarthmore in Pennsylvania.

Quakers are members of the Society of Friends, founded by George Fox and other Puritans in England in the 1660s. They believe that all Christians have the "inner light" of God within them, and do not need an organized Church. During their meetings, early Quakers often became very emotional, trembling and "quaking," which explains how they got their name.

Quakers were often persecuted. Their beliefs seemed dangerous to richer people, for the Quakers treated everyone as equals and refused to behave to them in a subservient manner just because they were upper-class. Quakers were often sent to prison in the 17th century if they did not attend Church of England services.

Some Quakers went to North America, where they could live and worship freely. William Penn founded the Quaker colony of Pennsylvania in 1681.

As time went on, Quakers lost their dangerous reputation. They lived simple lives, worked hard, and often did well in business.

Today Quakers worship by sitting quietly together in a "meeting house." They believe God is in every person, so they condemn all killing, especially in war. Many Quakers work for peace, and care for those in trouble. ◆

Quakers have established several organizations to work for peace and help the less fortunate. One of the best-known is the American Friends Service Committee (AFSC), which was founded in Philadelphia in 1917 to provide aid for victims of World War I. The AFSC received the Nobel Peace Prize in 1947 for its relief work during World War II (1939-1945) and its aftermath. Today the AFSC continues to provide aid throughout the world.

**▼ See also**

Christianity
Pennsylvania
Protestant Christianity
Puritans

**BIOGRAPHY**
Fox, George
Penn, William

# Quarantine

Quarantine is a way of stopping infectious diseases from spreading. People, plants or animals that may be diseased are held in quarantine until they are harmless.

Many countries used to hold people in quarantine. But it was easy to evade and not very effective. Nowadays people "in quarantine" for diseases like yellow fever simply report to a doctor until cleared.

Animals and plants are still quarantined in many countries. All mammals including pet dogs, entering the United Kingdom, for example, are held for six months until the authorities are certain they are free of the fatal disease rabies.

## LOOKING BACK

Quarantine was first used in Venice in the 14th century. Ships were isolated for 40 days (*quarantina*) to be certain that people or goods entering the country were disease-free. Other European countries used this system for several centuries.

From the 16th to the 19th centuries, ships could carry a "bill of health" to prove that their last port of call was "clean" (free from disease). By the early 20th century this practice had declined because of better understanding of communicable diseases and how they spread. ◆

In the past, houses in the U.S. were placed under quarantine by the local public health department if anyone living there had a serious communicable disease, such as diphtheria, smallpox or polio. This practice continued in many U.S. towns and cities until the mid-20th century.

**▼ See also**

Black Death
Diseases
Epidemics
Health
Influenza
Polio

# Quarries

**▼ See also**

Building
Mining
Roads and highways
Rocks
Sculpture

A quarry is a pit or hole in the ground from which stone or rock is obtained. Rock from quarries is used in the construction industry and in road building.

There are two main types of quarry. In one type, large blocks of stone are cut and trimmed by special machines. The rocks quarried in this way include granite, marble, limestone and sandstone. They are used for buildings and for making statues. Slate is also cut in blocks, which are then split into thin slices. It is used for roofs and for facing buildings.

The other main type of quarry produces *aggregate* (broken stone). In these quarries, explosives are used to produce large quantities of rock pieces. The larger fragments are crushed. Much of this aggregate is used for road building or for the "beds" on which railway lines are laid. Limestone from such quarries is often made into lime for use on farms and by the chemical industry. ◆

Marble is a type of metamorphic limestone. One of the most famous marble quarries is at Carrara in Italy. Its marble is pure white and has been used by sculptors since the Renaissance (15th–16th centuries).

# Quasars

The first quasar was identified in 1963. It is called 3C 273. That means entry number 273 in the Third Cambridge Catalogue of Radio Sources.

The most distant quasars are so far away that we are seeing them now as they were when the Universe was one-sixth of its present size.

When astronomers started to find strong radio signals from particular places in the sky, they looked at photographs taken of those places with ordinary telescopes. In some cases they found galaxies, but in others there was just a faint point of light. At first they called these "quasi-stellar radio sources," which means something sending out radio waves that looks like a star but is not. This was soon shortened to "quasars."

By studying the quasars' light, astronomers found out that some of the quasars are the most distant objects that we can see. Although they look faint, they are actually sending out more light than hundreds of ordinary giant galaxies put together. The most distant quasars are more than 10 billion lightyears away. Their light has been traveling to us for so long that it was halfway here before the Sun and Earth came into existence.

Quasars are embedded in galaxies. They shine so brightly that they swamp the fainter light of their parent galaxy. At the middle of the quasar is an extremely powerful source of energy, which astronomers believe is almost certainly a black hole. The gas and stars falling into the black hole give out huge amounts of energy, making the center of the quasar so bright that it can be seen over enormous distances. ◆

**▼ See also**
Black holes
Galaxies
Light-years

# Rabbits

**Distribution**
Throughout the world
**Size**
Head-and-body length about 35 cm (14 in), tail short
**Number of young**
Up to 12, suckled for about 4 weeks
**Lifespan**
Up to 9 years
**Subphylum**
Vertebrata
**Class**
Mammalia
**Order**
Lagomorpha
**Number of species**
21

Rabbits are gnawing animals, feeding on plants and usually living in groups and sheltering in burrows. When they feed, they do not move far from home, so a short dash can take them to safety. They rely on their good eyesight and senses of hearing and smell to warn them of enemies. They are hunted by many predators, including human beings.

Most rabbits produce a large number of young in the course of a year. Even so, only the European rabbit has become widespread and a pest, as it did after it was introduced in Australia. Most species are found in restricted areas, and some are endangered.

In some ways rabbits and hares are like rodents, but there are many differences between the two groups. One is that rabbits have four upper incisor teeth. There are two tiny ones behind the big incisors that you can see. These are completely covered with enamel, unlike the incisors of rodents, which have enamel only on the outer side. ◆

Some kinds of North American hare are often called rabbits or jackrabbits.

In the Middle Ages in England, rabbits were specially guarded in enclosures called "warrens" and were used for their meat and skins.

▶ Baby rabbits are blind and furless at birth. Though their mothers feed them only twice a day, they grow quickly. By the time they are eight days old (as here) they have some hair and their eyes are almost open. They are ready to face the outside world by the time they are three weeks old.

**▼ See also**
Domestication
Hares
Rodents

# Raccoons

▲ A group of North American raccoons feeding. Raccoons are more active in the twilight and evening hours than during the day.

▼ **See also**
Animal tracks and signs
Mammals
Pandas

Many people will know about at least one part of a raccoon: its long, furry, striped tail was an essential part of the fur caps worn by hunters of the American West, such as Davy Crockett. The rest of the animal is grayish-brown, apart from the black "bandit's mask" that covers the upper part of its face. Raccoons live only in the Americas. They are usually found in forests, near water, and can climb and swim well. They eat almost anything: wild fruit, birds' eggs and insects in the trees; worms, fish, frogs, young muskrats, crayfish and clams in the water. They have discovered that humans produce edible waste and often make their dens in areas near trash dumps It is difficult to keep raccoons out of most places. They have front paws like little hands, with long, mobile fingers that can undo catches and locks meant to deter them.

Normally raccoons live alone, and a male may have to travel a long distance to find a mate. Most females have a family of four or five young, born in a safe den in April or May. They develop slowly. At first blind and helpless, they do not leave the den until they are about 8 weeks old, and are not weaned until the end of the summer. Then they do not hibernate, but go to look for hunting grounds of their own. ◆

**Distribution**
North, Central and South America, now also Europe
**Size**
Head-and-body length up to 60 cm (2 ft), tail up to 40 cm (16 in)
**Weight**
2–12 kg (4–26 lbs)
**Number of young**
Usually 4 or 5
**Lifespan**
Rarely more than 5 years in the wild, over 20 in captivity
**Subphylum** Vertebrata
**Class** Mammalia
**Order** Carnivora
**Family** Procyonidae
**Number of species** 7

*N*ever play with wild raccoons—they may be carrying rabies, a potentially fatal disease.

*T*he name "raccoon" comes from "aroughcoune," a word used for the animal by the Native Americans of Virginia. It means "he scratches with his hands."

# Racism

In the past some scientists have divided human beings into different races by looking at things like size, skin color and other physical differences. Unfortunately this also led many people to hold racist ideas. They decided that some racial groups were superior to others, and this allowed "superior" races to ill-treat and discriminate against "inferior" races.

European settlers in Africa, Asia and South America took over the land belonging to the original inhabitants. In Australia and New Zealand, Aborigine and Maori people were massacred when they tried to resist the new settlers.

Nazi Germany was ruled on racist lines. Jews and Gypsies, and anyone else that Adolf Hitler decided was "inferior," were persecuted and put into concentration camps. Eventually this led to the Holocaust, in which millions of people were systematically put to death.

## Racism today

Racism did not die with the defeat of Hitler. The apartheid system in South Africa classified people into different races, and gave power to a white minority. It can still be difficult for people from ethnic minorities to gain full civil rights in democratic countries. Civil rights groups fight for laws to outlaw racist discrimination, and to promote equal opportunities for people of all ethnic groups.

In many countries, from Bosnia to Rwanda, people still die because they belong to the "wrong" racial group. There are also some political groups, in Europe and elsewhere, that are ready to preach the racist message and to encourage attacks on those who are different in some way from themselves. ◆

▼ **See also**
Aborigines
African Americans
Concentration camps
Ethnic groups
Holocaust
Human beings
Human rights
Ku Klux Klan
Maori
Nazis
Rwanda
South Africa

**BIOGRAPHY**
King, Martin Luther
Mandela, Nelson
Tutu, Desmond

# Radar

Radar (RAdio Detection And Ranging) can tell us the position of a moving or stationary object, even if it is too far away to see, or if it is dark or foggy. It is essential for air traffic controllers, who need to know the height and position of aircraft around busy airports. It also enables ships to travel safely without risk of collisions. Radar can detect objects as small as an insect or as large as a mountain.

Weather observation and forecasting are helped by radar, which can detect the approach of storms or hurricanes. Scientists use radar to find out about the atmosphere and other planets. It is essential for space travel, allowing controllers on the ground to track craft before they reach their orbits. Radar has many military uses, as it can warn of approaching missiles or attacking planes and ships. On the ground, police use radar to catch speeding motorists.

## How radar works

If you shout in a mountain valley, you hear an echo as the sound waves are reflected from a nearby cliff. Radar works in a similar way. It detects things by bouncing radio waves off them. The transmitter of the radar equipment beams radio waves into the sky. When they hit an object, some of the waves are reflected back. The reflected waves are detected by a radar dish or aerial. From the time it takes for these waves to travel to the object and back again, the radar equipment can work out how far away the object is. A signal takes 1/500th of a second to return from an object (for example, an aircraft) 300 km (186 mi) away. The signal appears as a bright spot or blip on a display screen. This gives the operator information about the position of the aircraft. The radar aerial rotates so that it can cover all of the sky.

Most large aircraft have on-board radar to warn them of other planes in the vicinity. It can also warn the pilot about storms ahead, since storm clouds are also detected and show up on the screen. The radar equipment on board ships beams radio waves out across the surface of the water so that they will be reflected back from any ships or hazards nearby.

## LOOKING BACK

In 1935 the British government asked a scientist, Robert Watson-Watt, to invent a "death ray" (a beam of destructive radio waves) to attack enemy aircraft. He said he could not, but while doing research on that project, he realized radio waves would bounce off an airplane and he invented the first radar system for detecting enemy planes. ♦

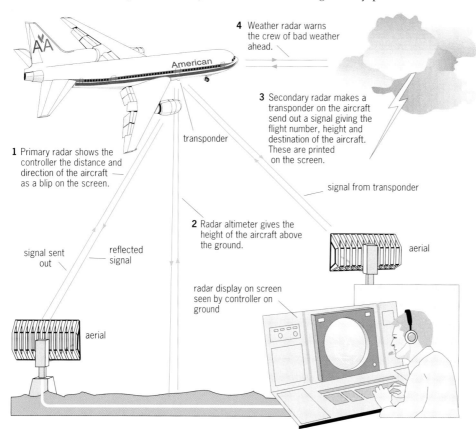

4 Weather radar warns the crew of bad weather ahead.

3 Secondary radar makes a transponder on the aircraft send out a signal giving the flight number, height and destination of the aircraft. These are printed on the screen.

transponder

signal from transponder

1 Primary radar shows the controller the distance and direction of the aircraft — as a blip on the screen.

2 Radar altimeter gives the height of the aircraft above the ground.

signal sent out

reflected signal

aerial

radar display on screen seen by controller on ground

aerial

◄ Four types of radar are being used by this aircraft and the controller on the ground.

▼ **See also**

Airports
Microwaves
Radiation
Radio
Weather

# Radiation

Radiation can be thought of as energy on the move. Some kinds of energy, such as radio signals and sound, travel about as invisible waves. Other kinds of radiation are tiny particles that shoot out from atoms at enormous speeds. Cosmic rays from space are particles. Radioactive materials can produce a mixture of radiations, some of which are particles and some of which are waves.

## Radioactivity

When people talk about radiation from nuclear power plants, they mean the mixture of particle and wave radiation that comes from radioactive materials. These materials are made up of atoms that change into a different kind of atom by throwing out tiny atomic particles.

There are two kinds of particles, called *alpha* and *beta*. Each beta-particle is an electron. Each alpha-particle is two protons and two neutrons. Radioactive materials also throw out gamma rays. These travel as waves, carrying a lot of energy. Scientists often use a Geiger counter to measure the nuclear radiation from radioactive materials.

## Useful radioactivity

Nuclear radiation has many uses. Doctors use it to kill the cells that make cancer growths. Radioactive materials can help doctors to find out how well the kidneys and other parts of the body are working. However, they have to be very careful not to use too much nuclear radiation because that would harm the patient. Space probes that travel far from the Sun use radioactive materials to make electricity. Radioactive materials are also used as portable sources of the powerful gamma rays that can be used to X-ray steel girders in buildings or bridges to locate cracks.

## Wavelength and frequency

Every type of wave radiation has a wavelength and a frequency, just like the ripples you see on water. Imagine you are standing in a pond. Someone drops a stone in so that tiny waves

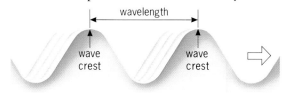

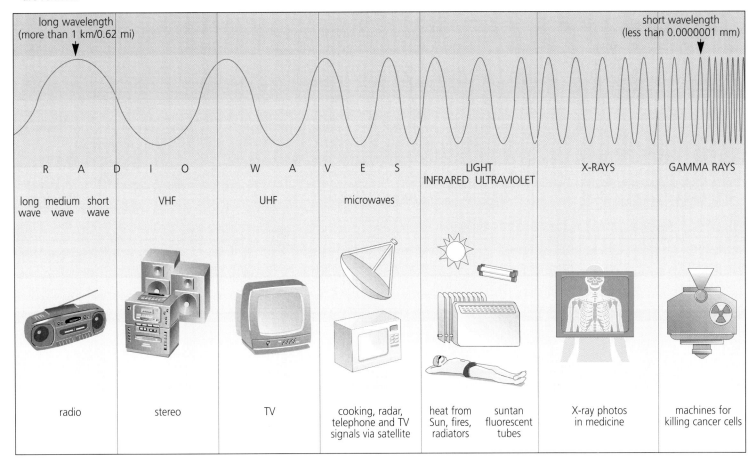

travel toward you across the water. The number of waves reaching you every second is called the frequency. The distance from one crest to the next is the wavelength. The more waves reach you every second, the closer together are the crests; the higher the frequency, the shorter the wavelength.

## Electromagnetic radiation

Most types of wave radiation belong to the same "family." They are electromagnetic waves. You can see the different types in the chart on page 45. They can all travel through empty space, which is why light and heat can reach us from the Sun. And they all travel at the same speed, the speed of light. But they all have different wavelengths and frequencies.

## Cosmic rays

Out in space, speeding around almost as fast as light travels, are cosmic rays. This kind of radiation is made up of tiny atomic particles. They carry a great deal of energy because they are traveling so fast. Astronomers think that many cosmic rays come from exploding stars called supernovas, though some come from the Sun, and some from other faraway galaxies.

## Danger from the Sun

We all enjoy a sunny day, but too much sunlight on our skin—from spending a day at the beach, for example—can be harmful. Sometimes the damage caused by the Sun's radiation is quickly obvious: people with fair skin can get a painful sunburn. But people who tan easily are also in danger from overexposure to sunlight. Radiation from the Sun can cause skin cancer, which often develops years after the skin has been burned or tanned.

To prevent Sun damage, apply protective *sunblock*—a lotion or cream, sold at most drug and cosmetics stores—to exposed areas of the skin whenever you go to a beach or swimming pool, or work outdoors when the Sun is shining. On very hot summer days, try to avoid being outside in midday, when the Sun's rays are most intense. And wear sunglasses and a brimmed hat to protect your eyes: too much bright sunlight can harm them, too.

## Sound radiation

Sound is a type of radiation. When you speak, sound waves radiate out from your mouth and are picked up by other people's ears. The sound waves are tiny compressions that travel through the air. They travel at a speed of about 330 m (1,083 ft) per second, which is nearly a million times slower than the speed of light.

Low notes have the lowest frequencies and the longest wavelengths. High notes have the highest frequencies and the shortest wavelengths. Sounds that are too high for the human ear to hear are called ultrasonic sounds.

## Radiation dangers

There are small amounts of nuclear radiation around us all the time that come from radioactive materials in the Earth. This is called "background radiation" and it normally does us no harm. However, scientists need to keep a close check on this, so that suitable precautions can be taken, for too much radiation can be dangerous. For example, a natural radioactive gas called radon leaks up through the ground in some places and can collect in houses. Pumps have to be fitted to get rid of it.

A nuclear bomb or an accident at a nuclear power plant would make enough radiation to kill people nearby. This radiation may cause cancer, often many years later. So nuclear power plants have huge concrete walls to keep the radiation from escaping, and people who work in them have to wear special clothing for protection.

**LOOKING BACK**

Although we have always been aware of heat and light, radioactivity and the invisible electromagnetic radiations have been known only for about 100 years. There are many sources of electromagnetic radiation—both natural and man-made. Heinrich Hertz discovered radio waves in 1887, and then in 1895 Wilhelm Roentgen discovered X-rays.

In 1896 Henri Becquerel found that uranium gave off radiation and called this radioactivity. Marie Curie looked for other radioactive materials that occur in nature and discovered radium and polonium. These discoveries helped scientists find out what the atom is like. ◆

**Protection from Radiation**

*Alpha-particles* are stopped by a sheet of paper.
*Beta-particles* are stopped by 3 mm (0.12 in) of metal or 6 mm (0.24 in) of wood.
*Gamma rays* are almost stopped by 5–10 cm (2–4 in) of lead or 30–60 cm (12–24 in) of concrete.

▲ Worker exposed to radiation wearing protective clothing.

# Radio

Radio is a system for transmitting sound over long distances by using radio waves. The word "radio" is used for both the transmission (broadcasting) system, and for the device that enables listeners to hear what has been transmitted (the broadcast).

## Radio waves

Radio waves have two characteristics. One is power, or *amplitude*. The other is *frequency*. One popular radio system modulates the wave by changing its power while keeping its frequency the same. This system is called *amplitude modulation*, or AM radio.

Another way to modulate the wave is to change its frequency while keeping its amplitude the same. This system is called *frequency modulation*, or FM radio.

## Broadcasting components

Radio broadcasting requires three components: a program, a means to transmit (broadcast) it, and a device to receive the transmission (broadcast).

*Program.* The program—the speaking or music to be transmitted—can be live or recorded. The speaking and music are translated by special equipment into electronic impulses.

*Transmission.* These impulses are sent into the transmission system. A transmitter sends out a constant wave, called the *carrier wave*, at a certain frequency, or number of cycles per second, called the *carrier frequency*. For example, an AM radio station at 1560 on the dial transmits its carrier wave at a frequency of 1,560 kilocycles per second. Carrier waves travel at the speed of light, approximately 300,000 km (186,000 mi) per second.

When the electronic impulses from speaking or music are introduced into the carrier wave

they change—or *modulate*—it. Those modulations are models, or *analogs*, of the speaking or music from the source, so the transmission system is called analog transmission.

*Receiver.* The receiver, commonly known as the radio, allows listeners to hear the broadcast. The radio antenna picks up the carrier frequency. Then it "reads" the modulations and reproduces the speaking or music that they represent.

## Paying for radio broadcasts

In many countries, the national government controls radio broadcasting, which is usually nationwide. It is paid for with taxes charged to listeners for their radio receivers. The U.S. has always been an exception: it has many different stations, most of which are privately owned and are supported by advertising.

In the U.S., local stations usually belong to private networks, such as the Columbia Broadcasting System (CBS) and the American Broadcasting Company (ABC). These networks provide them with certain programs, such as coverage of sports events and national news, which the local stations broadcast in addition to shows that they themselves produce.

National Public Radio (NPR) is an association of non-profit radio stations that do not broadcast any advertising. Their broadcasts are paid for by local contributors and by grants from the federal government.

## Other uses of radio waves

Besides AM and FM radio stations, radio waves are used for other types of communication. Police, fire, taxi and ambulance crews use two-way radios for communicating with their headquarters or with one another. Mobile phones are linked to main telephone networks by radio. Ships and aircraft use radio for

## Frequency

Transmitters send out many thousands, or even millions, of radio waves every second. The number of waves every second is called the frequency. It is marked on the tuning scale of a radio either in kHz (for kilohertz, meaning "thousand waves every second") or MHz (for megahertz, meaning "million waves every second").

Different stations use different frequencies, so you have to tune the receiver to select the one that you want to listen to. The more radio waves are sent out every second, the closer they are together. The distance from one wave to the next is called the wavelength. A high-frequency radio wave therefore has a shorter wavelength than a low-frequency radio wave. 200 kHz means that the transmitter is sending 200,000 radio waves every second. 100 MHz means that the transmitter is sending 100 million radio waves every second.

▼ Radio waves can travel thousands of miles around the Earth, bouncing between the ground and the ionosphere.

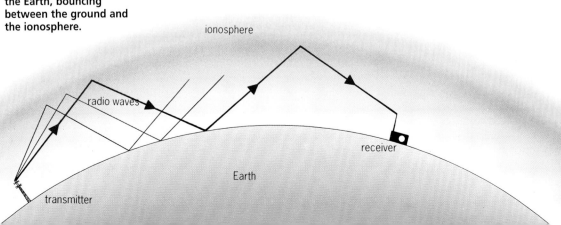

ionosphere

radio waves

receiver

Earth

transmitter

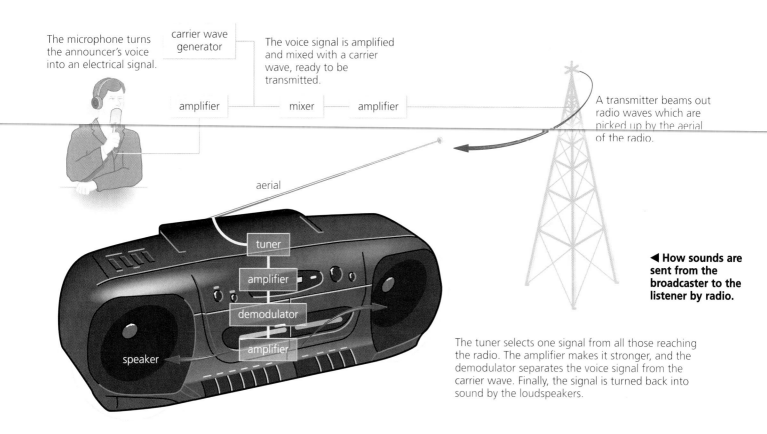

The microphone turns the announcer's voice into an electrical signal.

carrier wave generator

The voice signal is amplified and mixed with a carrier wave, ready to be transmitted.

amplifier — mixer — amplifier

A transmitter beams out radio waves which are picked up by the aerial of the radio.

aerial

tuner

amplifier

demodulator

amplifier

speaker

◄ **How sounds are sent from the broadcaster to the listener by radio.**

The tuner selects one signal from all those reaching the radio. The amplifier makes it stronger, and the demodulator separates the voice signal from the carrier wave. Finally, the signal is turned back into sound by the loudspeakers.

communication and for navigation: they can use radio signals to determine their location. Television uses radio waves for transmitting pictures and sound. Satellites receive and retransmit radio waves all over the world. Spacecraft can be controlled by radio waves, and so can toys such as model cars, boats and planes.

## LOOKING BACK

Many inventors in many countries contributed to the development of radio, but in 1895 Guglielmo Marconi was the first to send radio signals through the air. Those first transmissions traveled only about a mile, but by 1900 Marconi's "wireless telegraph" was being used to communicate with ships hundreds of miles from shore. In the beginning Morse code was used, but by 1906 human speech was being transmitted successfully.

In 1920, KDKA in Pittsburgh and WWJ in Detroit became the first commercial radio stations on the air, and during the next few years many more AM stations began to broadcast. In those early broadcasts, sound levels were so low that people could only hear them through special headsets. However, by the end of the 1920s, amplification equipment

## Digital Broadcasting

In recent years, new transmission systems have been developed that change the basic nature of radio transmission. While analog systems modulate carrier waves to transmit voice and music, digital systems translate the voice or music into data, information about the voice or music rather than a model of it. That data is transmitted over the carrier wave, and at the other end the receiver gets the data and uses it to reproduce the voice and music. Digital systems are more efficient than analog systems because they can transmit more information on a carrier wave.

had improved enough to enable people to listen through speakers. By the 1930s, as the U.S. suffered through the Great Depression, radio had become a popular source of entertainment.

The first experiments with FM radio were conducted by U.S. inventor Edwin Armstrong in the 1930s, and many FM stations went on the air in the 1940s and 1950s. By the mid-1960s FM transmission systems were strong enough to rival AM radio.

FM broadcasting was designed to deliver a higher quality of sound than AM broadcasting. Its modulation system permitted broadcasting in stereo, so it was a much better system for music programs. By the 1970s FM stations were attracting more listeners than AM stations, and this is still the case today. ◆

**U**.S. radio broadcasting is regulated by the Federal Communications Commission (FCC), a government agency created in 1934. Over the years the FCC has established a series of technical and programming regulations that all stations have to follow.

▼ **See also**

Atmosphere
Electronics
Loudspeakers
Microphones
Microwaves
Satellites
Sound
Telegraph
Television
Valves
Waves

**BIOGRAPHY**
Marconi, Guglielmo

# Railroads

The smooth metal tracks of railroads, also known as trains, allow heavy loads to be moved more efficiently than on roads. A single locomotive may pull a load weighing thousands of tons. The track it travels on is made of steel rails laid on concrete or wooden ties. The ties lie on a layer of gravel. This helps to take the weight of the passing train and keep the rails level. The two rails are laid a fixed distance apart, known as the *gauge*. In the U.S. and most Western nations, the gauge is 1.44 m (56.5 in). Russia, Finland and Spain use a wider gauge.

flange on wheel

steel rail

gravel

▶ Train wheels have flanges to keep them on the rails. The rails are mounted on ties embedded in gravel.

## Constructing railroads

When a railroad is to be built, engineers choose a route that is as level as possible. Any slope or gradient has to be very gradual, or the steel wheels of the locomotive will slip. Curves also have to be as gentle as possible, because a train cannot turn sharply at high speed. Viaducts are used to carry the railway across valleys, and tunnels are used to carry it through hills.

In mountainous countries where the slope of the track is very steep, a special extra rail is used between the outer rails. This is called a rack rail. It has teeth that point upward, and a powered gearwheel on the locomotive, called a pinion, engages the teeth. This allows the train to pull itself up a hillside without slipping.

When a track is laid, short gaps are often left between the lengths of rail. This allows the rails to expand when they warm up in summer. Without the gaps, the rails would bend out of shape. Sometimes extra long rails are used. These are fixed very tightly to the ties so they cannot expand in the heat. Railway tracks are regularly checked, often by trains with measuring instruments on board.

## Signaling

To avoid collisions, a railroad line is divided into sections with a signal at the beginning of each section. Signals are like traffic lights. A train can pass a signal only if it shows the right color or the right position.

The signals are operated from a signal box. In modern signal boxes, the positions of all the trains on the line are displayed by a computer. The computer ensures that only one train is traveling on each section of line.

The signal box also controls the route that each train follows. There is no steering wheel in a locomotive. Instead, trains are steered by special moving rails, called *points*. These are used to make a train change direction where tracks divide or where they join together.

## Types of train

The fastest modern trains can travel at speeds of over 300 km (186 mi) per hour. They are powered either by overhead electric wires or by diesel engines. High-speed passenger trains are widely used in Europe and Japan. There are even trains that use magnets to make them "float" above the track by magnetic levitation. These trains can go even faster because there is no contact with the track and thus no friction to slow them down.

The load that a locomotive pulls can be either passengers or freight. Commuter trains carry people to and from their work, transporting far more people than could be carried in cars or buses. Freight trains carry cargo. They are manufactured to carry such substances as oil, chemicals, clay, cars and iron ore. Some freight trains can be over 500 m (1,640 ft) long.

## LOOKING BACK

The first passenger railroad opened between Stockton and Darlington, England, in 1825. The Liverpool-to-Manchester railroad opened five years later. During the 1840s railroads

▼ A heavy freight train on the Alaskan Railroad being pulled by five locomotives.

▲ A French poster from 1842 celebrating one of the wonders of our time—railroads. *Le chemin de fer* is French for railroad; literally translated, it means "road of iron."

▶ A Eurostar train leaving Waterloo International Station, London. Shuttle trains like this carry cars, trucks and passengers between Britain and mainland Europe via the Channel Tunnel. This tunnel is buried 40 m (131 ft) below the seabed under the waters of the English Channel; it opened in 1994.

▶ An Amtrak train waits for passengers at the railroad station in Seattle, Washington. Amtrak is a company established by the U.S. government in 1970 to run the nation's intercity passenger railroads.

expanded very rapidly in England, and continued to grow throughout the century.

Public railroads opened in Belgium and Germany in 1835, and in the next 20 years construction started in many parts of the world. In 1863 two American companies, the Union Pacific and the Central Pacific, started to build a railroad across the continent, one company working eastward from the Pacific coast and the other westward from the Missouri River. Six years later the two lines met in Utah.

In the early days of railroad building, all the cuttings, embankments and tunnels were dug by hand. Teams of thousands of men, using pickaxes and other hand tools, worked

to move the earth and lay tracks.

Railroads brought great changes to the way people lived. For the first time in history, people could travel long distances every day to work. This meant that cities could grow bigger, with outer suburbs connected to the center by train. ◆

### Railroads in the United States

The first railroad in the U.S. was established by the Baltimore and Ohio (B&O) Railroad Company in 1830. Horse-drawn cars carried passengers between Baltimore and Ellicott City, Maryland, a distance of 21 km (13 mi). A B&O train drawn by a steam locomotive began service in 1831 between Baltimore and New York City.

Railroads developed rapidly in the eastern half of the U.S. in the following decades. In the early 1860s, the U.S. Congress passed legislation to build a *transcontinental railroad*—a railroad that would cross the U.S. and span the entire North American continent, from the Atlantic to the Pacific oceans. Construction began in 1863 and was completed on May 10, 1869. The U.S. transcontinental railroad was the first railroad line in the world to span an entire continent.

# Rain

When air rises, it becomes colder. As it gets colder, the water vapor molecules in the air change from gas to liquid.

There are very small solid particles in the air. These specks may be salt from the sea, dust or smoke. The liquid water molecules collect around these and soon a raindrop is formed. They fall from the sky when they are too heavy to stay in the air. They get bigger as they fall because other small drops join with them. Rain is caused by different conditions. Mountain barriers may cause air to rise, the air above the heated earth may rise, or storms may form.

Farmers and gardeners like rain, because without it their plants will not grow. But if there is too much rain, it may cause a flood, which can be damaging and dangerous. ◆

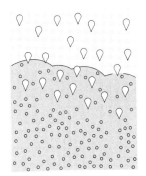

▲ Rain begins as tiny water droplets formed around particles in the air. Several droplets join to form heavier drops, which fall as rain.

▼ **See also**
Clouds
Floods
Monsoons
Water cycle
Weather

# Rainbows

White light from the Sun is really a mixture of colors. When a beam of light goes into water or glass, it slows down. So, if a beam enters at an angle, the part of the beam that goes in first slows down more than the rest. Scientists call this *refraction*. But blue light slows down more than green, and green more than red, so white light is split up into all the colors.

When a beam of sunlight goes into a raindrop, it is split up. It is then reflected from the back of the drop and is still further split up as it comes out. Only one color from each raindrop will reach any particular person's eye, but because there are thousands of raindrops we can see the whole bow. Each person sees light from many different drops, glinting different colors in the sunlight. A rainbow always seems to move away if you walk toward it, because the colors come from a different set of drops. ◆

For you to see a rainbow, the Sun must be shining behind you, and rain must be falling somewhere in front of you.

There is a picture of a rainbow in Volume 7, in the article on Zimbabwe.

▼ **See also**
Color
Light
Optics
Symbols

# Ranches

Some grain and fruit farms, as well as farms that raise small fur-bearing animals such as mink, are also called ranches.

Ranches that entertain tourists who pay for horseback riding and other outdoor activities are called *dude ranches*.

Cattle ranches have to be large because many acres of grassland are needed to feed a herd. Large ranches were first built in South America in the early 19th century. Today ranches are found in many parts of the world, but primarily in North America (the western U.S. and Canada), South America and Australia.

▼ **See also**
Cattle
Corn
Cowboys
United States of America

▼ Cowboys guard cattle at the King Ranch, in Texas. The King Ranch, which covers 825,000 acres (3,367 sq km/1,300 sq mi), is one of the largest cattle ranches in the world. It is bigger than the state of Rhode Island.

Ranches are large farms devoted mostly to raising and breeding herds of cattle, horses, sheep or goats.

Cattle ranching came to the American West in the middle of the 19th century and developed rapidly in the decades following the Civil War, which ended in 1865. Early American ranchers owned their cattle, horses and equipment, but not the land. They raised their livestock on public land called *open range* and hired workers called *cowboys* or *cowhands* to guard their herds.

When it came time to slaughter the cattle, cowboys formed large herds and, riding on horseback, "drove" them (moved them along) overland to the railroad in Kansas. A herd, consisting of several thousand cattle, could be "driven" 16–25 km (10–15 mi) a day. In Kansas, buyers purchased the cattle and shipped them by railroad to slaughterhouses in Chicago, St. Louis and eastern U.S. cities.

Public grazing lands shrank as more and more homesteaders settled in the West in the late 19th century. Sheep ranches also developed at that time. Today most ranchers own all or most of their land. (An average U.S. ranch covers 3,000–4,000 acres.) To fatten their cattle, many ranchers ship them by rail to farms in the Corn Belt (major corn-growing states in the Midwest) before they are sent on to the slaughterhouse. ◆

# Rastafarians

Rastafarians are both a religious group and a general movement for the dignity of black people wherever they are poor and oppressed. The movement began in Jamaica in the 1930s with the work of Marcus Garvey. To Rastafarians he is a prophet.

## Back to Africa

Garvey encouraged black people to return to Africa, particularly to Ethiopia, and to see Africa as the religious and cultural inspiration of their lives.

Rastafarians believe that everywhere outside Africa is like an exile for black people, and that the Ethiopian Orthodox Church is the only acceptable form of Christianity, so many Rastafarians have joined it. They have also developed separate religious ideas, but there are no Rastafarian churches. They believe that they are the true black Israelites, a chosen people, and that Emperor Haile Selassie of Ethiopia (1892–1975), was the expected Messiah and the living God, whom they call Jah. It is his name—*Ras* (prince) *Tafari* (of the house of Tafari)—that gives the movement its name.

## Lions' manes and reggae

One of Haile Selassie's titles was "Lion of Judah." This, and the proud walk and fearlessness of lions, are an important symbol for Rastafarians. They wear a hairstyle, called dreadlocks, which represents a lion's mane. They also wear knitted hats, called tams, with red, black, green and gold stripes. Red is the color of blood and reminds Rastafarians of the deaths of black slaves and others who have fought for black freedom. Black is the skin color of dignity and creativity. Green is for the rich vegetation of Africa and Jamaica. Gold is the color of the faith. Rastafarians have also developed their own music, reggae, and their own dialect of Jamaican English. ◆

The Rastafarian lifestyle may include following certain dietary rules, often vegetarianism. Because they believe so fiercely in the rights of the individual human being, many Rastafarians say "I and I" rather than "we" or "us."

Rastafarians have expressed themselves powerfully through reggae music and songs. Bob Marley was one of the most famous of their musicians.

▲ Marcus Garvey is commemorated on a postage stamp in his native Jamaica, where he is honored as a hero. Garvey (1887–1940) was the founder of the Universal Negro Improvement Association (UNIA), which worked for the fair treatment of black people.

▼ **See also**
Caribbean
Ethiopia
Jamaica
Reggae
**BIOGRAPHY**
Haile Selassie

# Rats

The rat family is a huge one, containing over a thousand different kinds of small-sized rodents including mice, voles, hamsters and gerbils. The animals generally called rats tend to be larger than most of the other members of the group. Most of these creatures have little contact with human beings, but the true rats, especially the black rat and the brown rat, have become major pests to humans.

**Distribution**
Throughout the world except in the coldest places or most remote islands
**Size**
Brown rat: head-and-body length 20–26 cm (8–10 in); tail 20–23 cm (8–9 in); weight up to 600 g (1.32 lbs); black rats are slightly smaller
**Number of young**
About 7 or 8, 4 times a year. Weaned by the age of 3 weeks, females may produce their first family at about 4 months of age.
**Lifespan**
Up to 4 years in captivity
**Subphylum**
Vertebrata
**Class**
Mammalia
**Order**
Rodentia
**Family**
Muridae (rat and mouse family)
**Number of species**
78 (true rats)

▶ The majority of animals called rats, such as this slender-tailed cloud rat, are forest dwellers, which feed on seeds and leaves. The cloud rat is not closely related to brown and black rats.

The word "rat" is often added to the name of a large rodent, whether or not it is really a rat. For instance, the muskrat is really related to the voles and lemmings, but because of its size it is called a rat.

▼ **See also**

Black Death
Gerbils
Guinea pigs
Hamsters
Mice
Rodents
Voles

The black rat came originally from Southeast Asia. It is a good climber, but needs warmth and so is most successful in countries with hot climates. Nowadays in cool places it often flourishes in centrally heated buildings, but it is not found in the open. The brown rat came from much farther north, probably from Central Asia, and can stand cold weather. It is a good swimmer. Its spread into Europe is said to have occurred in the early part of the 18th century, when large numbers swam across the River Volga. Since then it has colonized almost the whole world, helped by human beings who have often unintentionally carried rats with cargoes as they traveled from one place to another. Brown rats live in open country as well as in towns and do a great deal of damage in both these areas.

Both black and brown rats eat almost anything and often damage more than they eat. Both can carry diseases, some of which may be transmitted to human beings or domestic animals. The Black Death, which is said to have killed a third of the population of Europe in the Middle Ages, and later plagues were caused by organisms carried by the fleas of black rats. Today, plague is not found in Europe, but Weil's disease, which is carried by brown rats, is a danger that sewer workers must face. It is sometimes fatal to humans, and almost always kills any dog that catches it.

So-called brown rats have been tamed. They are often white or mixed white and brown, and make excellent pets, despite the bad reputation of their wild relatives. They are very clean and much friendlier than the more commonly kept rodents, such as hamsters and gerbils. ◆

Rats are very destructive animals. They are said to eat about one-fifth of the world's crops each year. Their success lies partly in the fact that humans have often killed animals, such as snakes and other small carnivores, that would naturally keep their numbers in check.

Rats' incisor teeth are so strong that they can cut through wood and some metals. They may cause structural damage to buildings and can damage the insulation on electrical equipment, sometimes causing fires.

A litter of rats usually contains about 8 young, but the record number is over 20. These are able to produce their first families at the age of 4 months. Their lifespan in the wild is about 18 months.

▼ The brown rat's intelligence and sharp senses of hearing and smell enable it to survive alongside humans, in spite of all efforts to exterminate it.

# Recording

Recording is a way of keeping sounds or video pictures so that you can hear or see them later. Sound is made by vibrations in the air. There is no way of keeping the vibrations themselves, so sound is recorded by representing the vibrations in some other way. On a cassette tape the vibrations are represented by magnetic patterns in the metal coating on the tape. On a CD (compact disc) they are represented by microscopic bumps on the surface.

A recording machine is needed to capture sound. A microphone turns the sound into tiny electrical signals, which represent the vibrations in the air. These signals are used to make the recording. A tape, CD or video player turns the recording back into electrical signals and then back to sound.

way, the signal is recorded as a magnetic pattern on the tape. Cassette tape recordings are analog recordings. Digital audiotape (DAT) records digital signals. The binary numbers 0 and 1 are stored as an on-and-off magnetic pattern on the tape.

Compact discs contain digital recordings. The 0s and 1s of the binary numbers are represented by microscopic pits in the surface of the disc.

## Recording studios

Simple sound recordings, such as those for news bulletins, are made with a single microphone and tape recorder. Music recordings are made in a recording studio. Different voices and instruments are picked up by different microphones and recorded separately. Each recording is called a track.

Video recording works in a similar way to sound recording. Moving pictures are turned into electrical signals by a video camera.

Most music recordings are made in stereo. This means that two tracks are recorded. Each track contains different parts of the original music. When the tape or CD is played, the sounds on the tracks come out of different loudspeakers. This makes the sound more real, because the instruments seem to be located in different places.

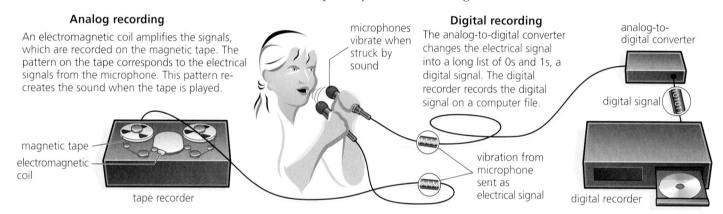

**Analog recording**

An electromagnetic coil amplifies the signals, which are recorded on the magnetic tape. The pattern on the tape corresponds to the electrical signals from the microphone. This pattern re-creates the sound when the tape is played.

magnetic tape
electromagnetic coil
tape recorder

microphones vibrate when struck by sound

**Digital recording**

The analog-to-digital converter changes the electrical signal into a long list of 0s and 1s, a digital signal. The digital recorder records the digital signal on a computer file.

vibration from microphone sent as electrical signal

analog-to-digital converter

digital signal

digital recorder

## Analog and digital

Recordings are made either in analog form or in digital form. An analog recording is a copy or image, such as the magnetic pattern on a cassette tape, of the signal from the microphone. To make a digital recording, the signal is coded by turning it into a long list of numbers. This process is called *digitization*. It is done by an analog-to-digital converter. The converter measures the strength of the analog signal from the microphone thousands of times every second. Each time it gives an answer as a binary number (a number represented by a combination of the two digits 0 and 1). The long list of numbers is called a *digital signal*.

## Tape and compact-disc recording

A cassette tape contains millions of tiny magnetic particles (they are a bit like tiny bar magnets). The electrical signal is sent to the recording head, which magnetizes the particles weakly or strongly as the signal changes. In this

Some studios can record up to 64 tracks. The different tracks are mixed together to make the final recording.

In an analog recording studio, tracks are recorded on wide magnetic tapes. In a digital studio, the signals are digitized and recorded on a computer. The sound engineer then mixes the tracks on a computer screen. Digital recordings can be copied exactly. Each time an analog recording is copied, it gets slightly distorted.

### LOOKING BACK

The first successful sound-recording machine was built in 1878 by the American inventor Thomas Edison. The machine, called a *phonograph*, recorded sounds by making a groove in a tin-foil or wax-covered cylinder. The recording was made mechanically, because there were no electronics at the time.

Flat discs (records) were first used in 1888, and vinyl records in 1948. Magnetic tape was developed in the 1930s, and compact discs in the early 1980s. ◆

▲ Differences between analog and digital recording techniques.

In a digital recording studio, the sounds are recorded and mixed using a computer, rather than on magnetic tape.

# Recycling

▶ Many towns have recycling centers, where people can leave materials such as newspapers, cans and bottles.

When we take waste products and turn them into useful materials, we are recycling them. Recycling materials saves energy and raw materials. It can also help to reduce damage to the environment. For every ton of waste paper collected and recycled, two trees can be saved. Recycling glass means that fewer sand pits and limestone quarries are needed, while recycling metals such as steel and aluminum similarly reduces the number of mines and quarries. As raw materials become scarcer and therefore more expensive, it will become increasingly necessary to recycle.

Trash from homes and factories contains useful materials that can be recycled. More than half of the contents of the average family garbage can could be retrieved, sorted and used again.

At present only 25% of the world's paper is recycled. This could quite easily be increased to 75%. Over 35 million trees could then be saved each year.

## Recycling glass

Glass is unique in that it can be used over and over again without any loss of quality. Broken or waste glass can be mixed with sand, limestone and soda ash, and used to make new glass.

## Recycling paper and cardboard

The world steel industry uses about 45% scrap metal to produce the iron it needs.

Paper and cardboard are made from pulped wood, and more than half of household waste is paper. Waste paper and cardboard are easy to

collect, and although recycled paper is not as good as the original, it still has many uses. Recycled paper and cardboard can also be used in the building industry, to make insulation materials and plasterboard.

## Recycling metals

Even before recycling became so economically important, there was a scrap-metal industry. People collected waste metal products, particularly iron, for sale to metal-producing firms. Some metals are easy to separate from rubbish. Most food cans are made of tin-plated steel, and they can be separated using magnets. The steel is of no great value at present, but the tin coating can be melted down and used again. Aluminum is also very valuable. Soft-drink cans, metal foil and disposable pie plates are all made of aluminum and can be separated out and melted down.

## Recycling plastics

It is possible to recycle plastic materials, but when a product contains a mixture of plastics, this may be difficult. However, scientists have developed "compatibilizers," which are special agents that are able to bond different plastics together, creating a recycled plastic "alloy."

## Other forms of recycling

It is possible to recycle road materials such as asphalt and concrete. They can be scraped off the road for heating and relaying. Even when trash is simply dumped into landfill sites, some recycling can be carried out. The trash, when compressed, can create methane for use as an energy source. ◆

▶ Beverage bottles at a recycling center.

▼ See also
Aluminum
Materials
Paper
Plastics
Trash

# Red Cross

At Solferino, the French under Napoleon III fought on the side of the Kingdom of Piedmont. The Piedmontese aimed to drive the Austrian rulers out of Lombardy and Venetia and form a united kingdom of all Italy. They eventually succeeded.

The headquarters of the Red Cross and Red Crescent Societies are still based in Geneva, Switzerland.

A business trip led to the founding of one of the finest charity organizations in the world. A 31-year-old Swiss businessman, Jean Henri Dunant, had traveled to northern Italy in June 1859, hoping to meet with the French emperor, Napoleon III. Instead, he became an unwilling spectator at the Battle of Solferino between the Austrians and the French.

Dunant spent several days caring for some of the thousands of wounded men who were left on the battlefield. Then he launched a campaign that led to a conference to set up a permanent aid society in 1864. It adopted as its emblem the Swiss flag with the colors reversed—and the Red Cross was born.

Today the organization is known as the International Red Cross and Red Crescent Movement. A crescent is used by Muslim countries because the cross is a Christian symbol.

The International Committee of the Red Cross acts as an intermediary between countries at war. Under a treaty called the Geneva Convention (1864), the countries that have agreed to it promise not to fire on people, hospitals and ambulances displaying the Red Cross. They promise to treat prisoners of war in a humane manner. The Red Cross also helps trace people who have been taken prisoner.

There are individual Red Cross and Red Crescent Societies in 146 countries. Their work is coordinated by the League of Red Cross and Red Crescent Societies, founded in 1919. National Red Cross Societies carry out their own programs. These often include teaching people basic first aid.

### LOOKING BACK

Henri Dunant spent so much time working for the new Red Cross that he became very poor. But in 1895 his plight was made public. He was given a pension, and in 1901 he shared the first Nobel Peace Prize with a Frenchman, Frédéric Passy. ◆

▼See also
Charities
First aid
Peace movement

**BIOGRAPHY**
Barton, Clara

# Reeds

Wherever you see reeds growing you know the ground is really wet. The reed is a very large member of the grass family and can grow over 3 m (10 ft) high. Reeds have tough, long-lasting stems that are used to make matting and screens. They are best known for their use in thatching and were extensively cropped in the Norfolk fens in England. Some wind instruments, such as the clarinet, have a piece of reed stem in the mouthpiece. When moistened it becomes soft and vibrates as air is blown over it: this creates a musical note. In ancient Egypt, the stem of papyrus (the paper reed) was used to make paper. Papyrus once grew along the banks of the River Nile.

## Other grass-like plants found in wet places

Rushes are spiky plants. The center of the round stem is filled with fluffy white pith (used by the Romans as a wick for candles and later used as an early form of toothpaste).

Sedges are grass-like plants with sharp-edged stems that are triangular in cross-section, and leaves growing out in three directions. ◆

Here is a way to remember the difference between sedges and rushes: sedges have edges and rushes are round.

Growing beds of reeds are now being used as biological filters to clean up sewage.

▼See also
Grasses
Paper
Wetlands

▼ Reed beds are home to large numbers of birds. This one is a bittern, a member of the heron family.

# Reformation

In 1500, Christians in Western Europe all belonged to the Catholic Church, with the pope in Rome at its head. Fifty years later, European Christians were bitterly divided into separate Churches. We call this change the Reformation.

## Problems in the Church

Some people had been critical of the Catholic Church long before the Reformation. Popes often behaved more like powerful kings than religious leaders. Bishops and abbots of great monasteries were often wealthy landowners and also royal advisers at court. But ordinary priests were often so poor and ignorant that they, too, could hardly do their job properly. Sometimes prayers to pictures, statues and "relics" of Jesus or saints seemed somewhat like magic spells.

|  | Protestant Churches | Roman Catholic Church |
|---|---|---|
| **Organization** | *Luther's churches:* Bishops and priests less powerful. No monks, nuns, friars, or pope.<br>*Calvin's churches:* Ministers chosen by the people for their church. | Pope, head of the Church, with cardinals, archbishops, priests, monks, nuns, friars. |
| **Churches** | Churches plain, without pictures and statues; the altar a simple table without cross or candles. | Churches rich with paintings and statues of Virgin Mary and saints. Altar elaborately decorated with cross and candles. |
| **Services** | Communion held in local language. Ministers wore plain black gowns. Long sermons preached to teach the Bible. | The mass celebrated in Latin. Priests wore vestments. |

**Protestant Branches**

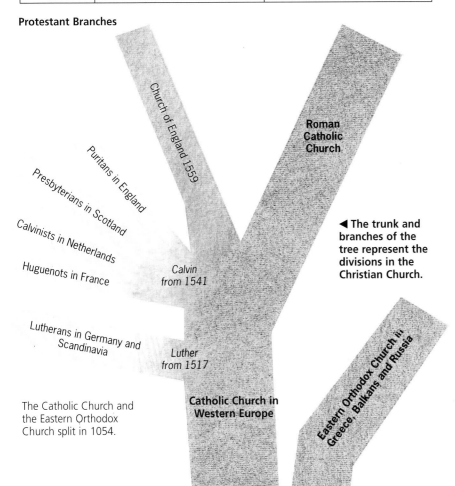

Church of England 1559
Puritans in England
Presbyterians in Scotland
Calvinists in Netherlands
Huguenots in France
Lutherans in Germany and Scandinavia

Roman Catholic Church

Calvin from 1541

Luther from 1517

◀ The trunk and branches of the tree represent the divisions in the Christian Church.

**Catholic Church in Western Europe**

Eastern Orthodox Church in Greece, Balkans, and Russia

The Catholic Church and the Eastern Orthodox Church split in 1054.

## Protest in the Church

The Church was further undermined by the row over indulgences (pardons for sins) that people could buy. In 1517, a German monk, Martin Luther, wrote a long list of reasons why he disagreed with indulgences, and pinned it on the church door in his hometown of Wittenberg in Saxony. Perhaps this would have been just a local quarrel if printing had not been invented. But Luther's list, and other churchmen's arguments against it, were printed throughout Germany. His ideas spread. The ruler of Saxony, and other German princes who wanted to be free of interference by the pope, backed Luther. They drew up a "Protest" in 1529. Soon the "Protestants" set up a separate Church. The nickname stuck.

## Different kinds of Protestants

Luther taught that people must work out their own faith in God from the Bible, so they did not need the pope or priests. Often Protestants had different ideas from each other. John Calvin set up a church in Geneva. Its members chose their own ministers, lived simple, strict lives and believed they were specially chosen by God. Calvin's teachings spread to France and Scotland. In 1534 Henry VIII of England made himself Supreme Head of the Church in England because the pope refused to grant him a divorce. Changes in belief came later. In 1559 Elizabeth I set up the Church of England, which was a "middle way" between Catholic and Protestant ideas.

## Counter-Reformation

The Catholic Church began to reform itself (the Counter-Reformation) and tried hard to win back Protestants. Both sides believed that they were right, and that those who disagreed with them would go to hell. Rulers did not want different Christian churches in their kingdoms because of possible conflicts. So, in the 16th and 17th centuries, there were terrible religious wars and persecutions in Europe. Many years passed before Protestants and Catholics began to respect and tolerate each other. ◆

# Refrigerators

Refrigerators are machines for keeping things cold. Most homes in Western countries have small refrigerators for storing fresh food (and perhaps some frozen food as well). Refrigerators can also be very large, like those in ships that transport perishable foods.

### How they work

Refrigerators work by evaporation. When a liquid changes to a vapor, it takes heat from its surroundings. If you wet your finger and then wave your hand, that finger feels coldest. The water takes heat from your finger as it evaporates. Refrigerators move heat, taking it away from the inside, which becomes colder, and giving it to the outside, which gets warmer. In refrigerators the cooling is done by evaporating a special substance called a *refrigerant*.

### Compression refrigerators

The refrigerant circulates around a sealed system of pipes. An electric pump compresses the refrigerant vapor, and this causes it to get hot. You get the same effect with a bicycle pump if you pump very hard.

The refrigerant leaves the compressor at high pressure. As it flows through the condenser pipes it gives out heat, cools down and condenses to liquid refrigerant. This section of pipe is always placed outside the refrigerator. Black cooling fins help the heat to be lost to the surrounding air.

The liquid then passes from this narrow pipe through a small hole or expansion valve. This leads to a larger evaporator pipe. The lower pressure causes the liquid to evaporate and take in heat from its surroundings. This pipe is inside the refrigerator, and so the food loses some of its heat and gets cold.

The refrigerant vapor now returns to the compressor and the cycle is repeated. A thermostat controls the temperature by turning the compressor motor on and off as necessary.

Not all refrigerators use a compressor. Some use the heat from a gas flame to circulate an ammonia refrigerant. Refrigerators like this have no moving parts and make no noise, but they are much less efficient than compression refrigerators and cost more to operate.

Refrigerators keep food at a temperature of about 5 °C (41°F). Freezers work in the same way as refrigerators, but are more powerful and give a greater cooling effect. In a freezer, food stays frozen at about –18 °C (0°F).

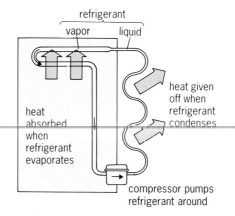

◀ Refrigerant substance is pumped around a circuit of pipes in a compression refrigerator.

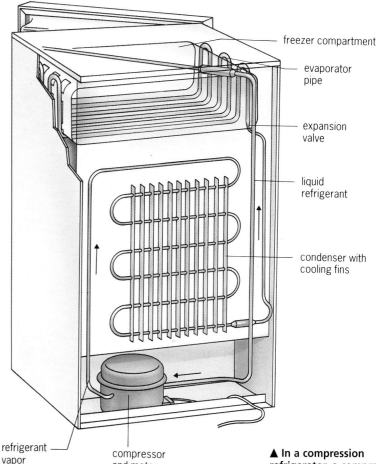

▲ In a compression refrigerator, a compressor pumps the refrigerant around. The liquid refrigerant turns to vapor when it passes through the expansion valve. This produces a cooling effect. The vapor turns back to liquid in the condenser.

### LOOKING BACK

Ice is one of the oldest methods of refrigeration and was used by the Chinese in 1000 B.C.

In 1748, in Scotland, William Cullen demonstrated artificial refrigeration for the first time, but he did not put the discovery to practical use. The first practical compression refrigerators were built in the mid-19th century. The earliest refrigerant to be used was ammonia, but this was poisonous, and corrosive if it leaked. Safer, synthetic refrigerants were not developed until the 1920s. ◆

▼ See also
Cold
Heat

BIOGRAPHY
Faraday, Michael

# Refugees

**M**any refugees, since the days of the Pilgrims, have come to the United States.

**T**here have been more than 40 million refugees throughout the world since the end of World War II.

Refugees are people who flee from their homes because their lives are in danger from war or famine, or because of persecution for their religion or politics. Those who register with the United Nations High Commissioner for Refugees are helped until they can return home or settle elsewhere. Officially, there are more than 14 million refugees, but there are millions of others who have fled to safety. Many are people who have moved to a distant part of their own country because of war, famine or persecution. Many others are not allowed to register or not accepted as being refugees, often because they cannot prove that their lives were in danger.

Most of today's refugees have left home because of famine or civil war. Thailand has many refugees from Cambodia. People have fled from civil war in Sudan to Ethiopia, Kenya and Uganda. When Soviet troops entered Afghanistan in 1979, many Afghans fled to Pakistan. Many people became refugees as a result of the tribal war between the Tutsis and the Hutus in Rwanda in 1995. Over the years of war in the former Yugoslavia, thousands of families were forced to leave their homes and became refugees.

Most refugees and displaced people arrive with nothing. They need food, clothes, shelter and medical care. Many have walked hundreds of miles, seen people die on the way, and become separated from the rest of their family. They probably cannot speak the local language, and they may not be welcome in an area that is already poor.

The United Nations High Commissioner for Refugees has a small staff to help organize refugee camps, but relies on many different organizations to give aid. In time, the refugees may be able to go home because a famine is over or a war has ended. But some will have to resettle because they cannot return to their own country. Many of the "Boat People" who fled from Vietnam in the 1980s have settled in North America, Europe or Australia, but others have lived in Hong Kong for years waiting for the chance to start a new life.

These people are mostly sure of a place to resettle, but those who arrived after June 15, 1988, have to go through screening procedures before they are accepted as genuine refugees. If they are rejected, they may be returned to Vietnam.

Camps for Palestinians in Israel became permanent settlements because no one wanted to give land to the refugees.

## LOOKING BACK

The French word *réfugié* was used to describe Protestant Huguenots who fled from Catholic France to England and other countries in 1685. Many Jews fled from Russia early in the 20th century, and from Germany during the 1930s, prior to World War II.

Millions of people became refugees during and after World War I and the Russian Revolution. In 1920s and 1930s, they were aided by the High Commission for Refugees and its successor, the Nansen International Office for Refugees; both organizations were created by the League of Nations, the predecessor of the United Nations. After World War II ended in 1945, millions of new European refugees were aided by a UN agency called UNRRA, later renamed the International Refugee Organization (IRO).

Millions more became refugees in the late 1940s, when Pakistan split from India and Palestine was divided into Jewish Israel and Arab Jordan. The UN Relief and Works Agency (UNRWA) was created in 1949 to help Palestinian refugees. In 1951, the Office of the UN High Commissioner for Refugees was created as a successor to the IRO to look after refugees in other parts of the world. ◆

▶ By January 1993, an estimated 130,000 Bosnians had been made refugees by the war between the countries of the former Yugoslavia.

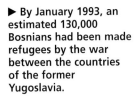

# Reggae

**See also**
Caribbean
Jamaica
Rastafarians

▼ Bob Marley's Rastafarian belief was central to his world-famous reggae music.

Reggae is a kind of pop music. It began in Jamaica in the 1960s, and quickly spread to other places where West Indians and, in particular, Rastafarians lived. The late Bob Marley and other musicians have now made reggae popular in many parts of the world. It has also influenced many mainstream pop musicians.

Reggae grew out of earlier Jamaican musical styles known as "ska" and "rocksteady." It has a characteristic rhythm, with a heavy beat on the second and fourth counts of every bar (one-*two*-three-*four*). Reggae words are in Jamaican dialect, and are often about Caribbean life and Rastafarian culture. Some reggae records are just a backing track with no vocals. This is "dub" reggae. At reggae discos, disk jockeys play "dub" reggae and "rap" over it, talking fast and rhythmically, quickly making up the rhymes as they go along. ◆

# Reincarnation

In ancient times many people believed in reincarnation. Plato, the Greek philosopher, believed that an immortal soul passed from one body to another.

**See also**
Buddhism
Hinduism
Sikhism

Members of some religions believe that when we die we are reborn as another human being or as an animal. This is called reincarnation, transmigration or rebirth. Hindus, Sikhs and Jains believe that we have immortal souls that go from body to body until they are finally free. Buddhists believe it is consciousness that travels from one life to the next, bearing the laws of cause and effect (*karma*). In whatever way rebirth happens, it is believed to be fair. The kind of life we have is the result of what was done, said or thought in previous lives. ◆

# Reindeer

Herds of reindeer (caribou) may migrate great distances to reach good summer feeding grounds in the tundra, where their calves are born. In winter they return to the shelter of the forests. Unlike all other kinds of deer, reindeer females have antlers, but they are smaller than those of the males. It is said that both sexes use their antlers for pushing snow from their food in the winter. Reindeer eat many kinds of plants, including a species of lichen that is known as reindeer moss.

Reindeer have been hunted by humans since prehistoric times. Their numbers are now greatly reduced. In parts of Northern Europe and Asia the reindeer have been domesticated. They still make their migrations, but they are followed by the Lapps (also called Sami, a people who live in northern Scandinavia), who use them for their meat, milk and hides. The Lapps also make things from their bones and antlers. In a few places reindeer are still ridden, or used to pull sleighs. ◆

**Distribution**
Tundra and northern forests of Europe, Asia and North America
**Size**
Head and body length up to 2.2 m (7.2 ft)
**Weight**
Up to 320 kg (700 lbs)
**Number of young**
1 (called a calf). It can outrun a man when it is a day old
**Lifespan**
About 5 years in the wild, may survive more than 20 years in captivity
**Subphylum** Vertebrata
**Class** Mammalia
**Order** Artiodactyla
**Family** Cervidae
**Number of species** 1

**See also**
Deer
Domestication
Horns and antlers
Migration

▼ Herding domesticated reindeer in Lapland. Reindeer have thick coats and large hooves to help them travel over snow.

# Relativity

The speed of light is about 300,000 km (186,000 mi) per second. According to relativity theory, nothing can travel faster than light.

At present even the fastest rockets can still travel at only a tiny fraction of the speed of light, so we cannot experience the change in the measurement of time directly.

In Einstein's mass-energy equation $E = mc^2$, $E$ stands for energy (in joules), $m$ for mass (in kg) and c for the speed of light (in meters per second).

▼ **See also**

Atoms
Black holes
Energy
Light
Mass
Nuclear power
Time

**BIOGRAPHY**
Einstein, Albert

Albert Einstein proposed his theory of special relativity in 1905. He developed it from two basic ideas. One was that all speeds are relative: they only tell you how fast something is moving *relative to something else*. A train may be traveling straight past a platform at 150 km (90 mi) per hour but inside the train, everything behaves as if the platform is traveling past the train. The second, much more difficult, idea was that relative motion has no effect on the speed of light. Light always passes you at the same relative speed, whether you are rushing toward or away from the light source.

Einstein linked these two ideas mathematically. He concluded that relative motion affects how we view other people's measurements of distance and time. For example, if you could see inside a rocket traveling past you at nearly the speed of light, any clocks inside would appear to be running slow. But, to the people in the rocket, time would be normal. Einstein also concluded that energy has mass. As things gain or lose energy, they also gain or lose mass. He expressed this idea in a famous equation, $E = mc^2$ (c stands for the speed of light). In this equation, $c^2$ is such a big number that the energy changes in everyday events produce no detectable changes in mass. However, when scientists first started to split atoms, they measured mass changes which made them realize that huge amounts of energy might be released. This ultimately led to the development of the atomic bomb and other forms of nuclear power.

In 1915 Einstein published his theory of general relativity. This includes the effects of gravity and acceleration on space and time. Scientists have used this theory to develop their ideas about collapsed stars called black holes. It has also made them think that space itself may be curved by gravity. ◆

# Religions

Many people ask "Where was I before I was born?," "Where will I go when I die?" and "Why do people suffer?"

These are all questions that religions try to answer. They teach that the meaning of life is not only in our friends and families, our interests and work, but in something that will not die or change and is beyond, as well as related to, our world. This might be called God, or an eternal state of peacefulness called nirvana. Believing in God, or following the teachings of great leaders like the Buddha, might change the way we behave. It does not mean that we take the world less seriously but that we see deeper meanings in things. Religions are also organizations of people who share the same beliefs or way of life. You may be born into a religion or you can join one from choice.

## Beliefs

Members of a religion share important ideas, such as belief in God, in reincarnation, in the teachings of prophets, and in heaven and hell. Christians believe that Jesus is the son of God, and Muslims that Muhammad is the last and greatest of the prophets. Buddhists believe that Gautama Buddha taught a path from suffering to peacefulness.

**Places of Worship**
Churches and chapels for Christians
Mosques for Muslims
Gurdwaras for Sikhs
Synagogues for Jews
Temples for Hindus, Buddhists, Jains

◀ A priest greets parishioners after Sunday mass.

◄◄ A Hindu meditates by the banks of the River Ganges.

◄ An African Muslim has marked out a sacred area with stones. Here he is reading the Koran, the holy book of Muslims.

▼ A procession of Sikhs carrying the *Guru Granth Sahib*, their holy book, on a throne at the opening of a new gurdwara (temple) in Kenya.

## Stories about reality

Teachers of all religions tell stories to help people understand the world and its meaning. These are sometimes called myths. Myths may be used to explain why the world exists, how it might end, and what are the best ways of living. The Hindu story of Rama and Sita in the Ramayana is a myth. So is the Jewish story of creation in Genesis, the first book of the Bible. Some Christians think that the story of the birth of Jesus is a myth that was created to help them understand who Jesus really was. Other Christians believe that the story of Christ's nativity is literally true.

## How to behave

Whether or not people believe that these stories or myths are true, they can still affect the way people treat each other. They set models of good behavior. All religions try to guide people, to show them the difference between good and bad, right and wrong. The story of Jesus' care for other people and his patient self-sacrifice on the cross have inspired Christians to love and serve others. Muslims are encouraged to live honestly and bravely as Muhammad did. Hindus, Buddhists and Jains teach that no form of life should be harmed since all life is a unity. Members of different religions find that they share common attitudes, including love, faithfulness in marriage, and peace.

## Communities

Every religion is a kind of extended family or community. Members feel a special relationship with, and a special duty toward, each other. Most religions have a place where their members can meet for worship and social activities. This becomes an important part of people's lives, whether it is a Hindu temple, Christian church, Sikh gurdwara, Muslim mosque or Jewish synagogue.

## Rituals

One of the reasons for which members of religions meet is for prayer and worship. People may use not only words but movements of the body, such as kneeling or bowing low to the floor, for prayers. Sometimes there are processions. All of these services are called rituals, rites or ceremonies. Usually they take place on a particular day of the week: Sundays for Christians, Fridays for Muslims, Saturdays for Jews. There might be religious music or chanting, which makes the ritual different from what you do at other times and in other places.

## Experiences

Some experiences of believers are out of the ordinary. St. Paul believed he heard Jesus' voice on the way to Damascus. Muhammad is said to have heard the Koran recited to him.

But many religious experiences are more everyday. People often find that their beliefs and the help of their community give them the strength to put up with illness and personal tragedy bravely and cheerfully. Others are able to make great sacrifices to nurse those who are dying or to argue with powerful governments about cruelty and injustice.

## Religion today

Members of different religious faiths are making efforts to talk to each other and understand each other better. They are sharing in projects to help people all over the world. There are peace pilgrimages, environmental projects, and organizations such as the World Congress of Faiths which are bringing members of different religions together. There is a sense of purpose, hope and beauty in much religious teaching that seems to satisfy a deeper human need than the desire for money, power and possessions. ◆

**▼ See also**
Bahaism
Buddhism
Christianity
God
Hinduism
Initiation ceremonies
Islam
Judaism
Myths and legends
Rastafarians
Rites and rituals
Shintoism
Sikhism
Taoism

# Renaissance

The word "renaissance" means "rebirth." It is the name used for the period of great discoveries in learning and art that reached its peak in late 15th- and 16th-century Italy. But the Renaissance spread far beyond Italy to France, Germany, Britain and most of Western Europe.

For centuries the Catholic Church had been the center of learning and art. But toward the end of the Middle Ages, educated people began to find out more about the old "classical" civilizations of Greece and Rome. This led them to discover many new ideas about themselves and their world. It became interesting and fashionable to learn Greek. It was an exciting time—people felt there was no limit to what they could discover or do. It all seemed like a new beginning, a rebirth.

In Italy people could see the impressive remains of beautiful classical buildings. There were rich and powerful cities: Rome, the center of the Catholic Church; Florence, whose riches came from banking and the production of silk, velvet and woolen textiles; Milan, where the best armor was made; and Venice and Genoa, which controlled the profitable trade routes from the East. The revival of interest in culture encouraged wealthy leading citizens to commission and employ artists and scholars.

## Artists discover space

Renaissance painters and sculptors studied old Greek and Roman works of art, as well as the world around them. They gradually learned how to make their own pictures and carvings more realistic.

The two pictures of Mary with the baby Jesus on the next page show how artists discovered new ways to make space in their pictures. Duccio painted his gentle mother and baby in the late Middle Ages. His picture is like a flat, beautiful pattern. You cannot look beyond the people into the background.

In the following centuries, Raphael and other Renaissance artists discovered how to make space and distance in their pictures by using the rules of perspective. This Mary sits on a solid throne, with steps you could walk up. You can look beyond the throne to a tiny glimpse of a distant countryside. The artist has used light and shadows to paint the chubby baby and the grown-ups, so that they look real and solid, too.

▼ Leonardo da Vinci was one of the greatest artists of the Renaissance. He was also a scientist, architect and engineer, and had many other interests. These two drawings are from his notebooks. One shows how he worked out the anatomy of the human figure; the other is an experimental flying machine.

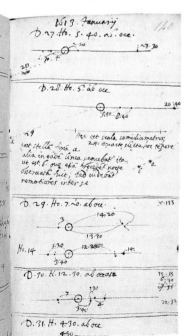

▼ In the Renaissance, scholars began to find out more about the world around them, and the Universe. Galileo was the first astronomer to use a telescope in his work. These are his notes on the movements of one of the planets he observed on January 28, 1613. Astronomers later determined that the planet was Neptune.

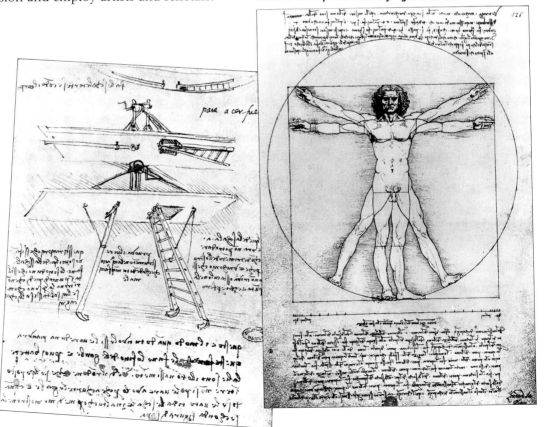

◀ The picture on the left is the Rucellai Madonna, painted by Duccio about 1285. The picture on the right is the Ansidei Madonna, painted by Raphael about 1504. You can see how much more realistic the people and the setting look in the later Renaissance painting.

## Architects solve problems

The citizens of Florence, inspired by the classical influences of the time, wanted their new cathedral to have a dome. But no one knew how to build such a big one. For over 50 years there was a great hole in the cathedral roof. Finally, there was a competition, won by Filippo Brunelleschi, a goldsmith. He studied some domes built long ago, including the Pantheon in Rome. This was a classical domed temple built by the Romans 1,300 years earlier. Then Brunelleschi began to solve the problems. The walls of the cathedral were so high and far apart that he had to design special scaffolding and a hoist to lift the building materials. He used brick (which is lighter than stone) with stone ribs for support, and built an inner and an outer dome in concentric rings. The dome was finished on August 31, 1436. It was the first dome built since ancient times, and it still soars above the city of Florence. ◆

◀ Italian Renaissance architect Brunelleschi amazed his contemporaries when he devised a way of constructing a great dome for the cathedral in Florence.

# Reproduction

All types of living things can reproduce to make young just like themselves. Lions produce lion cubs, and not tiger cubs. Blackbirds' eggs contain blackbird chicks and not sparrows. Acorns only grow into oak trees, and dandelion seeds always produce dandelion plants. This happens because of genes, the chemical instructions for making a living thing, which are passed from one generation to the next during reproduction.

Many creatures and plants reproduce sexually. In animals, a sperm cell from the male fuses with an egg cell from the female. In plants, pollen from the male part of a flower fertilizes an ovule (the plant equivalent of an egg) in the female part of another flower, to produce seeds that grow into next season's plants.

▶ A freshwater *Hydra* with bud. The bud is already catching its own food and will soon detach from its parent and become fully independent.

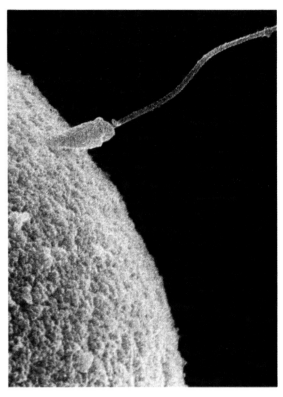

▲ This picture shows a male sperm joining with a female egg. The picture has been magnified many times. Millions of sperm cells enter the female body, but only one will succeed in fertilizing the much larger egg.

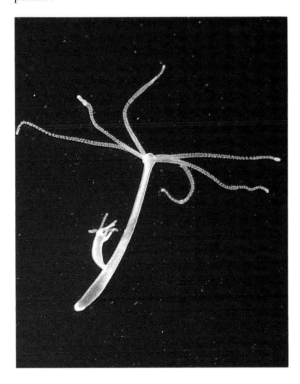

## Budding and splitting

Some organisms reproduce without sex. Amoebas simply split in two. Some sea anemones and their relatives, like *Hydra*, can reproduce by budding. A small bud develops on the side of an adult and grows into a new animal joined to the parent by a stalk. Then the stalk breaks and there are two animals where before there was one. Geraniums and many other plants can grow from a cutting. A stem cut from a big plant grows roots and becomes a new young plant.

## Sperms and eggs

Most animals reproduce sexually. The male produces millions of tiny swimming sperms. The female makes fewer, larger eggs. One sperm joins with an egg, either in water around the parents (*external fertilization*) or inside the female's body (*internal fertilization*). Most fish and frogs use the external method. Insects, reptiles, birds and mammals use the internal one. Fertilization brings together genes from both parents and starts the development of an egg into a new animal.

## Embryos and development

When an egg has been fertilized, it splits into two; the two parts into four; four into eight; and so on. This turns the egg into an *embryo*: a growing ball of cells that gradually changes and develops into a new animal. In fish, frogs, reptiles and birds, the embryo develops from an egg, using food called *yolk* stored in the egg. Embryo mammals grow inside their mother's body, using food supplied by the mother through the placenta. ◆

# Reptiles

▲ One of the 90 species of living turtles and tortoises. Like the others, this turtle has no teeth. Instead, it has a strong horny beak that it uses to crush insects and other invertebrates.

▼ **See also**
Alligators
Chameleons
Crocodiles
Dinosaurs
Lizards
Snakes
Tortoises and turtles
Warm- and cold-
  bloodedness

Crocodiles, snakes, tortoises and lizards all belong to the group of vertebrates (backboned animals) known as reptiles. Many have strong limbs, though most cannot move very fast for more than a short time. They use lungs to breathe, and have a tough, dry and usually scaly skin. They are "cold-blooded," which means they control their body temperature through their behavior—for example, by moving into cold places when hot and warm places when cold.

In the breeding season, males use dances or bright colors to attract females. After mating, the females choose a sheltered place or make a simple nest, where they generally lay a fairly small number of eggs. These usually have a papery or leathery shell, but are otherwise very much like birds' eggs. In most cases they are left to be hatched by the heat of the sun, but some reptiles remain near the nest, and a few kinds, such as crocodiles and some snakes, look after their eggs and young. The females of some reptiles, most of which live in cool parts of the world, hold the eggs inside their bodies until they are ready to hatch. The eggs are always laid on dry land, and the babies that hatch from them look just like their parents.

In the past, many kinds of reptiles flourished. The dinosaurs, which evolved from reptiles, included the largest known land-living creatures. Today there are only four surviving orders (groups) of reptiles:

*Turtles and tortoises* are all armored with a bony shell. Many swim well and live in water, but they must come onto land to lay their eggs.

*Rhynchocephalia* contains one living species, the tuatara, which lives on a few islands off the coast of New Zealand. It is the only survivor of a big group of reptiles that were important during the days of the dinosaurs.

*Lizards and snakes* are the best-known and the most abundant reptiles.

*Crocodiles and their relatives* are the bulkiest of today's reptiles, and all live in or near water, although they have to come ashore to lay their eggs. ◆

**Distribution** Mostly in the warmer parts of the world
**Largest** Estuarine or salt-water crocodile may grow to over 7 m (23 ft) in length
**Smallest** Two species of dwarf gecko from the West Indies are about 1.7 cm (0.66 in) long
**Number of young** Sea turtles may lay up to 200 eggs at a time. Most geckos (small lizards) produce only 1 or 2 eggs at a time.
**Lifespan** Big crocodiles and turtles may be 200 years old. Most reptiles have shorter lifespans.
**Subphylum** Vertebrata
**Class** Reptilia
**Number of species** About 6,000

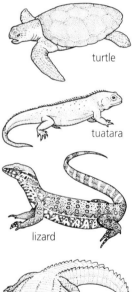

turtle

tuatara

lizard

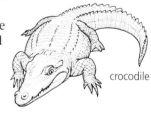

crocodile

---

# Republics

The word "republic" comes from the Latin phrase *res publica*, which means "the people's affairs."

Any country that does not have a king or other hereditary monarch as head of state is called a republic. Its head of state is usually a president. Strictly speaking, a republic is a country where the people, through their elected representatives, exercise supreme power, but many republics are ruled by dictators or by single political groups.

The Romans drove out their king and set up a republic in 509 B.C. It lasted for nearly 500 years. The next important countries to become republics were the United States of America, in 1776, and France, in 1792. ◆

▼ **See also**
Dictators
Kings and queens
Presidents
Rome and the Roman
  Empire

# Respiration

People usually think that respiration means breathing. But breathing is just one way of getting oxygen so that respiration can take place.

All living things need energy. They need it for movement, growth, repairing wounds and all the other processes necessary for life. Engines obtain energy from fuel, such as gasoline. The "fuel" that provides energy for living things is their food, and energy is released from food by a process called respiration.

windpipe

lung

one air sac

air sac covered with blood vessels

carbon dioxide breathed out

air sac

oxygen breathed in

blood vessel in lung

blood full of carbon dioxide

blood full of oxygen

blood vessel among body cells

body cell

blood full of oxygen

blood full of carbon dioxide

→ oxygen

⇒ carbon dioxide

▲ Aerobic respiration occurs in every cell and needs a constant supply of oxygen. Oxygen from air breathed into the lungs passes into the blood and is carried to the cells. Carbon dioxide produced by respiration passes into the blood and is carried to the lungs where it is breathed out.

## Respiration with oxygen

When an engine uses gasoline, it burns it with oxygen to produce energy, and there is a type of respiration that uses oxygen in a similar way. It is called *aerobic respiration*. Sugars and fats in food are combined with oxygen in a kind of controlled "burning" in cells all over the body. This process releases energy, water, and carbon dioxide, a waste gas.

Animals have special respiratory organs to obtain oxygen for aerobic respiration and to get rid of the carbon dioxide. The carbon dioxide is exchanged for oxygen in the respiratory organs. The gills of fish exchange carbon dioxide for oxygen in water. The lungs of humans and most animals with backbones exchange carbon

dioxide for oxygen in the air. Blood carries oxygen from respiratory organs to every cell in the body where respiration occurs. In these cells oxygen is combined with food to release energy. Blood then carries waste carbon dioxide back to the respiratory organs to be removed from the body. Respiration releases heat, and warm-blooded animals (birds and mammals) keep their body temperatures high by respiration.

## Respiration without oxygen

Some organisms can respire without oxygen. This is called *anaerobic respiration*. They include microbes living in thick mud, and parasites living inside an animal's intestine. Many plants can respire anaerobically for a while if covered by floodwaters. Your muscles respire anaerobically when you run very quickly. No matter how fast you breathe, or how fast your heart pumps blood, your muscles cannot get enough energy from aerobic respiration, so they get the extra energy they need anaerobically. This produces lactic acid as a waste product instead of carbon dioxide. The lactic acid gathers in your muscles and eventually makes them ache so much you have to stop. By rapid breathing, enough oxygen is breathed in to change the lactic acid into carbon dioxide. This is then breathed out of the body, and the pain is relieved. ◆

Plants also respire, so they also need oxygen. But plants make their own oxygen. It is another product of photosynthesis. Plants use energy from the Sun to turn carbon dioxide and water into glucose and oxygen.

▼ The scientific name for sea slug, *nudibranch*, means "naked gills." Sea slugs have flaps or finger-like projections, which provide a large area where respiration takes place. Unlike fish, their gills are on the outside.

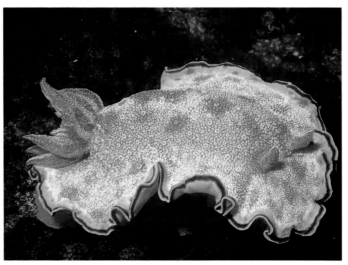

# Revolutions

"**R**evolution" is a word that can be applied to any far-reaching change in the political, social or economic structure of a society. It is not only used in reference to changes in government but also to social changes, such as agricultural revolutions, or the "high-tech" revolution of the 1970s and 1980s when the worldwide use of computers began.

**See also**
Agricultural revolutions
American Revolution
China
England
France
Industrial Revolution
Iran
Russia and the Russian
  Federation

A revolution occurs when people overthrow the government of their country, usually with violence, and completely change the society in which they live. Revolutions, such as those in America and France in the 18th century, take place when a large number of people feel that they must change the way their country is run.

Revolutions often happen when a country is ruled by a bad government, and when the ruling class is very rich and most of the people are very poor. This was the main cause of the Russian Revolution of 1917 and the Chinese Revolution of 1949.

A revolution happened in Iran in 1979 when the Shah was overthrown by Muslim fundamentalists led by Ayatollah Khomeini. ♦

# Rheumatism

Although rheumatoid arthritis can affect anyone, it is most common in women.

There is no single illness called rheumatism. Rheumatism is used as a general term to describe any disorder or illness in which the joints, muscles and connecting tissues of the body become inflamed, swollen and painful. Gout, osteoarthritis, rheumatoid arthritis and rheumatic fever are all called rheumatism. Gout and osteoarthritis usually occur in older people. Gout is caused when increased uric acid production makes crystals, which are deposited on the joints. The wearing away of the cartilage of the joints due to aging causes osteoarthritis. Rheumatoid arthritis can attack people of all ages. It can affect any joint, but usually attacks knuckles and wrists. Rheumatic fever is a disease of children. It usually follows an untreated infection such as tonsillitis. It can affect many parts of the body, including the heart and the joints, but recovery is usually complete, if it is treated properly with medicine and plenty of rest. ♦

**See also**
Arthritis
Bones
Muscles
Skeletons

# Rhinoceroses

Rhinoceroses are different from all other horned mammals in that their horns are not on the top of their head, but are toward the end of their nose. These horns are not like the horns of cattle, or the antlers of deer, but are made of compressed thick hairs.

Rhinos live in tropical grasslands and forests, always in reach of water, for they need to drink every day and also enjoy wallowing in mud. They feed entirely on plants, which black rhinos pick using a grasping upper lip. They have good senses of hearing and smell, but they are short-sighted. Apart from mothers with calves, they usually live alone, and are suspicious of strangers. As a result, they may attack intruders without real cause.

In spite of their heavy skin, rhinoceroses are plagued by ticks and other parasites. They are often seen with tick birds, which help the rhinos by feeding on the pests. Baby rhinos may be hunted by the big cats, but humans are the only enemies of the adults. In the past, dozens of types of rhinoceroses lived in many parts of the world. Today, only five species survive, and all of these have been hunted and poached to near-extinction. ♦

**Distribution**
Africa and tropical Asia
**Largest**
White (square-lipped) rhino, which may be up to 5 m (16 ft) in length and weigh up to 3,600 kg (8,000 lbs)
**Smallest**
Sumatran (hairy) rhino, which is less than 3.2 m (10.5 ft) in length and weighs less than 2,000 kg (4,400 lbs)
**Number of young** 1
The baby stays with its mother for about 2 years; then she usually gives birth to another.
**Lifespan**
Up to 50 years
**Subphylum** Vertebrata
**Class** Mammalia
**Order** Perissodactyla
**Family** Rhinocerotidae
**Number of species** 5

**See also**
Endangered species
Horns and antlers
Mammals

▼ White rhino female with calf. Unlike the other rhino species, white rhinos are mild-natured and very easily frightened off, although white rhino mothers will defend their calves.

# Rhode Island (U.S.A.)

Rhode Island is the smallest state in the nation. From its founding as a colony, it was known as a champion of religious tolerance and freedom of conscience. Its coastline has been a favorite of vacationers for many decades. Rhode Island is the home state of the Perry brothers, Matthew and Oliver Hazard, who were distinguished U.S. Navy officers in the early 19th century. It is also the birthplace of painter Gilbert Stuart (1755–1828), who earned a place in American history with his portraits of George Washington and other early U.S. Presidents.

## History

Rhode Island traces its origins to Roger Williams, a clergyman who was banished from the Massachusetts Bay Colony in 1635 for disagreeing with the religious views of its leaders. Williams made his way south through the wilderness, purchased a plot from the Narragansett Indians, and in 1636 established a settlement that he called Providence Plantation because he believed he had been led there by Divine Providence (God).

In 1638 other well-known exiles from Massachusetts, including Anne Hutchinson and her family, established a settlement named Pocasset (later known as Portsmouth) on Narragansett Bay's Aquidneck Island. A third settlement, Newport, was founded by exiles in 1639,

▼ The harbor at Newport is crowded with sailboats during the summer.

**Area**
3,189 sq km
(1,231 sq mi)
**Capital**
Providence
**Population**
990,000
**Entered Union**
1790
**Places to visit**
"The Breakers" and other mansions, Touro Synagogue, Newport; Slater Mill Historic Site, Pawtucket; Block Island
**Famous Rhode Islanders**
Matthew Perry, Oliver Hazard Perry, Gilbert Stuart

▼ **See also**

American Revolution
Chickens
Congress, U.S.
Constitution, U.S.
Thirteen Colonies
United States of America
Yachts

**BIOGRAPHY**
Perry, Matthew
Perry, Oliver Hazard
Williams, Roger

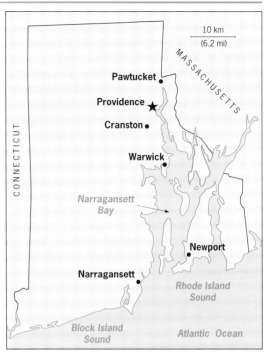

and a fourth was created at Warwick in 1642. Five years later the four towns joined to organize their own government. They adopted the name Rhode Island. This was a version of Roodt Eylandt ("red island"), the name given to the region by Dutch explorer Adriaen Block in 1614.

Williams's policy of religious freedom attracted many new settlers to Rhode Island, including a number of Jews and Quakers. All the early settlers followed Williams's example of buying land from the local Indians rather than taking it by force. During the 18th century, Rhode Islanders objected to England's harsh trade policies, and Narragansett Bay became a haven for smugglers defying English laws. In a famous act of defiance, Rhode Island patriots protested those laws by burning the English ship *Liberty* in 1769 as it lay at dock in Newport. On May 4, 1776, the colony formally renounced its allegiance to King George III of England.

Even after the triumph of the American Revolution, Rhode Island continued its tradition of independence. It opposed attempts by the Continental Congress to raise funds by taxing imports, and it refused to send delegates to the Constitutional Convention in Philadelphia in 1787. When it refused to ratify the new Constitution, the federal government threatened to cut trade ties with Rhode Island. It finally adopted the Constitution in 1790 by a very narrow margin.

Rhode Islanders strongly opposed slavery and backed the Union during the Civil War (1861–1865). Throughout the 19th century, the state welcomed new immigrants, including French Canadians, Portuguese, Irish, Poles and Italians. The growth of the textile industry led to the creation of so-called mill towns, where workers lived in houses owned by the company they worked for and had to shop in company-owned stores. The state's textile industry declined during the 1920s as mills began relocating to the southern states. Today, electronics and service-related industries have become the mainstay of Rhode Island's economy.

## Geography

Narragansett Bay is the most striking geographic feature of the state, cutting inland about 30 miles to Providence. In the bay lie several large islands, including Aquidneck (now called "Rhode Island"). The state's coastline is marked by sandy beaches, salt marshes and lagoons. Inland there are rolling hills with many small lakes and streams.

More than half the state remains covered by forests, and the bay is a rich source of lobster and other fish. The climate is seasonal though not extreme in either summer or winter, but many hurricanes have struck the state, causing considerable damage.

## What people do

Rhode Island is highly industrial. Jewelry and silverware manufacturing are its major industries, followed by electronics, plastic products and ship construction. State residents also engage in commercial fishing and small-scale agriculture, including dairy farms and poultry raising. The development of the Rhode Island Red chicken in the state in the mid-19th century marked the beginning of the U.S. poultry farming industry.

Tourism remains one of the state's largest industries. An important historic site is Newport's Touro Synagogue, built in 1763; it is the oldest synagogue in use in the nation. Newport is also the site of a number of elegant mansions that are open to visitors; many of them are on Cliff Walk, a path along the Atlantic coast. These mansions were the summer homes of American millionaires in the late 19th and early 20th century; among the most famous is "The Breakers," the home of the Vanderbilts. The International Tennis Hall of Fame is also in Newport, where the game first became popular in the U.S.

Block Island, in the Atlantic Ocean about 16 km (10 mi) off the southwest coast, includes a large nature preserve; the island welcomes visitors who enjoy the natural beauty of an unspoiled seashore. During the summer, the waters of Rhode Island teem with boats of all descriptions. There are annual yacht races off Newport, where the annual America's Cup Race was held from 1930 to 1983.

Providence is the site of the first indoor shopping mall in the U.S., the Arcade, built in 1828 and still in existence. The Slater Mill Historic Site in Pawtucket commemorates one of the first textile mills in the U.S.; it was built in 1793 by Samuel Slater, who is considered the founder of the American textile industry. ◆

# Rice

Rice is a grain crop that is eaten as a staple food in many parts of the world. Brown rice is very nutritious, because it contains carbohydrate for energy, a little protein, some minerals, vitamin E and the B complex vitamins. The vitamins are mainly concentrated in the skin and are lost when the rice is polished to make white rice.

Rice grows in all those parts of the world where there is a high rainfall, a hot temperature and fertile soil. Most rice is grown in flooded fields called paddies. The sowing, transplanting and then harvesting of rice are usually done by hand and are back-breaking jobs. In some wealthier countries, airplanes are used to sow the seeds and spray the plants.

After harvesting, the rice is dried and threshed and the grains are cleaned. The outer husk is removed, leaving brown rice. To make white rice, the grains are milled and "polished" to remove the outer skin.

## Types of rice

There are more than 14,000 different varieties of rice. Long-grain rices, such as Indian Patna and Basmati and American rice, are quite dry and fluffy when cooked. Medium-grain rices, such as Italian risotto rice, are a little more sticky. Short-grain rices, such as pudding or Carolina rice and Japanese sticky rice, can be extremely sticky. There are brown versions of all these rices. ◆

Rice has been cultivated in China since about 5000 B.C. China is still the major rice-growing country. It produces about 190 million tons a year.

Rice is a member of the grass family. There are many varieties—more than 4,000 are known in India alone.

Rice has been grown in the southern U.S. since the late 17th century. South Carolina was once the largest producer of rice in North America, and so-called Carolina rice was famous. Today the top rice-growing states are Arkansas, California, Louisiana, Texas and Mississippi.

Rice is unique among grains because it is the only one to be grown standing in water.

◀ Rice grows best in swampy conditions. The seedlings are planted out into flooded paddy fields like this one in Indonesia. Rice probably feeds more people than any other grain.

▼ See also

Food
Grain
Vitamins

# Rites and rituals

The term "rites of passage" was first used by the French anthropologist and folklorist Arnold van Gennep in 1909. He used it to draw attention to the similarities, across different cultures, among the ceremonies that mark new stages in a life.

There are four points in life when people pass from one stage to another, and the ceremonies associated with them are called rites of passage. The word "rites" here refers to the form of words and set of actions that are used on these occasions.

The four main stages of life marked by rites of passage ceremonies are: birth, coming of age, marriage and death. The ceremonies help everyone to understand and accept the important adjustments that have to be made when a baby is born; when someone grows up; when a couple get married; and when someone dies. Many of these ceremonies are very ancient. Each society in the world has developed traditions that have been passed on from generation to generation. Rites and rituals (ceremonial acts) are usually an important part of religious practice.

Jews, Hindus, Muslims, Sikhs and Christians all have ways of welcoming a baby into the religious community and giving it a name. When a boy or girl reaches puberty there may be a formal initiation ceremony, such as Bar and Bat Mitzvah for Jews and confirmation for Christians. For many people marriage is the most important ceremony of their lives. For Muslims the rite of marriage involves the signing of a legal contract.

When someone dies, some arrangements have to be made to bury or cremate the body with respect and help the relatives and friends. A funeral is the most important rite for Buddhists.

Most religions have set rituals for worship. These may involve priests who are trained to read from holy books, pray in a sacred language or bless the worshippers. People may wear special clothes and kneel or bow down to show respect. Communities often use a special greeting as part of their rituals and share ritual meals. ◆

In some societies a child is given one name at birth, and other names are added later in life.

In prehistoric times and in ancient Egypt people were buried with things from this world which they could use in the next.

▼ **See also**

Baptism
Funerals
Initiation ceremonies
Puberty
Weddings

# Rivers

Rivers provide many different places for plants and animals to live. Some live on the river bed, others in the open water, among the underwater weeds or the plants growing in shallow water near the river bank, or on the river bank itself. Herons, kingfishers and otters hunt for fish in the river, and swallows and bats swoop over the water to catch mayflies.

Dead plant and animal material washes into rivers from the land, and leaves and seeds blow into the water. This rotting material provides food for microscopic plants, worms, water snails, shrimp and mussels. These creatures in turn are food for fish, crayfish and turtles, and these animals may be eaten by otters, crocodiles and alligators.

## Adaptations to river life

In very muddy water, it can be difficult to search for food. Fish like the sturgeon use feelers on

▼ Rivers have been a major means of transportation in many parts of the world for thousands of years. This South American Indian, like many generations of his ancestors, travels on the Amazon River by dugout canoe.

their chins that are sensitive to touch and taste to locate food. Electric catfish and electric eels use tiny pulses of electricity to detect the presence of objects, including prey, in the water.

River animals must avoid being washed away. In slow-flowing rivers worms, mussels and insect larvae burrow in the mud. Where the current flows faster, the bottom is covered in stones or gravel, so animals can use claws or suckers to hang on. Freshwater limpets cling fast to the rocks. Water beetles and mayfly nymphs have flattened bodies for hiding in crevices, and caddis-fly larvae weigh themselves down with cases made of tiny stones. Lampreys use sucker-like mouths to cling to rocks.

Fish usually swim facing upstream, so they stay in the same place, and can take in food that is swept toward them. Trout and salmon cover their eggs in gravel to prevent them from being washed away, while sticklebacks make nests of weed. Dragonflies and snails glue their eggs to underwater plants.

## Large river animals

Water can support an animal's body, and some river animals grow very large. Nile crocodiles can measure 6.5 m (21 ft). One of the largest freshwater fish, the South American arapaima, is over 3 m (9.8 ft) long and can weigh 140 kg (300 lbs). In some tropical rivers there are large mammals, such as river dolphins, manatees (sea cows) and hippopotamuses. Hippos use the river to keep cool, staying in the water until the cool of the evening before going onto the bank to graze.

## What is a river?

A river is formed when water flows naturally between clearly defined banks. The water comes from rain or snow. When rain falls or snow melts, some of the water runs off the land down the steepest slope, forming trickles of water in folds of the land. These trickles

◄ The lush vegetation along this riverbank is home to many insects. Many of them produce larvae that live in the water. Water voles, shrews and otters burrow along the bank.

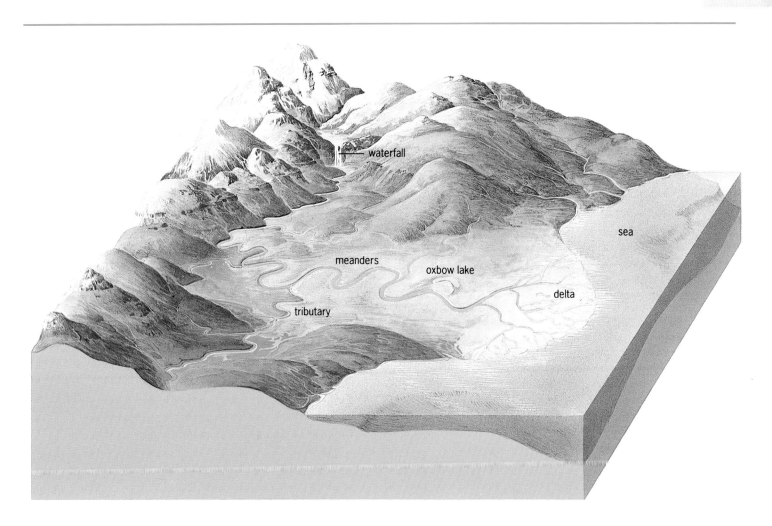

waterfall

sea

meanders

oxbow lake

delta

tributary

▲ The course of a river from its source in the mountains to its estuary at the sea. The curve called a meander is also known as an oxbow. An oxbow lake is a small, curved lake created when a river cuts across the loop of a meander during a flood, leaving the main river to run a shorter course.

Rivers carry about 8 billion tons of sediment into the oceans every year. The Huang He (Yellow River) in China is the world's muddiest river. Each year it carries 2,113,000,000 tons of sediment, which colors the river yellow.

Most river basins are worn down by about 1 m (3.3 ft) every 30,000 years.

eventually merge together to form streams, which join up to form rivers. The streams that join the main river are called tributaries. Some of the rainwater also sinks into the ground, and seeps down through the rocks until it meets a layer of rock that cannot hold any more water. Then the water runs out at the surface to form a spring.

A river gets bigger and bigger as it flows toward the sea, because more and more tributaries join it. It becomes deeper, broader and slower. The area of land that supplies a river with water is called its drainage basin.

## Rivers wear away rocks

Rivers cut into the land and create valleys and gorges. Rushing water has tremendous force. A cubic meter (1.3 cu yds) of water weighs a ton (910 kg/2,000 lbs). Water can split rocks just by pounding them. But more important is the load of sediment (stones and sand) the river carries. Rocks and soil are swept along by fast-flowing water, scouring the riverbed and banks. Large boulders are bounced along the riverbed, scouring out a deeper and deeper channel.

The rate at which water wears away land depends partly on how hard the rock is, and partly on the slope of the river. The steeper it is, the greater its power to erode (wear away). Where the land is rising or the sea level is falling, rivers can cut down through the rocks very fast. The mountains of the Grand Canyon in Arizona were rising as the Colorado River cut down through it. The river has cut a gorge 1.5 km (1 mi) deep.

The faster a river flows, the larger the rocks and the greater the load of sediment it can carry. When the river's flow is slowed down, it drops some of the sediment it is carrying; the largest pebbles go first, then the sand, and finally the fine silt. This happens when the river enters the still waters of a lake or the sea, or when the valley floor becomes less steep as it leaves the mountains.

## The river's upper course

Near its source, the river is well above sea level and is flowing very fast, so it has its greatest cutting power. The water sweeps along boulders and pebbles, especially during floods. The boulders grind against each other, gradually breaking down into smaller pieces of gravel, sand and mud. The river is still small, and quite shallow. Its bed is full of boulders. Where pebbles get trapped in small hollows, they swirl round and round, creating potholes.

## The river's middle course

Here, the river is not flowing so fast. It contains more water, so its bed is wider, and is lined with sand, small pebbles and water weeds. The river is not powerful enough to rush over large obstacles, so it flows around them, and its course winds among the hills. Where the water swings around a bend, the water on the outside of the bend has to flow farther than the water on the inside, so it flows faster. It cuts away the bank on the outside of the bend, widening the valley.

## The river estuary

As the river nears the sea, it becomes wide and sluggish, making huge curves (called *meanders*) around the slightest obstacles. As it spreads out and slows down, it sheds its load of sediment. It wears away tiny cliffs on the outside of the meanders and deposits little beaches of sand on the inside of the bends. When the river floods, it flows over its banks, spreading mud and sand over the surrounding land. As it enters the sea, it builds out a fan-shaped delta of mud.

## The World's Longest Rivers

1. Nile (Africa; 6,670 km/4,140 mi)
2. Amazon (South America; 6,450 km/ 4,010 mi)
3. Yangtze (China; 6,380 km/3,960 mi)
4. Mississippi and Missouri (U.S.; combined length 6,020 km/3,740 mi)
5. Yenisey and Angara (Russia; combined length 5,550 km/3,445 mi)
6. Huang He (China; 5,464 km/3,395 mi)
7. Ob and Irtysh (Russia; combined length 5,410 km/3,360 mi)
8. Zaire/Congo (Africa; 4,670 km/ 2,900 mi)
9. Mekong (Asia; 4,500 km/2,795 mi)
10. Amur (Asia; 4,400 km/2,730 mi)

# THE STAGES OF A RIVER

**A river has three stages, from its beginnings in high ground to its joining with the sea.**

◄ The fast-flowing upper course of a river.

◄ In its middle course a river flows more smoothly, often through a wide valley.

◄ The sluggish final stage in a river's life as it meanders towards the sea. The wide mouth of the river where it joins the sea is its estuary.

▲ An aerial view of the Mississippi Delta, a region of rich farmland along the lower Mississippi River.

## Seasonal changes

Many rivers have very different flows in summer and winter. In cold regions, the upper part of the river may be frozen in winter, so flow decreases. Melting snow and ice may cause spring floods. Rainfall may be seasonal—the annual floods of the River Nile, before the building of the Aswan Dam, were caused by heavy summer rainfall in the Ethiopian highlands. In arid lands, some rivers exist only for a brief period after heavy rain, when water rushes off the bare, baked soil, carrying huge boulders and cutting deep gorges called *wadis*. Other desert rivers vanish long before they reach the sea. As the river meanders across the desert, the water simply evaporates or sinks into the sand.

## Rivers and settlements

Rivers have provided important routes for humans to reach inland areas. Roads and railways follow river valleys. Large rivers can be used to transport food, fuel and goods. People have always settled along rivers. Dams, waterfalls and water wheels supply electricity for industry and domestic use. The water is also used for drinking, washing, and to irrigate fields. The silt deposited over floodplains by large rivers provides some of the most fertile soil in the world. ◆

# Roads and highways

Think about your recent journeys. You probably made many of them on roads. A road is often the best route from one place to another. But it will not always be the most direct way. Sometimes natural obstacles like rivers or hills have to be avoided. Modern roads often bypass town centers or residential areas to avoid traffic jams or being a nuisance to residents. Country roads twist and turn around people's property.

Traffic needs to travel safely and efficiently on our roads. There are rules about which side of the road we use and how fast we can go. Lights, signs and road markings help control traffic. Direction signs help us find our way.

Many people feel that when new roads are built, they bring in more traffic, which causes pollution. Clearing the land to build highways means that trees are cut down, plants are destroyed and the wildlife loses its habitat. People who feel strongly about this may get together to campaign against building new roads.

## Types of roads

Highways have several lanes in each direction separated by a central reservation. They have no sharp bends, steep hills, crossroads or cloverleafs. Traffic can travel a long way at high speeds without stopping. Many countries have highway systems that link up the major cities. In the U.S. highways are also called freeways. In Italy this kind of road is known as an autostrada, and in Germany it is called an autobahn. In the U.K. highways are called motorways.

Urban bypasses provide routes around city centers to improve traffic flow. Residential areas are served by networks of smaller roads. In country areas narrow, winding roads often follow the routes that people made hundreds—or, in Europe, thousands—of years ago.

## Road construction

Before a new road is built, the best route has to be chosen. Ground surveys and aerial photographs are used. The damage to the countryside, the inconvenience to people who live near, and the cost all have to be considered. Surveyors mark out the chosen route ready for the earth-moving vehicles to come in. These huge, expensive machines do

▼ This photograph shows the early stages of construction of a highway. The crushed rock will be off-loaded from the trucks and spread on the surface of the earth to form the lowest level of the foundation. In the background a bulldozer is leveling the surface.

the work of many people. A machine called a *scraper* loosens the top layer of soil, which is pushed aside by large bulldozers.

The road has to be as level as possible, so cuttings are made through hills and the soil used to fill in small valleys and form embankments. Bridges and tunnels may also be needed. The engineers then lay foundations of crushed rock to make sure the road can carry the weight of the predicted traffic. Sometimes cement or bitumen is added to the soil to form a solid base. Then a layer of concrete, called the *base course*, is put on the foundations. A machine called a spreader adds the top layer of asphalt or concrete slabs joined by bitumen. The concrete is often strengthened with steel mesh. Finally markings and signs showing the new road's number are added. The road can now be opened and shown on maps as ready for traffic.

## LOOKING BACK

The first roads were tracks used by people and pack animals. They were often bumpy, twisting, narrow routes. Hard and smooth roads were needed once the wheel had been invented. The first paved roads were built in Mesopotamia (now Iraq) in about 2200 B.C.

Two thousand years later the Romans built hard, straight roads all over Europe and North Africa. By the height of their power, the Romans had built nearly 85,000 km (53,000 mi) of road, connecting the capital with the farthest parts of their empire. They needed these roads so that soldiers could travel quickly throughout the empire. Roman roads were paved with stones and they sloped to

◄ This autobahn in Germany is raised on concrete stilts high above the ground. The engineers have planned it so that it does the least possible damage to the farmland below and so that the hills are less steep for traffic.

The first U.S. freeway was the Pennsylvania Turnpike, which opened in 1940.

either side to let rainwater drain away. In Great Britain, these roads were not used much after the Romans left, and many became overgrown.

When the Incas of South America built their empire in the 15th and 16th centuries, they created a network of highways and minor roads. One long road went along the coast and another one ran parallel to it over the Andes Mountains. There were many connecting roads between them, and they were all linked to the capital city.

For hundreds of years roads in Europe were neglected. In the 18th century more and more horse-drawn stage coaches were traveling between towns. They needed better roads, and so in England new roads were built and maintained privately. Travelers were charged tolls to use the roads.

A British engineer named John McAdam invented a new method of building roads. The ground beneath the new road was drained. A layer of egg-sized stones was laid and covered in smaller stones. The pounding of horse-drawn coaches ground these together and the gaps between became filled with dust and dirt. These roads were no good for the rubber-tired vehicles that appeared in the 20th century. A coating of tar or bitumen was added to seal the surface. Today "macadamized roads" are found in all Western nations. ◆

◄ A huge intersection of freeways in Los Angeles, California. Movement in and around the city depends on a complex system of such freeways. Damage to the roads caused by the earthquake of 1994 virtually brought the city to a standstill.

▼ **See also**
Automobiles
Transportation
Trucks

# Robots

A robot is a machine that does a job instead of a person. Most robots are nothing like the robots you might have seen in the movies. Instead, they are machines that work in factories, doing jobs that would be boring, dangerous or very tiring for people. These robots are called *industrial robots*. They work completely automatically, spraying cars with paint, cutting out car parts, stacking up heavy boxes, or welding pieces of metal together.

Robots are moved by electric motors, hydraulic power or pneumatic power. Smaller robots normally have electric motors. Robots that need to lift heavy objects normally have hydraulic power.

▶ Robby the Robot was a leading "character" in the classic Hollywood science fiction movie *Forbidden Planet* (1956).

## Parts of an industrial robot

An industrial robot's arm is attached to a heavy base. At the end of the arm is a wrist where the tool that the robot is using is attached. The tool could be a welding torch, or a screwdriver, or a simple gripper. The arm and wrist have joints that bend and twist to move the tool to where it is needed.

Different industrial robot arms move in different ways. Some arms are designed to act like human arms. They have a waist joint, which swivels from side to side, and a shoulder and elbow that bend up and down. Other robots

▶ A new car being welded by robots on an auto production line.

have a waist and shoulder, and an arm that gets longer or shorter. Most robot wrists can bend from side to side and up and down, and twist around as well.

## Controlling a robot

A robot's movements are controlled by computer. The computer sends instructions to each of the robot's joints, telling them which way to move, and how far. Inside the joints are sensors that the computer uses to check that the arm is in the correct position. Even the largest robots can be positioned accurately enough to thread a needle. The job the robot does can easily be changed by changing its tool and the instructions in its computer.

Before a robot can do a job, such as spraying paint onto a car body, it must be taught the movements it needs to make, and when to turn the spray gun on or off. The robot is taught by an engineer, who holds the spray gun and carries out the movements. The robot's sensors detect the movements, and the computer remembers them so that it can repeat them exactly over and over again.

## Robot senses

Robots that pick things up have touch sensors that tell the computer when they are gripping tightly enough. Otherwise, the robot could crush things—or drop them. On a production line, where several robots work together, there are also sensors on conveyor belts to make sure the objects the robots are working on are in the correct place. All the robots and sensors are linked together by computer to make sure everything runs smoothly. If something goes wrong, the computer stops the robots and alerts

an engineer.

Some robots have a video camera, which gives them sight. This allows the robot to pick out shapes and work out which way around they are. A robot that does packing might have a vision sensor so that it can turn things the correct way around to fit into a box.

## Robot vehicles

Robot vehicles work in places that are too dangerous for people or too difficult to get to. Some robot vehicles, such as robot submarines and bomb disposal robots, are remote-controlled by an operator. In some car factories, car parts are collected and delivered by automatic robot vehicles, which follow lines drawn on the factory floor. Robots like this have bump sensors that stop them if they run into anything.

## Intelligent robots

Walking, talking androids—robots that look like humans—can only be seen at the movies. They are still a thing of the future. Think how clever a robot would have to be to do all the things you might do in a day! Making a robot that can find its way about and identify objects with video eyes is very difficult. Robotics researchers are using artificial intelligence techniques to try to solve the problems. With artificial intelligence, the robot's computer brain gradually learns from its mistakes. For example, maze-solving robots try to find their way out of a maze. Each time they try, they get a bit better at it, and eventually they can do it perfectly. ◆

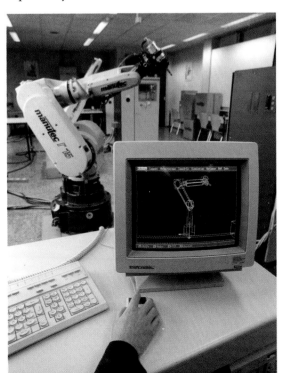

◀ An industrial robot's "working envelope" is the space it can reach with its arm. This robot can stretch only to the dimensions of the surfboard it is making.

The first industrial robots were designed in the 1950s in the U.S. and were used in factories. Robots with interchangeable tools were developed in the 1960s.

◀ This computer is being used to program the movements of the robot in the background.

**See also**
Computers
Hydraulics
Mass production

# Rockets

▶ A rocket used to launch communications and other satellites into orbit. It can launch two or three at the same time.

Most rockets are very expensive because they are used only once, but with the space shuttle only the fuel tank is wasted. The rest returns to Earth and is used again.

Long-range missiles are rockets that carry nuclear bombs over enormous distances to their targets.

**Saturn 5 rocket**
*Height*
110 m  (361 ft)
*Weight*
At liftoff 3,000 tons; 90 percent of this is fuel
*Power*
First-stage engines: the same as 160 jumbo jet airplane engines

▼ **See also**
Astronauts
Missiles
Satellites
Space exploration

**BIOGRAPHY**
Braun, Wernher von

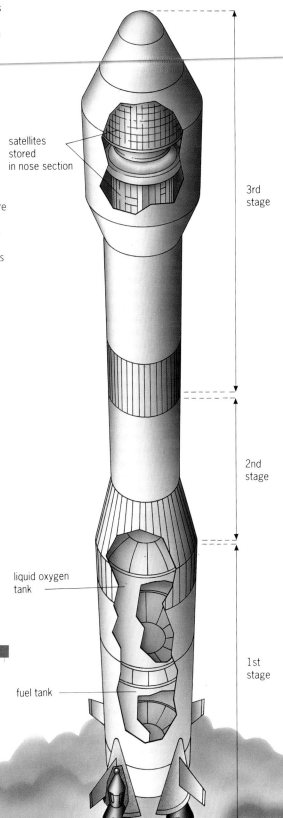

satellites stored in nose section

3rd stage

2nd stage

1st stage

liquid oxygen tank

fuel tank

engines

The huge rockets that go into space work in exactly the same way as the firework rockets you see on the Fourth of July. They are full of fuel, which burns to make a lot of hot gas. This expands rapidly, and the force of the expansion pushes the gases downward and the rocket upward. You can see how this works if you blow up a balloon and let it go. The air rushes out and the balloon shoots away. It goes all over the place because it is soft and the air can escape in any direction. Space rockets go in one direction because nozzles direct the gases.

## Space rockets

Space rockets have to be very powerful to escape from the strong pull of the Earth's gravity and send a spacecraft or satellite into space. They usually have several stages; they are really two or three rockets stacked on top of each other. The first stage, at the bottom, lifts the rocket off the ground, thrusting it up until the fuel runs out. It then falls away, and the second-stage engines take over, and so on. This means that the rocket does not carry unnecessary weight into space.

## Rocket fuels

In some space rockets the fuel is a rubbery solid. Solid-fuel rockets are often boosters, extra rockets fixed to the side of the main rocket. However, most space rockets use more powerful liquid fuels, which are stored in huge tanks inside the rocket. The fuel will not burn without oxygen, so a second tank carries an oxygen supply. Rockets are the only engines that will work in space, where there is no air to supply the oxygen. The jet engines on aircraft use oxygen from the air, so they will not work in space.

## LOOKING BACK

The first rockets were made nearly 1,000 years ago in China. They were like the firework rockets of today and were used in battles, fixed to arrows. Rockets were later used as distress signals, to save lives. Guided military rockets were used in the Napoleonic wars. In 1926 Robert Goddard launched the first rocket with an engine that burned liquid fuel. The German V=2 war rocket, designed by Wernher von Braun and made in 1942, was the first rocket powerful enough to reach space, but it was not until 1957 that a Soviet rocket launched the first satellite into space. In 1969 the giant American *Saturn 5* rocket launched the first astronauts to land on the Moon. ◆

# Rock music

Rock music—also called "rock and roll"—began in the U.S. in the mid-1950s. It developed from traditional black music—especially rhythm-and-blues (r&b) and gospel music. R&b songs sung by black performers had become popular among white teenagers in the early 1950s, and white artists began copying the style in new music that they called "rock and roll."

## Bill Haley and Elvis Presley

The first popular rock performing group was Bill Haley and the Comets. Their song "Rock Around the Clock" became the biggest hit of 1955 and is now a rock classic. The biggest rock star of all time was Elvis Presley (1935–1977), who recorded his first hit song, "Heartbreak Hotel," in 1956. During his 20-year career, Presley had no less than 77 hit songs; 33 made it into the top ten songs on the pop charts, and 14 of these were number-one hits. At one point Presley had 14 consecutive records that sold at least a million copies. Presley was one of the most successful artists in music history, and his popularity has continued since his death.

## The Beatles and the Stones

In the 1960s, a number of British rock groups who were already stars in Europe became popular in the U.S., including the Beatles, the Rolling Stones and the Who. In 1967 the Beatles released one of the most popular rock albums every recorded: *Sgt. Pepper's Lonely Hearts Club Band*. Popular American rock performers of the 1960s included the Beach Boys, who sang about surfing, and Bob Dylan, whose style incorporated elements of folk music. Black singers Wilson Pickett, James Brown and Otis Redding developed a new style of r&b called "soul music."

## Rock since the 1970s

New forms of rock music developed in the 1970s. One new style, which incorporated some elements of classical music, was called "progressive," played by such bands as King Crimson, Rush and Yes. "Heavy metal" bands also developed in the 1970s, including Led Zeppelin and Black Sabbath. "Punk" rock, still another form of rock music, was pioneered by such groups as the Sex Pistols, Clash and the Talking Heads.

Rock music in the 1980s was represented by Madonna and Michael Jackson. A British group called Police was briefly popular, but the group disbanded in

1983 and its lead singer and bassist, Sting, has since pursued a successful solo career. A new style of soul music arose in the 1980s as well: "rap," made popular by Run DMC and Public Enemy.

In the 1990s the new wave of rock music was "grunge," and its leading performer was Kurt Cobain and his group Nirvana. His career was brief, however: he committed suicide in 1994. ◆

The term "rock and roll" was used for the first time by Cleveland disk jockey Alan Freed in 1954.

A famous early performer of rock music was Buddy Holly and his band, the Crickets. Holly was one of the first white performers to write his own songs. He had seven hit songs during a two-year career that ended with his death in a plane crash in 1959. Other artists popular in rock's first decade included the Everly Brothers and Jerry Lee Lewis.

One of the most memorable events in rock music history was the Woodstock Music and Art Fair, a three-day festival held in upstate New York in August 1969. More than 300,000 people braved torrential rains to listen to performances by the Grateful Dead, Jimi Hendrix, Janis Joplin and other rock stars.

▶ Formed in Liverpool, England, in 1959, the Beatles became the most popular group in British rock music. International fame came in 1964 after their tour of the U.S.

Among the most famous rock events was Live Aid, two simultaneous concerts held in London and Philadelphia in 1985. Famous rock performers such as Led Zeppelin and the Who donated their talent to Live Aid, a benefit for famine relief in Africa.

The Rock and Roll Hall of Fame opened in Cleveland, Ohio, in September 1995.

▶ Elvis Presley is considered by many to be the "King of Rock and Roll."

▼ **See also**

Blues
Country music
Folk music
Gospel music
Music

# Rocks

Rocks are the substances that make up the Earth. We see rocks every day: sandstone, granite and marble, in the walls of large buildings, the cliffs along the seashore, and the broken pieces of stone in the tarmac on the road.

There are three main types of rocks. *Igneous* rocks were formed at very high temperatures from molten liquids, either deep within the Earth, or at the surface, from volcanoes, for example. *Sedimentary* rocks are formed from sand, mud or limey mud, laid down on land or in ancient rivers, lakes or seas. These form sandstone, mudstone and limestone. *Metamorphic* rocks are formed from either sedimentary or igneous rocks that have been buried and heated up or put under great stress.

## Igneous rocks

Igneous rocks are generally very hard, because they are formed from a molten mass of rock material called *magma*. The magma, which can be seen on the surface of the Earth as *lava*, consists of complex mixtures of chemicals. As the magma moves through cracks in the Earth's surface, it cools around the edges. It may cool completely deep within the Earth, or at the surface.

◄ Erosion of the cliffs along the coast of Iceland in the north Atlantic Ocean has exposed these striking basalt formations, formed when molten lava cooled. Iceland lies on the mid-Atlantic ridge, a line of active volcanoes where new crust is forming on the Earth's surface.

There are 8 elements that make up more than 98% of the world's rocks. They are (in order of the most to the least abundant): oxygen, silicon, aluminum, iron, calcium, sodium, potassium, magnesium.

The kind of igneous rock formed depends on the composition of the magma and the rate at which it cools. On cooling, the chemicals in the magma form crystals. These crystals, like grains of salt or sugar, have particular shapes depending on their chemical composition, and

**Igneous Rocks**
basalt
gabbro
granite
lava
obsidian
peridotite
pumice

▲ Granite is a coarse- or medium-grained igneous rock, rich in quartz. It was formed when the magma cooled deep below the surface of the Earth, and it is the most common type of rock in the Earth's crust. Granite used to be a popular paving and building stone.

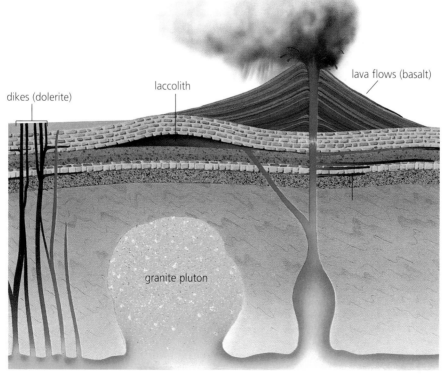

dikes (dolerite)

laccolith

lava flows (basalt)

granite pluton

◄ Only a small proportion of the molten lava that forces its way up through the Earth's crust eventually solidifies on the surface. Most cools within the crust, squeezed between existing rocks. The strange shapes that cool underground are often exposed millions of years later, as weathering wears down the surface of the Earth.

The land here is made from sediments deposited by the river during the last 5,000 years.

Sediment deposited by the river when it reaches the sea.

▲ A river carries sediment to the sea. Sediment builds up at the mouth of the river, spreading wider and becoming thicker. Eventually the sediment hardens to form sedimentary rock.

The igneous rock called pumice began as volcanic lava filled with gases. As the gases escaped, they left tiny holes that filled with air. As a result, pumice is so light it floats on water.

▲ Millstone grit is a coarse sandstone. The grains of sand can easily be seen without a magnifying glass. This rock was once used to make millstones for grinding corn and has often been used as a building stone.

the longer it takes them to cool, the larger they become. The solid crystalline forms are called *minerals*.

Igneous rocks formed deep in the Earth's crust are called *plutonic* rocks. A common type is granite, which contains many large crystals of the common mineral quartz. Igneous rocks formed nearer the surface in dikes or sills include dolerite, which contains smaller crystals of other minerals, but hardly any quartz. *Volcanic* rocks —those formed at the surface— include basalt, a common rock type, like dolerite, but very fine-grained, because it cooled faster in the air.

### Sedimentary rocks

Sandstones, mudstones and limestones were once soft and moving sands and muds on the bottom of rivers, lakes and seas.

These sediments form part of the great cycle of erosion and deposition that is going on all the time. The rocks on land are eroded by the action of rain, streams, wind, ice and plant roots. Small rock fragments in the form of sand or mud are blown away or washed down into rivers or lakes where they may sink to the bottom. Over the years, millions of sand grains may be deposited in one place, and thick layers build up.

The largest areas of deposition are in the sea. Sediment is brought in from all the great rivers, and it is also eroded from coastlines by the sea itself. These grains of sand and mud may be deposited in shallow waters, within a few miles of the coast, or they may be swept well out into the oceans. Over millions of years, the sediment may build up to be many hundreds of feet thick.

**Sedimentary Rocks**
chalk
clay
coal
coral
flint
limestone
sandstone
shale
travertine

Rocks are usually too hard to be bent or squeezed out of shape. However, it is possible to bend thin slabs of itacolumite, a rare type of sandstone, by hand. This is due to its unusual crystalline structure.

## From sediment to rock

For the sediment to form rock, two main changes take place. First of all, water is lost. As the layers of sediment build up, the deeper sediment is pressed down by the weight of sand or mud above. The grains press closer and closer together, and water moves up and toward the lake or sea above.

The second stage is the formation of a kind of cement. After many years, sometimes thousands of years, the remaining water around the grains contains solutions of minerals. Further loss of water causes these mineral solutions to form crystals in the spaces between the rock grains.

## Metamorphic rocks

The word "metamorphic" means "later, or changed, form." These are rocks that have been altered either by heat, or by heat and pressure together.

When magma forces its way up in the Earth's crust, it heats the surrounding rock for a distance of several yards. If it is passing through sandstone, this may be baked into hard quartzite. Limestone may be baked into marble. This type of metamorphism can only affect small amounts of rock close to the passage of the magma.

Large-scale metamorphism can take place when mountains are forming. For example, when major plates of the Earth's crust collide, there are great pressures, and sediments on the ocean floor, such

◀ Slate splits into thin sheets. However, cutting roof slates by hand is skilled work. Fewer stonemasons have this skill today because roofs are now usually covered with asphalt shingles in the U.S., and clay tiles in other parts of the world.

**Metamorphic rocks**
gneiss
marble
quartzite
slate
soapstone

as mudstones and sandstones, may be altered over wide areas into slates and schists. Both pressure and heat are involved.

## Changing crystal direction

When a metamorphic rock forms, the pressure forces all the crystals in a rock to line up. In mudstones and sandstones, all the mineral crystals lie in a random arrangement. When great forces act on these rocks, the grains line up at right angles to the direction of the pressure.

## New minerals

New minerals are often created in metamorphism. The great heat can melt the original rock into a liquid, and impurities may then come together and form new minerals such as tourmaline or garnets on cooling. A very unusual example of this is the formation of diamonds in coal layers that have been heated by igneous rocks. ◆

▶ Gneiss is a coarse-grained rock with irregular bands of different colors. Gneisses often glitter because they contain the mineral mica. They were formed from rocks changed by great heat and pressure.

**See also**
Earth
Erosion
Geologists
Minerals
Plate tectonics
Sculpture

# Rocky Mountains

▶ Until the discovery of minerals there in the late 19th century, the only people who ventured into the Rockies were hunters. Now national parks in the Rockies, like Grand Teton in Wyoming, are popular with many visitors.

The highest peak in the Rocky Mountains is Mount Elbert in Colorado, at 4,399 m (14,433 ft).

▶ Over millions of years, water and ice have worn the rocks of Utah's Bryce Canyon into strange shapes.

The Rocky Mountains, or Rockies, is a name given to a series of mountain ranges running down the west-center of North America from Alaska to Mexico. Their proper geological name is the Cordilleran Province. Some mountains have gentle slopes with rounded tops, but others are tall with jagged rocky peaks. Many of them are more than 4,000 m (13,000 ft) above sea level. Between the snow-capped peaks lie wide valleys, plateaus, lakes and rivers. In some places there are hot springs, such as the geysers in Yellowstone National Park. The range contains some of the most dramatic scenery in North America. The roads and railways that cross them go through spectacular passes.

The Cordillera started to form 190 million years ago, and is still slowly rising. As the land rises, rivers cut deep valleys and canyons in places. The mountains form the Continental Divide in North America, separating rivers flowing east, such as the Missouri, from those flowing west, like the Colorado River.

## Life in the mountains

The region is home to 5 million people. There are deposits of metals such as iron, silver, gold, lead and zinc, as well as uranium, phosphates and other salts. There is also coal, oil and natural gas. Some rivers have been dammed to produce hydroelectric power. Other places suffer from a shortage of water. The winds blowing from the west bring rain to the western slopes, leaving the central and eastern slopes dry.

The alpine meadows are full of wild flowers. Below the meadows, there are forests, and cattle and horses graze on the grassy lower slopes. Many large mammals live in the mountains and forests: grizzly and brown bears, cougars (also called pumas or mountain lions), deer, Rocky Mountain goats and wild mountain sheep. One of the most important sources of income is tourism, including skiing, fishing and walking in the many national parks. ◆

# Rodents

**Distribution**
Worldwide
**Largest**
The capybara: head-and-body length up to 134 cm (52 in); weight up to 66 kg (145 lbs)
**Smallest**
Pygmy mouse: head-and-body length may be as little as 4.5 cm (1.8 in) and weight as little as 2.5 g (0.09 oz). There are many other mice that are only very slightly larger.
**Number of young**
Variable, but many in most litters. Many species produce a series of litters in the summer.
**Lifespan**
Up to 20 years in beavers and marmots, but very short in most small species. Wild mice rarely survive for much more than a year.
**Subphylum**
Vertebrata
**Class**
Mammalia
**Order**
Rodentia
**Number of species**
About 1,700

Almost half of all of the known kinds of mammals are rodents. They are found in almost every part of the world, from hot tropical forests to deserts and cold tundras. Mice, rats, beavers, squirrels and porcupines are all members of the rodent order. (Hedgehogs, which are often confused with porcupines, are not rodents at all but are members of the insectivore order.)

Rodents are sometimes called gnawing animals, for in the front of their mouths they have only two incisor teeth in the upper jaw and two in the lower jaw. These are different from the incisors of most other mammals, for they continue to grow throughout the animal's life. But they do not just get longer and longer. They are worn down by the tough food that rodents eat, and so they stay the same length. The incisors have a covering of enamel on the front only. Because this is extremely hard, it stands up a little above the dentine behind it. The constant wear sharpens it to a razor-like edge. In the back of their mouths are grinding teeth, which are necessary because rodents feed mainly on plants. However, many rodents eat insects and other small

creatures as well.

Most rodents are small animals, but their appearance varies greatly. Some, like the porcupines, have spines. Others such as beavers and coypu have soft fur, while some of the mole rats have only a few hairs sticking out of their naked bodies. Some have huge ears and long tails; others have tiny ears and no tails.

Their ways of life are equally varied. Many protect themselves by living in burrows; others are climbers. Some can run and some leap. Many are good swimmers and live in or near water. Many flesh-eating mammals and birds feed on rodents, so most rodent species survive only by producing large numbers of young. ◆

▲ Pacas are shy creatures that live by streams in the forests of South America. In the daytime they hide in burrows or holes in the ground. At night they come out to feed on many kinds of plants and fallen fruit.

**See also**

Beavers
Gerbils
Guinea pigs
Hamsters
Mice
Porcupines
Rats
Squirrels
Teeth

# Roller skating

Roller skates were invented by Joseph Merlin, a Belgian musical-instrument maker, around 1760, but early skates were difficult to stop or turn. In 1863, an American, James L. Plimpton, produced a practical four-wheeled skate that enabled the skater to move in a curve by leaning to one side. Roller skating became popular with ice skaters who wanted to practice on land. In 1866 Plimpton opened the first roller-skating rink, in Newport, Rhode Island.

Roller skating is the sport of gliding swiftly across the ground on roller skates. Roller skates are boots with built-in wheels. Speed skates have a longer, lower wheelbase than other skates.

Roller-skate wheels have been made out of clay, wood, steel and aluminum, but today they are usually made out of polyurethane, which gives a better grip. An innovation in the late 20th century is the in-line or Rollerblade skate, in which a row of four wheels, one behind the other, replaces the old rectangular arrangement.

There are several kinds of contests for men, women and relay teams in the U.S. and Europe. In speed skating the skaters race around an oval track. Roller Derby is a roller speed-skating contest for teams of men and women. They race around the track and gain points for lapping other skaters (finishing at least one circuit ahead of them). The sport can be violent, with skaters allowed to barge and shove as much as they like. Roller hockey is the roller-skating equivalent of ice hockey. Artistic skating includes figure skating, free skating and dance skating. There are also international contests. ◆

**See also**

Hockey, ice
Ice skating

# Romania

**Area**
237,500 sq km
(91,699 sq mi)
**Capital**
Bucharest
**Population**
22,922,000
**Language**
Romanian, Hungarian
**Religion**
Christian
**Government**
Republic
**Currency**
1 leu = 100 bani
**Major exports**
Agricultural products

▼ **See also**
Europe
Ottoman Empire

▼ This grandiose palace
was built during the rule
of the dictator Nicolae
Ceausescu. Fine old
buildings and streets
were pulled down to
make space for his
ambitious plans for
reconstruction.

Romania is a country in southeast Europe. The forested Carpathian Mountains and Transylvanian Alps are in the west; the east is lowland and the Danube River forms the southern boundary. In Romania the Danube is used for transport and for hydroelectric power. The Danube reaches the Black Sea in a huge delta, which is a nature reserve. Romania has a short coastline on the Black Sea, with tourist resorts. Summers are very hot, except in the mountains, but winters are cold in all parts of the country. The average winter temperature in Bucharest is around −2 °C (28°F).

Most of Romania is farmland. Large farms grow wheat, maize (corn), sunflowers and sugar beets. Romania's resources include oil, natural gas and lignite (soft brown coal). Industry has developed rapidly in recent years. Chemicals and iron and steel are important industries.

## LOOKING BACK

The name of the country means "Roman": this area was once part of the Roman Empire, and the Romanian language developed from Latin and is similar to Italian. Most Romanian Christians belong to the Orthodox Church. For many centuries, Turkey ruled Romania as part of the Ottoman Empire, but it became independent in 1861. From 1945 Romania had a Communist government. In 1989 the Communist leader Ceausescu was overthrown in a popular uprising and executed, but the Communist Party, renamed the National Salvation Front, remained a strong force in government. ♦

# Rome and the Roman Empire

From a small tribe of farmers, called the Latini, there grew a great empire that stretched from Britain to the land of the Arabs, from North Africa to the borders of Russia. These Latin-speaking people took over the town called Rome from its Etruscan kings in 509 B.C. The Romans spread their way of life, their laws and their language throughout Italy and then over the Mediterranean area and much of Europe.

## Everyday life

Wherever the Romans went as conquerors, they established their own way of life. Although many local customs survived, it is possible to talk about "Roman everyday life" throughout the empire. Archaeologists often find the same sorts of evidence, either buildings or things that people used, all over the Roman world.

In the big towns and cities many people lived in blocks of apartments above stores or small workshops. Those who were rich enough lived in private houses with rooms for slaves and a secluded garden. Our word "family" comes from the Latin *familia*, which meant a household of parents, children, other relatives and slaves or servants.

A big town house might have two dining rooms, to catch the light at different times of the year. Romans liked their food with lots of spices, and the main meal of the day (eaten at about four o'clock in the afternoon) usually had three courses. Many people, especially those who lived in apartments, ate takeout meals from hot-food shops. There were many stores that sold clothes and jewelry. Both men and women wore brooches and rings.

## Town planning

Roman towns were usually well planned, with straight streets dividing the town into regular blocks, like some modern American towns. A block of houses was called an *insula*, the Latin for "island." Inside the town there would

### The Myth of Romulus and Remus

In Roman mythology, Romulus and Remus were twin gods, the sons of Mars, the god of war, and Rhea, the daughter of king Numitor of Alba Longa. When they were babies, their uncle usurped their throne, put the babies in a basket and floated it down the Tiber River. He hoped that the babies would drown. But the basket bobbed to shore. A she-wolf heard the babies crying and let them feed from her breast. Soon afterwards, a shepherd rescued them and brought them up as his own sons. When they were grown, they killed their wicked uncle and claimed back the throne. Then they began building a new city. But they quarreled before it was finished, and Romulus killed Remus. So the new city was called "Rome," after Romulus. He ruled for 40 years, and when he died he was taken into heaven and became a god.

| 500 B.C. | 400 B.C. | 300 B.C. | 200 B.C. | 100 B.C. |
|---|---|---|---|---|
| Etruscans expelled from Rome | 390 Celts attack Rome and settle northern Italy | Rome fights Carthage | 146 Carthage defeated | Civil wars |
| Latini establish republic in Rome | Romans gain power over Etruscans and Greeks in Italy | Conquers Sicily and Spain | North Africa conquered<br><br>Roman armies fight in East | Julius Caesar defeats Celts, conquers Gaul<br><br>Egypt conquered |
| | | | | Augustus first emperor |

▼ Pompeii, south of Naples, had all the expected services and buildings of a provincial town: various bath houses, theaters, an amphitheater, lots of stores, marketplaces, and government buildings. The townspeople abandoned Pompeii and its neighboring town Herculaneum after the volcano Vesuvius erupted in 79 A.D. The ruins of Pompeii and Herculaneum were excavated in the 19th century by archaeologists and can be seen today. Many artifacts from the two towns have been sent to museums in Europe and the U.S.

also be buildings for entertainment and local government offices.

## Water and sewage

Roman towns usually had regular supplies of water and an efficient system of sewage disposal. Water pipes, of lead, wood or pottery, brought supplies from aqueducts to private houses, to businesses, and to fountains and public basins in the streets. Water was also needed for the many public baths.

## Fun and games

The Romans liked entertainment, and a town might have a theater, a stadium (for chariot racing) and even an amphitheater. Most Romans probably enjoyed a day at the amphitheater. One of the spectacles was a cruel sport in which trained men, called gladiators,

fought to the death in single combat. Sometimes animals were chased and killed in the arena, or even human beings. At various times, persecuted people, such as the Christians, were "thrown" to wild animals. Very large numbers went to all sorts of entertainment. The amphitheater at Pompeii could hold 20,000 spectators.

## The Roman army

At first the citizens of Rome raised an army and navy only when it was necessary to go to war. Later a professional army was formed; that is, men joined up and were paid to be soldiers all the time, so that they could be ready to fight at any time. Soldiers were organized into units called *legions*. Each legion was made up of about 5,000 men and had a name and a number. The men trained and fought in groups of 80 with a *centurion* (the name for a commander of about 100 men) in charge of each. The legionary soldiers were well armed and fought on foot. Other army units, called the cavalry, fought on horseback. Some were trained to use artillery weapons such as catapults. Some were engineers.

## The provinces

The army helped create the Roman world by conquering peoples, building forts and roads and keeping Roman-run countryside secure from attacks. Boundaries to the Roman world were established, sometimes using rivers, mountains or seas as a barrier. In many places the Romans had to build a barrier; for example, their great northern defense stretched from the Rhine River to the Danube River. Inside the boundaries the Romans created provinces.

## Towns and countryside

In the provinces the Romans encouraged the newly conquered peoples to live just like Romans. Many of the peoples in these new territories saw properly laid out towns for the first time. The new Roman citizens soon wanted to live in "Roman-style" houses, with mosaics and hypocausts (underfloor heating).

| 1–100 A.D. | 100 A.D. | 200 A.D. | 300 A.D. | 400 A.D. |
|---|---|---|---|---|
| 43 Britain occupied | 98–117 Emperor Trajan | Germans and other barbarian tribes invade | 330 Emperor Constantine moves capital to Byzantium | 410 Visigoths sack Rome |
| 70 Jerusalem destroyed | Empire at its most powerful | | | 476 Last western emperor resigns |
| 79 Vesuvius erupts | 117–138 Emperor Hadrian | | Franks, Goths, Huns, Visigoths and Vandals attack | |

They also came to expect local government services, places for entertainment and plenty of water for baths and fountains.

The countryside often changed, too. The central government in Rome wanted farmers to work as much land as possible. New farmhouses and estates appeared. The Romans called these *villas*. Villa owners, too, expected Roman comforts on their farms such as underfloor heating, mosaic floors and their own bath houses.

The Romans introduced their religion into the provinces and built temples to gods and goddesses such as Jupiter, Minerva and Juno. Quite often, though, people in the provinces worshipped their own gods, too. Celtic gods and goddesses were still worshipped in Roman Britain and in Gaul.

## The republic

When the Latin people threw out their Etruscan kings they created a state that they called a republic. Some people (men who owned property) were allowed to vote for the politicians who formed the government. At the head were two men, called consuls. Each year one was elected to lead the government and one the army. They were the chief judges as well. A sort of parliament, called the senate, discussed the way the state was governed and made new laws. A number of other elected officials carried out government business such

as the treasury and public works.

## The empire

In the 2nd century B.C. politicians began to fight each other for power and in the next century civil war broke out. Julius Caesar, who had conquered new provinces in Gaul (now France) and Germany, fought a civil war with a rival politician, Pompey. In the end Caesar won and made himself a dictator. He was murdered and another civil war began. The winner this time was Octavian, who in 27 B.C. made himself an emperor and called himself Augustus. This

▲ The green area shows the Roman Empire in the 2nd century A.D., with some of the provinces. The names of many modern countries are derived from their Latin names.

◀ A Roman mosaic fish from North Africa.

▶ This coin shows the Emperor Hadrian. The letter U on Roman coins and carved inscriptions is always shown as V. Hadrian lived from 76 to 138 A.D. and was proclaimed emperor (Augustus) in 117 A.D.

▼ See also
Byzantine Empire
Dark Ages
England
Etruscans
Greece
Italy
Mosaics
Slavery

BIOGRAPHY
Augustus
Caesar, Julius
Constantine the Great
Nero
Virgil

was the beginning of the period in Roman history called the empire.

Although men could still vote for their leaders it was not a proper democracy. The emperor decided who should rule and handed out jobs to people he could trust. The emperor's family now became the "royal" family. When an emperor died (sometimes he was murdered) his heir took over, unless the army decided they wanted someone else to rule.

Some emperors were good rulers who fought for a strong and protected empire (Hadrian, for example). Others were cruel and cared more about themselves and their own wealth than the Roman people. Under the rule of the emperors, Rome gradually conquered even more of the known world, as the map in this article shows.

## The end of an empire

Eventually the vast Roman Empire was divided in two, with one capital city in Rome and the

▼ A modern artist's reconstruction of a Roman street.

other in Byzantium. Byzantium was established by the Emperor Constantine as his capital in 330 A.D., and renamed Constantinople, the "city of Constantine."

By the 5th century A.D. the western part of the empire had been overrun by Goths, Huns and Vandals. The eastern empire became the Byzantine empire and survived until 1453 A.D., when it fell to the Ottoman Turks.

### Roman survivals

In many parts of Europe, the Mediterranean countries, North Africa and the Middle East, you can still see the ruined buildings of the Roman Empire. There are aqueducts in Spain, theaters in Cyprus, villas in France and fortresses in Israel. The Latin language developed into many European languages spoken today, including Italian, Spanish and French. Roman law is the basis of the laws of many European countries. The English names for the months are Roman. The English alphabet is Roman and Roman numerals are often used. ◆

The great amphitheater in Rome was completed in 80 A.D. and held about 50,000 people. It later got the name "Colosseum" from a gigantic statue of the Emperor Nero that stood close by. (The word *colosseum* is Latin for "huge.") The wooden floor has long since rotted away, showing the underground tunnels used to bring dangerous animals to the arena.

▼ This theater was built in the 1st century B.C. in what is now Tunisia, in North Africa. The seating capacity is about 3,500, so it was relatively small, compared to the great buildings in Rome and Pompeii.

# Roots

Roots are found at the base of the main stem in most flowering plants. They spread out to support the plant and anchor it firmly in the ground. Their other vital function is to absorb from the soil the water and mineral salts needed by the plant.

## Root systems

In a *fibrous root* system, numerous small roots branch out from the base of the stem, spreading widely but not very deep into the soil. In a *tap root* system, the radicle (seed root) becomes the main root with all others branching from it. Sometimes this root swells with stored food, as in carrots and

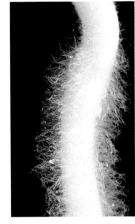

▲ Roots anchor a plant in the soil and absorb the water and minerals it needs through tiny root hairs. The growing tip of a root is protected from sharp soil particles by a root cap.

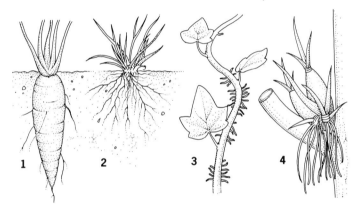

1    2    3    4

radishes. Some trees like oak and pine also have tap roots.

Not all roots grow below soil level. *Climbers*, like ivy, have tiny roots attaching their stems to the surface on which they are growing. *Aerial roots*, able to absorb water from the air, may develop in plants with poor root systems.

## Root structure

Roots are continually growing at a point just behind the tip, which is protected by the root cap. Farther back, a band of tiny root hairs encircles the root. These hairs grow from the root surface and absorb water and mineral salts from the soil. In the center of the root is the special conducting tissue that carries the water up into the main body of the plant. ◆

▲ A tap root (1) grows straight down and has smaller side branches called lateral roots. A fibrous root (2) has many branches about equal in size. Many climbing plants have roots that stick to the surface of a support (3). Aerial roots of tropical tree-growing orchids take in moisture from the steamy jungle air (4).

Members of the pea family develop lumps on their roots called *nodules*. Bacteria living inside these use nitrogen from the air to make nitrates, a form of natural fertilizer.

▼ **See also**
Bulbs and corms
Plants
Trees

# Rope

A rope is a long thick cord that is made up of fibers that have been twisted together. Most ropes today are made of synthetic fibers, such as nylon, polyester and glass fibers. These are glued together with resin to make long strands, and the strands are then twisted together to form the rope.

The material used to make the rope will depend on what the rope is for. Rope used for water-skiing is made of polypropylene. This is because it floats and does not get tangled. Mountain climbers use rope made of nylon, which is strong and firm.

Some ropes are made of steel wire. These are called *cables*. Twisted steel cables used to be used in suspension bridges. Newer bridges use cables that are made by clamping parallel strands of metal wire together. These steel ropes may be more than 30 cm (1 ft) in diameter, and they can carry loads of up to 400 tons.

## Natural-fiber ropes

At one time all ropes were made from natural fibers, and some ropes are still made in this way. The fibers used include sisal, which comes from leaves; hemp, which comes from stems; and coir, which comes from the husks of coconuts. The hair-like fibers are collected and

◀ This heavy-duty rope is marine hawser, used on large boats.

then combed and straightened in a machine. They come out of the machine in a sliver (a continuous ribbon). Several slivers are then twisted together to form yarns. These yarns are in turn twisted together to form strands, and three or more strands are finally twisted together to form the rope. ◆

▼ See also
Cables
Fibers
Knots
Synthetic fibers

# Rowing

Rowing is a sport in which men and women propel boats across water, using long paddles called oars. In rowing, each oarsman has one oar. In sculling, another form of the sport, the scullers have one smaller oar in each hand.

Rowing boats have crews of two, four or eight oarsmen. Eights have an extra person called a cox who steers the boat. Pairs and fours are "coxed" or "coxless." Sculling boats are single, double or quadruple, which is sometimes coxed. In addition to open events for all these boats, there are races for lightweight crews.

Rowing boats are light, streamlined craft. The oarsmen sit on sliding seats, and the oars are fixed in rowlocks on outriggers (projecting brackets). This increases the leverage of the oar. The boat is steered with a rudder, operated by the cox or an oarsman using his feet.

Events are held on lakes, rivers and coastal waters. Big meetings are called *regattas*. In the U.S., many colleges and universities have rowing teams and competitions. Rowing is also an Olympic sport.

## LOOKING BACK

Rowing is an ancient form of water transportation, and the galleys of early Mediterranean civilizations were propelled by crews of hundreds of oarsmen more than 3,000 years ago. The earliest reference to rowing races comes from the Roman poet Virgil some 2,000 years ago.

The sport as we know it began in 1715 in southern England, where Thames River boatmen who had just finished their apprenticeship took part in the Doggett's Coat and Badge sculling race. This event is still held today. ◆

The most famous rowing regatta is at Henley, on the Thames River in England. It has been held every year since 1839.

▼ See also
Boats
Olympic Games
Sports

# Rubber

**The History of Rubber**
*1770* English scientist Joseph Priestley experimented with a substance that would rub out pencil marks. He called it rubber.
*1823* Scottish chemist Charles Macintosh made a waterproof material with a layer of rubber between two layers of cloth. He used it to make the first "mackintosh" (raincoat).
*1839* U.S. inventor Charles Goodyear discovered how to make rubber harder when he accidentally spilled some rubber and sulphur on a hot stove. The process is called *vulcanization* and is used to make tires.

**▼ See also**
Tires

Natural rubber is made from latex, the juice of a fig-like tree that grows well near the Equator. The tree (*Hevea brasiliensis*) originally grew in Central and South America. Seeds from Brazil were grown in England, and the seedlings planted in Sri Lanka and Malaysia. Most natural rubber now comes from Southeast Asia.

Work on a rubber plantation begins early in the morning, when the latex is flowing best. A rubber tapper makes a sloping cut half-way round the tree. Each tapper cuts over 300 trees in three hours, then returns to collect the latex. The tapper will return to the same trees for 15 days in a month, making the cut on the same side but a little lower each time. After three or four years, the bark on the opposite side of the tree is started. In the plantation factory, the latex is cleaned, rolled, squeezed and dried. It is then packed into bales and sent to Europe or America.

Synthetic rubber is made from oil, gas and coal. In World War II, the Japanese invaded Southeast Asia when the armies of Europe and America desperately needed rubber. So synthetic rubber became very important at that time. ◆

▼ Sheets of rubber hanging out to dry on a rubber plantation in Thailand. From there the dried rubber will be sent to Europe or the U.S. for processing into such products as tires, tubes, boots and gloves.

# Rugs and carpets

In the U.S., nearly all rugs and carpets are now made by *tufting*. In this process, a machine pulls clusters of yarns through a thick backing material.

Georgia produces more rugs and carpets than any other state.

In the Thirteen Colonies, settlers made rugs by braiding cloth. They also made hooked rugs, which are created by drawing pieces of yarn through holes in a piece of strong backing material such as canvas or burlap.

The earliest "rugs" were probably animal skins used by prehistoric people on the floors of caves. Other early floor coverings were woven from grasses and reeds.

Rugs and carpets are floor coverings made of various fabrics. A rug covers part of a floor and can be picked up and moved, while a carpet extends over an entire floor (as in "wall-to-wall carpeting") and is attached to the floor.

Woven fabric rugs originated in the Middle East several thousand years ago. In the early Middle Ages, many were brought back to Europe by returning Crusaders. The Spanish began making rugs in the 13th century, and the craft later spread to England, France and other European countries.

Most rugs were created by hand-weaving on looms until the mid-19th century, when rug-weaving machines were introduced in Europe and America.

Today most woven rugs and carpets in Western countries are created by machines.

Among the most prized hand-woven rugs are so-called Oriental rugs, which are made in the Middle East and Asia by hand-knotting yarns onto a woven backing. Today machines can weave rugs and carpets in Oriental rug designs, but these are never as beautiful as handmade ones. ◆

**▼ See also**
Spinning
Weaving

▼ An Oriental rug maker in Turkmenistan spins wool. It will be dyed and then woven into a rug like the one displayed beside her.

# Running

Running is not simply walking fast. It is a quite different action. When you walk, you have at least one foot on the ground all the time. But when you run, you spend some of the time with both feet off the ground. Watch people running and you will notice that they bob up and down, as well as move forward. After each foot has landed, the runner uses it to push downward and backward on the ground. This makes the body move upward and forward.

## A spring in the foot

As the foot touches the ground again, the heel comes down first. The foot then rocks forward so that the ball of the foot is ready to push off again. The Achilles tendon at the back of the heel acts like a spring. It coils up as the heel touches down. Then it uncoils as the foot pushes off.

## Going even faster

Four-footed animals often have several different ways of running. When walking, only one foot is off the ground at a time. The other three feet act like a tripod, keeping the animal's center of gravity safely within the triangle of its three legs. As it speeds up, the animal does not spend long enough in one position to overbalance, and eventually all four feet come down at different times, giving a smoother motion. This is trotting. When the animal gallops, all four feet may be off the ground at the same time.

## Running races

Running has been a very popular competitive sport for thousands of years. Long-distance runners were used to carry messages and news over great distances before the use of horses. The longest races today are the marathons, which are 26 miles 385 yards (42.195 km) long. Variations on distance racing are steeplechases, in which the runners have to leap over hurdles at set intervals along the course, and relay races, where the race is run by teams, each member running in turn. ◆

▲ This picture shows how a runner uses the front foot to propel the body into the next stride.

◄ Very fast animals like the cheetah bend their spines so that the back legs swing past the front legs, giving them a very long stride when running.

The maximum speeds reached by humans during a world record sprint are 43 kmph (27 mph) for men (Carl Lewis, 1988) and 40 kmph (25 mph) for women (Florence Griffith Joyner, 1988).

▼ See also
Marathons
Olympic Games

# Russia and the Russian Federation

Russia is almost the size of the U.S. and Canada combined. From east to west it is about 8,000 km (5,000 mi) and includes 11 time zones. To cross the country by rail takes eight days.

## People

Russians make up the large majority of the population, but there are more than a hundred other nationalities and languages. Most Russians live in the European part of the country. Moscow and St. Petersburg, which used to be called Leningrad, are two of Europe's biggest cities. In the far north there are people who follow more traditional ways of life. Peoples such as the Nenets, Yakuts and Komi keep reindeer herds or live by fishing. The best farmlands are in the west, and wheat is one of the main crops.

Not all of the nationalities in the Russian Federation want to stay

**Area**
17,075,000 sq km
(6,592,800 sq mi)
**Capital**
Moscow
**Population**
147,370,000
**Language**
Russian
**Religion**
Christian, Muslim
**Government**
Parliamentary republic
**Currency**
1 rubel = 100 kopeks
**Major exports**
Minerals, timber

▶ In Moscow, St. Basil's Cathedral looks like a fairy-tale castle in the night sky.

▶ The towered red-brick walls of the Kremlin enclose an historic area covering 70 acres in the heart of Moscow. The Kremlin, which means "fortress," was originally built in the 12th century; the present brick structure dates from about 1500. The Kremlin includes government buildings, museums and churches. This is a view of the south side of the Kremlin, along the Moskva River. In the center is the Cathedral of the Archangel, built in 1505–1508. Partially visible to the left is the Great Kremlin Palace, which dates from the early 19th century.

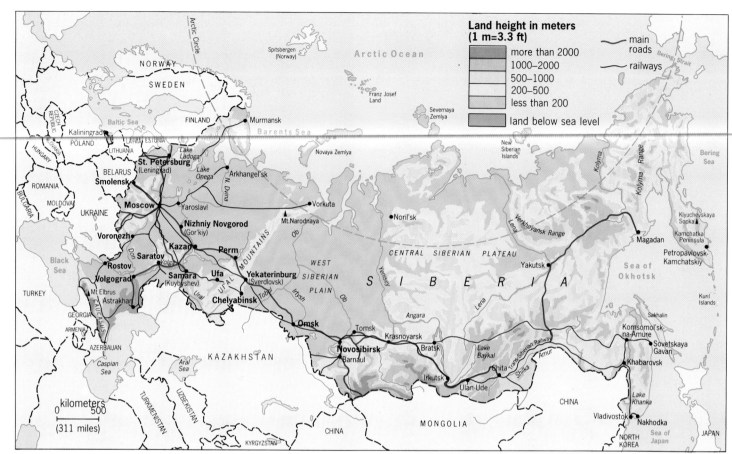

part of it. Some want the same kind of independence that was won by the former republics of the Soviet Union. The Chechens are Muslims who live in the Caucasus mountains region. They have been fighting the Russian army for self- government.

## Rivers and mountains

The Ural Mountains separate European and Asian parts of Russia. They are not very big: the highest peak, Mount Narodnaya, is about 2,000 m (6,560 ft) high. The largest mountains are on Russia's southern borders and in the Far East, along the Kamchatka peninsula. These mountains contain Russia's only active volcanoes. The highest one, Kluchevskaya Sopka, is 4,750 m (15,584 ft) high.

Several of the world's longest rivers flow through Russia. The Ob and the Lena flow north to the Arctic Ocean. In winter the Ob is frozen solid. The Amur River forms the border with China as it flows toward the Sea of Japan.

## Mineral wealth

Russia is very rich in most of the minerals used by modern society. Along with timber from the vast forests which cover a third of the country, they are Russia's main exports. Some of the oil

and gas fields are found in the Arctic Circle. Here it is very cold all year round and the ground is frozen. Machines sometimes do not work in the cold, and factories have to pay high wages to attract workers. Leaks from oil pipelines cause great damage to the environment. Gold, silver and diamonds come from Siberia, as well as vast coal deposits around Kuznetsk. These minerals have helped make the Volga River region one of the world's major centers of industry. Factories get power from the many hydroelectric power stations on the Don and Volga rivers.

## RUSSIAN HISTORY

Over 1,400 years ago there were tribes of Slav people living in parts of Central and Eastern Europe. In the 6th century A.D. some of them began to migrate farther eastward. They found themselves upon a great plain with no barrier in their path until they reached a mountain wall in the east or an ocean in the far north, the Arctic.

## Kiev Rus

This bleak plain was open to the cold eastern winds and snow for half the year, and to attacks from Huns, Scythians and Goths. At the first sign of danger the Slavs would spread out over

Russia has the second-longest rail network in the world. (The U.S. has the largest.) It has 154,000 km (95,700 mi) of track. Its railroads carry the most freight in the world: 2 billion tons a year.

Lake Baykal, near the border with Mongolia, is the deepest lake in the world; at one point it is 1,620 m (5,315 ft) deep. It contains one-fifth of the planet's fresh water.

The name "Russian" probably comes from a Norse word meaning "oarsmen" or "sailors."

the endless steppe (grasslands) or go deeper into the forest. Some settled down as farmers. Others became pioneers opening up new territory. From the 6th to the 9th century, Vikings from the north made trips for trade and adventure along the great Dnieper and Volga rivers to Kiev, Novgorod and other cities.

Kiev also traded with Greeks in the south, and it was from the Greeks that the Russians took their Christian religion. In 988 Grand Prince Vladimir of Kiev was converted to Christianity. The Russians adopted an alphabet based on the Greek rather than the Roman alphabet.

## The Golden Horde

▼ The map shows Kiev Rus and the routes used by Vikings, Greeks and Mongol-Tartars.

Kiev Rus was destroyed in 1240 by the Golden Horde of Mongol-Tartars. The Horde had come from the Gobi Desert, in what is now Mongolia, to overrun Russia. It occupied the country for

Viking adventurers and traders
Greek missionaries and merchants
Golden Horde of Mongol-Tartars

0 kilometers 500
(311 miles)

In 1812 Napoleon invaded Russia with a large army and captured Moscow, but he could not make the Russians surrender. The army was forced to retreat through the bitter Russian winter, and thousands of lives were lost.

about 250 years, cutting it off from important events elsewhere.

But the princes of Moscow gradually beat them off, and in the 16th century Ivan the Terrible finally defeated the Tartars at Kazan. He had himself crowned *czar* (emperor) in the capital city of Moscow in 1547. After that the country turned more toward

Europe than to Asia.

## Rise of the Russian Empire

After Ivan died, there were quarrels over the throne until Mikhail Romanov was made czar. The Romanov family ruled Russia from 1613 until they were overthrown in 1917. Mikhail Romanov's grandson Peter was the greatest of all Russian czars. He opened "a window to the West" by gaining a port on the Baltic Sea and building a grand new capital in marshes where the Neva River meets the Baltic. He called the city St. Petersburg.

With the help of many foreign craftsmen, Peter the Great set about modernizing his country. He built a modern navy and army, made Russia a world power, and introduced many reforms to westernize the nation. But the changes put an unbearable burden on the peasants, who were serfs with no land of their own. They were the property of the landowners. Peter also forced the *boyars* (nobles) and Church to obey his rule. Russia grew under his reign as he added Estonia and part of Latvia and Finland to the territories under Russian control.

In 1762, nearly 40 years after Peter's death, a young German princess took the Russian throne. She became known as Catherine the Great and ruled for 34 years. At first she tried to use liberal Western ideas to govern Russia, but she was scared by peasant revolts and the French Revolution of 1789. Her government became more brutal during the last years of her reign. It used secret police to arrest people who disagreed with its policy, and exiled some prisoners to Siberia.

Russia grew much larger during the reign of Catherine. The empire expanded eastward toward the Pacific Ocean, southward to the Crimea and Black Sea, and westward to occupy Lithuania and much of Poland. This vast empire was almost impossible to govern, at a time when transportation was by horseback or sleigh.

## Russia in crisis

By the middle of the 19th century Russia was in crisis. She fought against England and France in the Crimean War and, later in the century, England stopped her from taking over Afghanistan. At home the serfs had rebelled against the landowners, and many Russians wanted to modernize the country. Czar, Alexander II saw no alternative but to free the serfs and give them land. He did this in 1861, and many of the former serfs and their families built up successful small farms. Russia produced famous writers like Anton Chekhov and Leo Tolstoy. The composer Tchaikovsky also lived at this time. However, most Russians were still very poor and there was a lot of discontent.

A group of reformers, called the Narodniks, went to the people in the countryside to teach them to read and write. Others became terrorists and used bombs to attack Russia's leaders. Czar Alexander II, even though he had freed the serfs, was assassinated in 1881. The situation worsened in the reign of Nicholas II. In 1905, the first Russian Revolution occurred as workers went on strike and peasants revolted. The czar created a lawmaking body called the Duma to meet some protesters' demands, but this reform was not enough, and unrest continued.

## The 1917 Revolution

Russia's entry into World War I increased the nation's hardship. Two million men were killed, two million wounded and four million were taken prisoner. Riots by starving people in February 1917 quickly spread. Nicholas II was so incompetent in running the war and dealing with problems at home that he gradually lost all support. Forced to give up his throne, he and his family were shot the next year by the Bolsheviks. For eight months a temporary government ruled, but it was overthrown in October by the Bolshevik Party led by Lenin. Russia then became a republic inspired by the ideas of Karl Marx. The Communist Party ruled, everything was owned by the state, and religion was outlawed.

## Civil war

The hopes of peace were short-lived. Civil war broke out and the new republic was invaded by foreign troops, including British and Americans. Millions of people died. At the end of the civil war the Communist government divided the territories of the old empire into republics; the Republic of Russia was by far the largest of these territories.

In 1922 the new nation was named the Union of Soviet Socialist Republics (U.S.S.R.). After 70 years of Communist rule the Soviet Union collapsed in 1991. Boris Yeltsin became the first president of the new Russian Federation, consisting of 21 autonomous (self-governing) republics, various territories, provinces, and a Jewish autonomous region. Yeltsin organized the Commonwealth of Independent States, which was joined by all former Soviet republics except the Baltic states. Negotiations began with Ukraine over the Black Sea fleet and nuclear weapons.

РАБОЧИХ и ЛЕНИНА
СОЕДИНИЛА В СВОЕМ ПОРОХОВОМ
ДЫМУ

РЕВОЛЮЦИЯ 1905 г.

◀ A Soviet poster celebrating the Revolution of 1905, a large-scale uprising that preceded the 1917 Revolution. Posters were frequently used in the Soviet Union as propaganda (art that presents a message, often a political one). This poster, designed many years after the event it portrays, presents Lenin as the strong defender of the working man in 1905. In fact, his role in the uprising was very minor.

In 1903 the Russian Social Democratic Workers Party had split into two groups: the Bolsheviks and the Mensheviks. The Bolsheviks, led by Lenin, believed that a small group of party activists should work closely together to bring about a revolution. The Mensheviks wanted change to come more slowly. The Bolsheviks led the revolution of October 1917, and took power.

In 1991 rebels in one of the republics, Chechnya, which has a large Muslim population, demanded independence, at a time when its neighbors Azerbaijan, Armenia and Georgia had successfully done so. Civil war lasted until 1994, when Russian troops moved in to "re-establish order," and bombed the capital, Grozny. Rebels fled to the mountains, but renewed the fighting in 1995 and 1996. Yeltsin's period as president has been a troubled one, with violent political clashes in Moscow and a steep drop in the standard of living of most Russians.

## Life after Communism

Since 1991, life for Russians has changed rapidly. They have more freedom to say what they want, to vote for the many different political parties and to travel abroad. Industrialists and business people have been able to buy their factories from the state and make money for themselves. But poorer people have not always been so lucky. Many have lost their savings or found that their state pensions are no longer enough to live on. Workers such as coal miners have not been paid. In addition, Russia has not received as much aid and help from the rest of the world as it had hoped for. ◆

# Rwanda

Rwanda is a small, crowded African country. In the west is a hot, broad valley containing Lake Kivu. A mountain range overlooks the valley. But most of Rwanda consists of hilly grasslands, with some lakes in the east. There are three main groups of people. The Hutus make up more than 90 percent of the population; the Tutsis are a tall people who rear livestock; and there are a small number of pygmies, the Twa.

Germany ruled Rwanda from 1897 until 1916, when Belgium conquered the area. Rwanda was once ruled by Tutsi kings, who treated the Hutus as slaves. The Hutus rebelled in 1959 and overthrew the Tutsi monarchy. Rwanda became independent in 1962 and many Tutsis went into exile.

In 1990 there was an invasion from Uganda by a Tutsi army (the Rwandan Patriotic Front, or RPF), and civil war developed. In 1994 many Tutsis were murdered by Hutus, and the RPF carried out revenge attacks. Some 5 million people (mostly Hutu) fled, many into Zaïre. Nearly a million died in the massacres of 1994 before a new Tutsi/Hutu government was formed and a fragile peace restored. ◆

**Area**
26,340 sq km
(10,170 sq mi)
**Capital**
Kigali
**Population**
7,750,000
**Language**
French, Kinyarwanda
**Religion**
Christian, traditional, Muslim
**Government**
Republic
**Currency**
1 Rwanda franc = 100 centimes

▼**See also**
Africa
Burundi
Pygmies

---

# Sahara

The area of the Sahara is about 9,065,000 sq km (3,500,000 sq mi).

The Sahara is the world's largest desert. It covers most of northern Africa and is divided among 13 countries. It is crossed in the east by the world's longest river, the Nile, but there is hardly any rain in the desert.

The Sahara holds the record for the world's highest shade temperature and for the most sunshine. But the nights can be quite cold. About a tenth of the Sahara is sandy; the rest is gravel or rock. There are several mountain ranges, including the Hoggar and Tibesti ranges. The Atlas Mountains mark the northern edge of the desert in Morocco.

The Sahara is not completely deserted. Farmers live in the oases. There are artificial oases for people drilling for oil or mining iron ore and other valuable minerals. Among the Sahara's residents are the Tuareg people. They control the few remaining camel trains, which carry salt. There are roads across the Sahara now, and most goods travel by truck. Nomads move their flocks and herds along the edge of the desert and near the oases.

## The Sahel

The southern edge of the Sahara Desert is known as the Sahel. The desert does not suddenly stop; it gradually changes. As the amount of rainfall increases, more grasses and other plants grow. The Sahel stretches from northern Senegal to southern Sudan. This is an area that expects some rain, but only during four months of the year. ◆

Sahel is an Arabic word meaning "edge."

Between 1950 and 1967 the rainfall seemed to increase in the Sahel. Land was ploughed up, new crops were planted, and nomads took their animals farther into the Sahara. But the good years were followed by a succession of bad years, beginning in 1968. Animals died, crops failed, and there was a famine. The land had been over-used in the good years and badly eroded in the drought, making the Sahara even bigger.

▼**See also**
Africa
Deserts
Nomads
Oases

▼ The Tuareg people of the Sahara were once warriors. The name "Tuareg" means "People of the Veil." It is the men who veil their faces, not the women. Some Tuareg are nomads; others live in villages.

► A sail is pushed sideways when the wind blows across it. Sailors can use this effect to make their boats go in almost any direction they like.

# Sailing

Sailing boats use the force of the wind on large sheets called *sails* to push them along. Sails used to be made of canvas, but synthetic materials such as nylon are now normally used. To move in a particular direction, the line of the sails is changed so that the wind blows across them. A sail acts rather like the wing of an aircraft. As the air flows across it, pressure builds up on one side. By angling the sail, the sailor can use the sideways pressure to push the boat forward. The keel (centerboard) stops it from moving sideways. The boat can sail with the wind behind it, to the side of it, or even slightly ahead of it. By tacking (zigzagging), it can move against the direction of the wind. ◆

The first person to sail around the world alone was an American, Joshua Slocum (1844–1909), who left Massachusetts aboard his ship the *Spray* in 1895 and returned three years later. Slocum wrote a famous book about his voyage, called *Sailing Alone Around the World* (1900).

▼ **See also**
Boats
Sailing ships
Water sports
Yachts

**BIOGRAPHY**
Magellan, Ferdinand

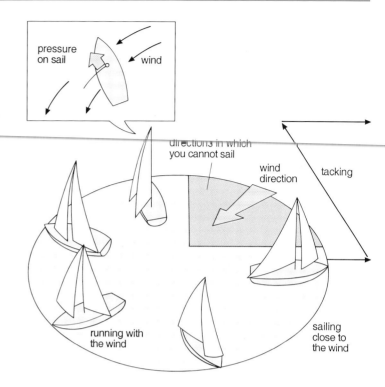

pressure on sail

wind

directions in which you cannot sail

wind direction

tacking

running with the wind

sailing close to the wind

# Sailing ships

Before the days of steam and diesel engines, merchant ships and warships had to rely on sails and the power of the wind to move them about. The earliest sailing ships had just one mast and sail. But as ships grew larger, more masts were added, masts became taller, and several sails were carried on each mast.

On a sailing ship, the ropes and spars that support the masts and sails are called the rigging. Some ships had sails that lay along the direction of their length; they were fore-and-aft rigged like modern yachts. However, most large sailing ships had sails that lay across the direction of their width; they were square-rigged. The square-rigged clippers were the fastest sailing ships of all. Their name came from the way they could "clip" time off their sailing schedules. In the 1850s, a clipper could carry a cargo of wool from Australia to England in just over two months.

Small sailing ships are still used for trading in many parts of the world. For example, dhows are used in the Middle East and junks in the Far East. Large, square-rigged sailing ships no longer carry cargo, but some still survive in museums or are used for training young people at sea.

The first steamships carried sails to assist their engines. Today, ship designers are starting to look at this idea again as they search for ways of saving fuel and cutting pollution from engines. ◆

▼ **See also**
Boats
Sailing
Ships
Yachts

In the years between 1840 and 1860, many U.S. clipper ships set speed records. One of the most famous was the *Flying Cloud*, built by Donald McKay. In 1854 it sailed from Boston around Cape Horn (at the tip of South America) to San Francisco in 89 days, eight hours. (Before the Panama Canal was built in the early 20th century, all ships sailing between the East Coast and the West Coast of the U.S. had to go around South America.)

The largest sailing ship ever built was the *France II*, launched in 1911. It weighed 5,900 tons (nearly 12 million lbs).

▼ This modern Japanese tanker has sails as well as an engine. The use of wind power can make substantial savings in the fuel needed to power the engines.

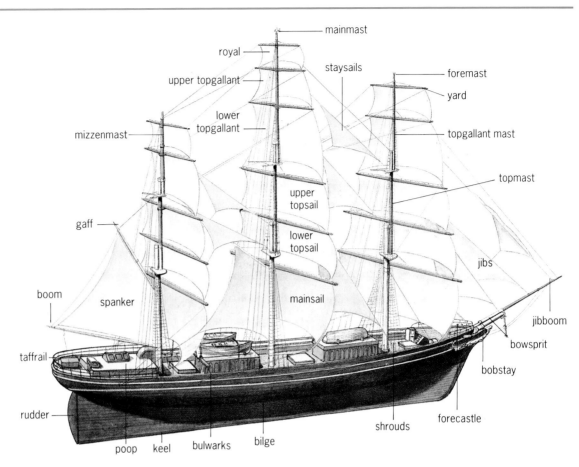

▶ Full-rigged clipper of the 1850s. Although iron steamships were being developed rapidly at this time, the wooden clippers were still the fastest vessels of their day.

The last big sailing ships were used until 1914 to carry fertilizer from South America to Europe around Cape Horn.

## Sailing Ships Through the Ages

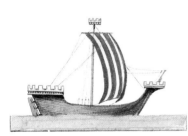

**Cog (13th century).** The sturdy wooden cog was developed in Northern Europe and used as a trader and as a warship. Early vessels were steered with a large oar at the back. Later ships, like this one, had rudders.

**Galleon (16th century).** Galleons were used by both the British and the Spanish fleets at the time of the Armada. They were also used to carry gold and other booty from the Americas back to Europe.

**Dhow (20th century).** The Arabian dhow was developed many centuries ago and is still used for fishing and coastal trading today. The sail arrangement is called lateen rigging.

**Junk (20th century).** Junks have been used in China and the Far East for many hundreds of years. The fore-and-aft rigged sails have wooden spars to support and reinforce them.

**Three-masted barque (1890s).** Barques have fore-and-aft rigging on their mizzenmast (rear mast). Some were built of steel. Some are still used today as training ships.

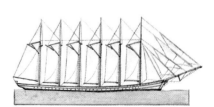

**Six-masted schooner (early 1900s).** Schooners have fore-and-aft rigging on all masts. The use of steel for masts and cables made it possible to build huge schooners with large sails.

# St. Lucia

St. Lucia is a Caribbean island lying between Martinique and St. Vincent. It was formed by volcanoes, but none are now active and they are covered in lush tropical forest. The island gained independence from the U.K. in 1979, but the Queen is still head of state and appoints a governor-general.

Farming and tourism are the main economic activities. St. Lucia produces tropical crops such as bananas, coconuts, breadfruit and mangoes, but farmlands were devastated by a tropical storm in 1994. Aid money has been spent on flood control and irrigation to produce a wider range of crops and to help make sure there is not so much damage on the island when there are hurricanes. ◆

**Area** 610 sq km
(236 sq mi)
**Capital** Castries
**Population** 141,000
**Language** English
**Religion** Christian
**Government**
Constitutional monarchy
**Currency** 1 East Caribbean dollar = 100 cents

▼ **See also**
Caribbean
West Indies

▲ St. Lucia's skyline is dominated by Gros Pilon and Petit Pilon, two conical peaks formed by the hard cores of volcanoes.

# Saints

Members of other religions sometimes use the English word "saint" for a member of their religion who is special in some way.

The Roman Catholic Church still canonizes people. It is only done after they are dead.

Saint is abbreviated as St.

Throughout history and in many different religions, people who have led particularly good lives have been recognized as saints.

Followers of the ancient Chinese philosopher Confucius recognize certain "holy rulers" from ancient times as saints. Buddhists believe that monks or others who attain *Nirvana* (a state of peacefulness that comes from following the Buddha's rules for living) are saints. Some Buddhists think that all people are capable of becoming saints. In the Hindu religion, holy people are often called *sadhus* ("good ones"). Other people, including some saints from other religions, are believed to be avatars—gods living on Earth in human form.

Christian saints provide particularly good examples of how God wants everyone to live. In the New Testament of the Bible the word refers to all Christians, but now it is used just for special people, usually after they are dead.

Christian saints usually model their lives on Jesus. They are unselfish and give up a lot to help other people. Many of them have died for their beliefs. They are then called *martyrs*. St. Paul traveled great distances to teach. St. Francis of Assisi spent his time with the poor, and with lepers and animals. Teresa of Avila wrote about her experience of God.

Many famous Christians have been officially *canonized* (declared to be saints) by the Church. These are the people that we speak of with the word "Saint" in front of their names.

▼ **See also**
Buddhism
Christianity
Hinduism
Monasteries

**BIOGRAPHY**
Augustine of Hippo, St.
Cabrini, St. Francis Xavier
Confucius
Francis of Assisi, St.
Joan of Arc
John the Baptist, St.
Patrick, St.
Paul, St.
Peter, St.
Seton, St. Elizabeth Ann
Teresa of Avila, St.

## Some Famous Saints

**Andrew** One of Jesus' apostles. Patron saint of Scotland.

**Bernadette** Saw a vision of the Virgin Mary at Lourdes.

**Bernard** Abbot of the Cistercian monastery of Clairvaux. Patron saint of travelers.

**Catherine of Alexandria** Killed for her faith on a spiked wheel, now called a "Catherine wheel."

**Francis of Assisi\*** Founded the Franciscan order of friars. Patron saint of animals.

**George** A soldier who killed a dragon and rescued a king's daughter. Patron saint of England.

**Joan of Arc\*** Defeated the English and saved France. She was burned at the stake.

**Mary Magdalene** Follower of Jesus. Her life was completely changed by him.

**Nicholas** Bishop in 4th-century Turkey. Patron saint of children and sailors, and of Russia.

**Patrick\*** Preached Christianity to the Irish; patron saint of Ireland.

**Paul\*** Missionary traveler and writer of many letters (epistles).

**Peter\*** One of Jesus' apostles. The first pope.

**Stephen** First Christian martyr; stoned to death.

**Teresa of Avila\*** Spanish Carmelite nun and mystic.

\* These saints are in the Biography volume, Vol 8.

◀ Two of the most famous Christian saints are Peter and Paul. This 15th-century Italian fresco shows St. Paul (right) visiting St. Peter in jail.

◀◀ Buddhists who have reached Nirvana (Enlightenment) are often considered saints. *Bodhisattvas* are Buddhists who have reached Nirvana but choose to remain on Earth to help others. This painting of a bodhisattva was made in China about 600 A.D.

◀ St. George, shown here in a 15th-century sculpture by Donatello, lived in the 3rd century A.D. He was a Christian martyr who was killed by Romans in Palestine. In the following centuries, many legends were told about him. According to the most famous legend, he converted thousands of people to Christianity after slaying an enormous dragon that was terrorizing them. During the Middle Ages, St. George was regarded as the model of a Christian knight. He became the patron saint of several cities and countries, including England.

# Salamanders

▲ Some salamanders, like this tiger salamander, have bad-tasting or poisonous flesh. They usually advertise this fact to their enemies with bright warning colors.

**Distribution**
Throughout the Northern Hemisphere and South America
**Largest**
Chinese giant salamander, up to 114 cm (3.7 ft) long; weight up to 30 kg (66 lbs)
**Smallest**
Pygmy salamander, as little as 3.7 cm (1.4 in) long
**Lifespan**
Giant salamanders live for over 50 years
**Subphylum**
Vertebrata
**Class**
Amphibia
**Order**
Urodela
**Family**
Salamandridae
**Number of species**
About 90

▼ **See also**
Amphibians
Frogs
Toads

Salamanders are amphibians, like frogs and toads. They have long narrow bodies, long tails and short legs with webbed feet for swimming. They use their powerful tails to propel themselves through the water. Like frogs, salamanders have moist skins and live in damp places. They feed on worms and insects. Some salamanders use their tongues to catch their prey. Most salamanders spend their adult lives on land, but some live mainly in water.

Some salamanders lay their eggs in water. These eggs hatch into tadpoles, which feed on small water animals. Other salamanders lay their eggs on land, in damp hollows under old logs or stones. The tadpole stage takes place inside the eggs, so tiny salamanders eventually hatch out from the eggs. A few kinds of salamander give birth to live young.

A few salamander tadpoles never really grow up. An adult axolotl is like a giant tadpole and has feathery gills on the outside of its head.

Most salamanders produce poisonous slime from glands in their skin. This wards off predators. These salamanders may be brightly colored to warn of their poison. ◆

# Salt

To most people, the word "salt" means the substance we use in cooking and on food. But to a scientist, it is used to describe a large number of chemical substances, of which common salt (table salt) is just one. Salts are formed when the hydrogen in an acid is replaced by a metal. All salts are made up of crystals. In the case of common salt, these crystals are white and cube-shaped.

## Common salt

Sodium chloride (common salt) is the most widely used mineral in the world. It has been estimated that there are 16,000 uses for it. Apart from being used in cooking and to make other chemicals, common salt is used in the food industry to preserve meat, fish and vegetables. It is also used to make foods such as margarine and butter. Salt is used in the manufacture of dyes, paper, pottery, leather and many medicines. Salt is also essential for keeping roads and pavements free of ice and snow in winter. The salt melts the ice and snow, and keeps it from freezing again. Pure water freezes at 0 °C (32°F), but the melted ice and snow freeze at a much lower temperature.

▼ **See also**
Chemicals
Crystals
Minerals
Rocks

**R**oman soldiers were paid a *salarium* (allowance of salt). The modern word "salary," which means a regular payment for work done, comes from this word.

**T**he United States mines more salt than any other country in the world. The leading salt-producing state is Louisiana.

▼ Rock salt is mined in underground caverns, using giant cutters like this.

In addition, salt is essential, in small quantities, for the proper working of the body. We have to eat salt because the body loses it all the time. For example, sweat contains salt, which is why it tastes salty. To stay healthy we need only about half a gram of salt a day, providing we are not rushing about and sweating a lot. But on average, adults consume between 5 and 20 grams (0.175–0.7 oz) of salt a day, about 20 times more than we need. The kidneys filter the extra salt and it leaves the body with the urine.

### Rock salt

There is plenty of salt in the world, but it is not always easy to get at. "Rock salt" is salt that is mined from huge layers deposited underground. These were formed long ago when prehistoric seas dried up. Often rock salt is mined by digging for it underground. Sometimes it is collected by pumping water or steam down the mine, forming brine. This is pumped to the surface, where the water is evaporated, leaving the salt.

All the oceans and seas of the world have such a high concentration of salt that their water cannot be drunk unless it has been *desalinated*—had the salt removed.

▼ Sea water evaporates from these shallow terraces in Tripoli, Lebanon, leaving sea salt behind to be collected.

### Sea salt

Sea water contains about 100 g (3.5 oz) of salt in every 5 liters (5.3 qts) of water. In some countries with hot sunshine, salt is obtained by trapping sea water in shallow pans or lagoons. When the sea water evaporates, "sea salt" is left behind. ◆

# Salvation Army

In 1861 a Methodist minister, William Booth, felt he must do more to help the very poor people of east London. He gave up his post and, with his wife, started the East End Revival Society, later renamed the Christian Mission. It combined preaching with social work.

Booth became convinced he was fighting a war against poverty and moral problems, and in 1878 he again renamed the mission. He called it the Salvation Army, and organized it along military lines, with ranks such as colonel, captain and corporal. He became the Army's general.

In 1890 Booth published a book, *In Darkest England*, which brought to the attention of the British public the terrible living conditions endured by the poor.

Today the Salvation Army has branches in nearly 100 countries, including the U.S. It has more than 25,000 officers, organized in over 14,500 corps. It runs nearly 5,000 social service centers, institutions, maternity homes, children's homes and schools. A feature of its work is the money it raises to help poor people everywhere. ◆

▼ **See also**
Charities
Poverty

**BIOGRAPHY**
Booth, Catherine and William

A feature of the Salvation Army since its early days has been its bands, which lead the hymn singing at meetings.

The weekly newspaper of the Salvation Army is called the *War Cry*.

# San Marino

San Marino is one of the smallest countries in the world. It is about 13 km (8 mi) long and is situated on the slopes of Mount Titano in central Italy, on the side bordering the Adriatic Sea. Its capital, San Marino, sits high up on the western side of the mountain and has to be reached by cable railway. It is a hilly region cut through by mountain streams and forested with trees such as olive, pine and fir. Farmland dominates the landscape but tourism is increasingly important. In recent years, manufacturing industries producing ceramics, paints and chemicals have begun to invade the countryside. ◆

**Area** 61 sq km (24 sq mi)
**Capital** San Marino
**Population** 25,000
**Language** Italian
**Religion** Christian
**Government** Republic
**Currency** 1 lira = 100 centesimi

▼ **See also**
Europe
Italy

# Satellites

Satellites are launched by rockets or the space shuttle. The shuttle can only reach heights of a few hundred miles, so it can only place satellites in low orbits. A small rocket motor attached to a satellite can then be used to move it to a higher orbit.

The International Telecommunications Satellite Organization (Intelsat) is a union of over 110 countries that pay for a network of communications satellites in geostationary orbit above the Atlantic, Pacific and Indian oceans.

The National Oceanographic and Atmospheric Administration (NOAA), a U.S. government organization, has weather satellites that fly in polar orbits and provide most of the cloud pictures seen on TV weather forecasts. Meteosat (European satellites) fly in geostationary orbit above West Africa.

A satellite is an object that travels around a larger object. The natural satellites of planets are often called moons. There are also many artificial satellites traveling around the Earth. The word "satellite" on its own often means an artificial one.

## Satellite orbits

A satellite's orbit is the path it travels in space. It can be a circle or an oval shape. A satellite keeps going around and does not fly off into space because the planet's gravity holds on to it.

A satellite 300 km (186 mi) from Earth goes around in about 90 minutes, while one that orbits at a height of 36,000 km (22,320 mi) goes around in 24 hours. A satellite at this height, in a circular orbit above the Equator, will always stay directly above the same spot on the Earth's surface, because it moves around the Earth in exactly the period of time that the Earth takes to spin around its axis. This is called a *geostationary orbit*. Other satellites travel in a north–south direction. This is called a *polar orbit*. Each time the satellites come around, they pass over a different part of the Earth's surface.

## Satellites of different kinds

Most artificial satellites get their power from panels of solar cells that turn sunlight into electricity. Many have small gas jets to turn them around and sensors to check that the solar panels stay facing the Sun.

◀ The Solar Maximum Mission satellite. The two large blue rectangles are solar energy panels that provide power to the satellite's instruments.

Some satellites are space stations where the crew can do experiments. Other satellites have no crew. There are various different kinds. *Communications satellites* send telephone, television and radio signals between the continents. *Navigation satellites* send out radio signals that help ships and aircraft to find their way. *"Spy" satellites* take photographs of the ground for military use. *Weather satellites* photograph cloud patterns and movements to help forecast the weather. Other satellites use special instruments to identify different kinds of vegetation and minerals. Satellites can look down at the Earth or out into the depths of space. *Orbiting telescopes*, such as the Hubble space telescope, can see much more clearly than telescopes on the ground because they do not have to look through the atmosphere, which blurs the view.

Satellites can also detect radiations (waves) that cannot get down to ground level, such as gamma rays, X-rays, and ultraviolet and infrared light. ◆

The Global Positioning System (GPS) is a network of satellites that allows people on land, at sea or in the air to fix their positions to within 30 m (100 ft).

Sputnik 1, the first artificial satellite, was launched by the Soviet Union in 1957.

Tiros 1, the first weather satellite, was launched in 1960.

Telstar carried the first live television pictures across the Atlantic Ocean in 1962.

▼ **See also**
Gravity
Moon
Navigation
Planets
Space exploration

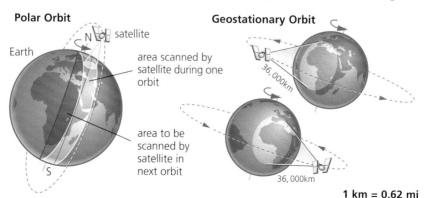

**Polar Orbit**

Earth — satellite — area scanned by satellite during one orbit — area to be scanned by satellite in next orbit

**Geostationary Orbit**

36,000km — 36,000km

**1 km = 0.62 mi**

▶ A satellite in a polar orbit travels around the Earth in a north–south direction while the Earth turns around beneath it. Each time the satellite comes around, it scans a different strip of the Earth's surface.

◀ A geostationary satellite goes around the Earth in the same time as the Earth itself spins around. It always stays above the same point on the Earth's surface. Three geostationary satellites spread out evenly above the Equator can "see" nearly all of our planet.

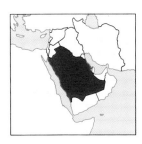

# Saudi Arabia

**Area**
2,149,690 sq km
(829,995 sq mi)
**Capital**
Riyadh
**Population**
17,451,000
**Language**
Arabic
**Religion**
Muslim
**Government**
Monarchy
**Currency**
1 Saudi riyal = 100 halalas
**Major exports**
Oil

Saudi Arabia is a giant desert kingdom bigger than the states of Alaska and California combined. It is also the richest country by far in the Middle East, because beneath the thousands of square miles of empty desert lie the biggest known reserves of oil in the world. The huge wealth from oil has been used to build modern cities, including Riyadh, Jeddah and Dammam, which are connected by an internal airline network.

Saudi cities are modern, but the country's society remains extremely traditional. The Saudi royal family comes from an Islamic desert tribe, and their traditions have been maintained. Women are rarely seen in public, and when they are, their heads and bodies are covered in black. Women are not allowed to drive cars. Men and boys wear the traditional cool, loose-fitting white

robes and white headdresses. The country was never governed as a colony by a European power, as happened to most Arab states. The cities of Mecca and Medina, where the prophet Muhammad founded the Muslim religion, are in Saudi Arabia, and several million pilgrims visit Mecca each year. ◆

◀ The 300-year-old city of Jeddah is the main Saudi Arabian port for pilgrims arriving to go to Mecca.

The kingdom of Saudi Arabia was formed in 1932. The Saud family had been expanding its territories for over 100 years.

The Saudis have kept alive traditional desert pastimes such as hunting with falcons and camel racing. On special occasions the Saudis hold feasts in the desert. A sheep, roasted whole, is the main delicacy.

▼ **See also**
Arabs
Islam
Middle East
Oil

**BIOGRAPHY**
Muhammad

# Scandinavia

The weight of the ice sheet that covered Scandinavia during the last ice age pushed the land down. As the ice retreated, the land slowly came back and, 10,000 years later, is still rising at 1 cm (0.39 in) a year.

Scandinavia is a region of Northern Europe that includes Norway, Sweden, Denmark, Iceland, the Faeroe Islands and Finland.

The northern part of Scandinavia is in the Arctic Circle, but the cold climate is softened by a warm oceanic current called the North Atlantic Drift. The western side consists of rugged mountains, some of which hold glaciers. Along much of the Norwegian coast, the mountains are indented by long, deep inlets called fjords. Inland, the ancient rock mass is divided by the Baltic Sea and covered in thousands of lakes.

Large areas of Norway, Sweden and Finland are covered in forests, while Iceland and the Faeroes are almost treeless. Acid rains are threatening the forests, while the Baltic Sea suffers from a buildup of industrial and agricultural chemicals. ◆

▼ **See also**
Acid rain
Denmark
Fjords
Finland
Glaciers
Ice ages
Iceland
Norway
Sweden

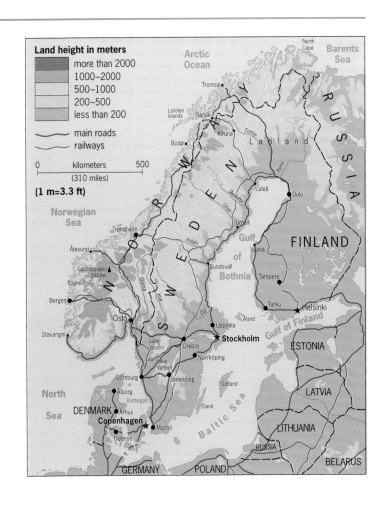

# Scanners

▶ A woman having an MRI scan. A computer linked to the scanner converts signals from the scanned area into an image and displays it on a monitor.

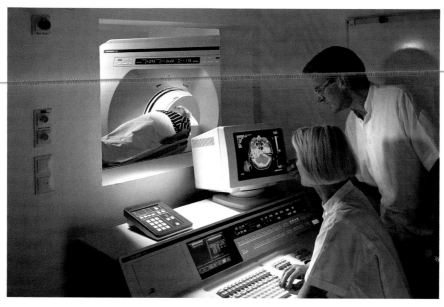

With an ultrasound scanner, it is possible to see an unborn baby in its mother's womb. This method is much safer than using X-rays, which might harm the growing baby.

Machines that scan prices of products at supermarket check-outs are also called scanners.

Scanners are machines used to record information by scanning it electronically. The term "scanner" is usually used to refer to hospital machines that take pictures of the inside of a person's body. Such scanners produce pictures with more detail than an ordinary X-ray photo. They do not look at the whole body at once: they "scan" it often in cross-section, one strip at a time.

*CAT (Computerized Axial Tomography) scanners* X-ray a thin "slice" of the body from many different angles. A computer processes all the information, and produces a picture of the slice. Patients lie on a special bed that moves slowly through the scanner while the X-ray beam and its detector rotate around them. The beam is made as weak as possible because X-rays are harmful.

*MRI (magnetic resonance imaging) scanners* also take pictures of slices of the body, but without using X-rays. They use the fact that all parts of the body have hydrogen atoms in them but that these are more concentrated in some parts than in others. The scanner puts a very strong magnetic field through the body, then sends out powerful pulses of radio waves. This makes the hydrogen atoms wobble and give out their own radio waves. From the signals detected, the computer builds up a picture of each slice of the body. CAT and MRI scanners are bulky and expensive.

*Ultrasound scanners* give less detailed pictures, but are much cheaper, and far more convenient for some jobs. They work by using very high frequency sound waves—sounds that are too high for us to hear. A small probe is used to beam the sound waves into the body. These reflect from different layers inside and are picked up again by the probe. As the probe is moved around, the computer builds up its picture. ◆

▼ *Position computed tomography (PCT) is another way of taking pictures of the inside of a person's body. Here it is being used to produce maps of the brain, enabling doctors to look at which parts of the brain allow us to see. The scans show which areas (arrowed) are affected by visual stimulation. Initially the patients eyes are closed (left), but when they are open mental activity increases as shown (middle, right).*

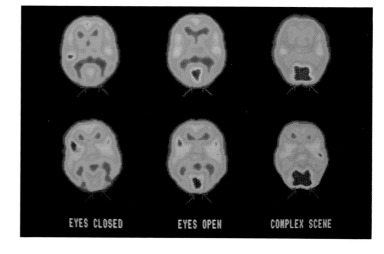

EYES CLOSED      EYES OPEN      COMPLEX SCENE

▼ **See also**
Sound
X-rays

# Schools

Today every country has state-run (public) schools that are free to attend. Children start full-time school at different ages in different countries—for example, at 5 in England, at 6 in the U.S. and at 7 in Russia, though many children in those countries attend nursery school or kindergarten first. Most nursery schools are privately run in the U.S. but are state-run in many other countries. There are both public and private kindergartens in most countries, including the U.S.

The years of schooling in many parts of the U.S. are still divided into "grade," or primary, which students attend from the ages of 6 to 13, and secondary, or high school, from 14 to 18. However, in many areas, primary school now ends at the age of 8 or 9, and children then enter middle school, where they remain until high school begins. Other countries have different ways of dividing these age groups.

## Compulsory schooling

In the U.S., children are required to attend school until the age of 16, but most students remain to graduate from high school, usually at the age of 18. England also requires children to stay in school until they are 16, which is when they normally graduate from secondary school.

In Russia, children must attend school until the age of 15. Most students in Japan must attend school until the age of 18.

State-run schools are paid for and run in different ways. In the U.S., local taxes support public schools, which are administered by locally elected school boards. In France and England the national government operates the schools; in Germany the individual states administer their educational system.

Some of the poorer countries in Africa and Asia can afford to offer only five years of free schooling. In China, all children go to primary school, but only one in three continues in school.

## Private (independent) schools

Most Western countries have private as well as public schools. In the U.S. there are private schools from nursery school through secondary school. Private secondary schools are often called "prep" (preparatory) schools.

Some private schools are boarding schools, where students live while they are being taught. In England, middle- and upper-class children are sent away to boarding schools as a matter of course, usually at the age of 6.

Private schools are sometimes run by religious denominations. The Roman Catholic Church, for example, has schools in communities throughout the U.S.

## The curriculum

What is taught in schools is called the curriculum. In most countries this is usually decided by the central or regional government, and students study the same curriculum throughout the country, using identical textbooks. England, for example, has a nationwide plan of study called the National Curriculum. The U.S. has no nationwide curriculum; what students study in public schools and the books they use are decided by local school boards and teachers. However, in many states local schools must follow curriculum guidelines established by their state government.

A school curriculum usually requires children to read and write their regional or national language. For many minority children in countries throughout the world, this may not be the language they speak at home.

The curriculum also includes mathematics, science, history or social studies, and often another language. Art, music and physical education are often taught as well. In Muslim countries, such as Iran and Pakistan, religious leaders (*imams*) influence the curriculum, which must include learning to recite the Koran. Religious education is also compulsory in the United Kingdom. In China, Communist politics and history are taught.

## Examinations

In most U.S. schools, both public and private, students take tests that are graded by their teachers. Periodically they also take standardized "achievement tests" that are given in schools throughout the region, state or nation to compare student performance; such tests are provided by a private testing service, which also grades them. Some states, such as New York, require that students pass a comprehensive test before receiving a high school diploma.

Other countries have compulsory nationwide testing programs. In England, children are tested to determine what kind of secondary school they will attend (usually academic, which prepares them for a university, or vocational, which teaches them job skills). Other European countries have similar systems. ◆

For centuries, schools in Europe were run by church authorities. The movement for free public education began in the 19th century. The U.S. led the way: public schools in America began in the early 1800s in New England. State-run schools in Europe began later in the century.

In the 19th and early 20th centuries, "one-room schools" were common in rural areas in the U.S. Children of all ages were taught in such schools, usually by just one teacher.

In many U.S. public schools in large cities, which often have a number of immigrant minority children, English is taught as a second language (ESL). Some of these schools offer *bilingual education*, in which children are instructed in basic subjects in their own language while they learn English; later, they move into classes that are taught in English.

In America, the term "public school" means a day school that is operated by local authorities, is usually open to both girls and boys, and is free to attend. In England, "public school" means something very different: a privately run boarding school for boys for which tuition is charged. One of the most famous English "public schools" is Eton, which was founded in 1440. Some of England's most distinguished leaders have attended Eton. Prince William, the son of Charles, the Prince of Wales, and grandson of Queen Elizabeth II, enrolled at Eton in 1996.

Sunday schools—schools run by churches on Sundays to teach religion to children—began in Wales in the late 17th century.

▼ **See also**
Colleges and universities
Teachers

**BIOGRAPHY**
Mann, Horace
Montessori, Maria

# Science fiction

Science fiction is a label (often shortened to SF or sci-fi) for books and films that ask the question "What if?" The "ifs" are usually about a scientific advance or a major change in the environment. SF aims to disturb our perceptions of what is real and normal by taking us into other worlds. It is often more interested in ideas than people, and reflects the great impact of technology on the modern world.

The first triumph of science fiction was Mary Shelley's *Frankenstein* (1818), and the genre was later developed by Jules Verne (*Journey to the Centre of the Earth*, 1864) and H. G. Wells (*War of the Worlds*, 1898). These writers showed a serious concern with the problems arising from the use of new technologies which has remained to this day, even attracting genuine scientists such as Isaac Asimov and Arthur C. Clarke to write science fiction books.

Science fiction stories have provided plenty of material for movies and television, particularly those dealing with space travel, as for example the films *Star Wars* and *Alien*, both of which were followed by successful sequels. Some of the most popular television shows, such as *Star Trek*, have been science fiction.

Computers are playing an increasingly important role in SF stories. One major recent development has been the arrival of cyberpunk. Cyberpunk stories are set in cyberspace, a world within the interlinking worldwide network of computers, which humans can enter and participate in through virtual reality. ◆

**Some Famous Authors of Science Fiction**

Isaac Asimov (*David Starr, Space Ranger*, 1952)
Ray Bradbury (*Fahrenheit 451*, 1953)
Arthur C. Clarke (*2001: A Space Odyssey*, 1968)
Robert Heinlein (*Stranger in a Strange Land*, 1961)
Jules Verne (*20,000 Leagues Under the Sea*, 1870)
H. G. Wells (*War of the Worlds*, 1898)

▼ **See also**

Books
Movies
Robots
Virtual reality

**BIOGRAPHY**

Lewis, C.S.
Orwell, George
Shelley, Mary
Verne, Jules

# Scientists

Scientists want to learn about everything in the Universe. Chemists investigate all the different substances in the world and also make new ones. Physicists are interested in atoms and the particles that make up the matter of the Universe; they also study different forms of energy, such as heat, light, sound, electricity and magnetism.

Biologists study living things. Geologists look at what our planet Earth is made of. Astronomers are interested in stars, planets and galaxies.

Scientists ask questions about the subject that interests them. They then set up experiments and make careful measurements to try to find answers. From their observations they develop theories on what is happening and how things work. They test these theories by setting up different types of experiment. ◆

▼ **See also**

Astronomers
Biologists
Biotechnology
Chemists
Genetics
Geologists
Physicists
Technology

# Scorpions

Scorpions live mainly in the warmer parts of the world. They are rarely seen—they are solitary animals that hide during the daytime and come out at night to hunt.

They feed chiefly on insects and other small creatures, which they kill using their large claws and the poisonous sting at the end of their tails. The sting is also used in defense against larger enemies such as monkeys. Their poison can be dangerous to human beings as well.

During the breeding season scorpions have an elaborate pattern of courtship before mating. This looks like a dance as the male guides the female over his sperm. ◆

**Distribution**
In many habitats in warm parts of the world
**Largest scorpion**
About 18 cm (7 in) long
**Smallest scorpion**
About 1 cm (0.39 in) long
**Phylum**
Arthropoda
**Class**
Arachnida
**Order**
Scorpiones
**Number of species**
About 700

▶ Female scorpions produce living young, keeping their eggs inside their bodies until the babies are born. The young ones clamber onto their mother's back, and she cares for them until after their first molt (shedding of their exterior surface).

▼ **See also**

Invertebrates
Spiders

# Scotland

Scotland is in the British Isles, in the northern region of the island called Great Britain. It is one of the four parts of the United Kingdom. Once it was a separate kingdom, and it still has its own national Church, legal system and education system, which are different from those in England and Wales. In international sports, Scotland usually competes as a separate country. Some Scots today feel that Scotland should have more independence from England, or even become a separate country again.

## Highlands

The Highlands in the north are mostly mountainous, with many islands to the west (the Hebrides). Farther north are the Orkney and Shetland islands. In the past, many people spoke Gaelic here, but it is now heard only in the northwest and in the islands. But Gaelic place names are found in most of Scotland.

The traditional Highland occupations are fishing and farming. Cattle and sheep graze on the hills; crops are grown along the valley bottoms and on the coastal plains. Farming was often in crofts, small pieces of land whose tenants could keep animals on the hills. Today crofters usually need a second job, often in tourism or some other service. Spectacular Highland scenery brings many visitors.

Fishing is important around much of Scotland. An efficient modern fleet catches mackerel, herring, cod and other fish. These are often deep-frozen as soon as they are landed, and exported worldwide. Fish farming grew in the 1980s. North Sea oil has changed life for many Highlanders and other Scots, especially around Aberdeen, where there are jobs working on oil rigs and supplying them by ship and helicopter.

## Lowlands and Southern Uplands

Most of Scotland's people and industry are in the Lowlands. People used to mine coal here but now most of the mines have closed. Other traditional industries such as steelmaking are in danger. But there are newer industries: chemicals, electronics and light engineering. The chief Scottish cities are Edinburgh and Glasgow. Edinburgh is the capital and an important financial city. Each summer there is an internationally celebrated arts festival. Glasgow, an industrial and commercial city, is much bigger than Edinburgh, though its population is falling now. Glasgow used to be world-famous for heavy engineering, especially shipbuilding.

The Southern Uplands are more fertile than the Highlands. Crops grow in the Tweed Valley, and livestock farms are scattered throughout the region. In towns like Hawick and Galashiels people use local wool to make knitwear and tweed cloth.

## LOOKING BACK

The earliest residents of Scotland were hunter-gatherers and Neolithic (New Stone Age) farmers and fishermen thousands of years ago. A series of settlers from other parts of the British Isles, as well as Viking invaders from Scandinavia, came to Scotland over many centuries. Warring tribes occupied much of the region in the 1st century A.D., when Roman invaders came from southern Great Britain to take over the region, which they called Caledonia. Technically the Romans ruled Scotland for four centuries, but the region and its inhabitants were so wild and warring that the Romans tried to keep it separate from the rest of Great Britain (Britannia). In fact, the Romans built two large walls to do just that: Hadrian's Wall and the Severtine Wall.

In the 5th century A.D. the Romans abandoned Great Britain and it was again ruled by various tribes. Scotland was converted to Christianity in the 6th century A.D. by Columba (later St. Columba), an Irish monk. Various tribes united to form the kingdom of Scotland in 1018. Invaders from England were defeated by William Wallace in 1297 and by Robert Bruce in 1314. In 1603, King James VI of Scotland, son of Mary, Queen of Scots, succeeded to the English throne as King James I. More than a century later, in 1707, the Act of Union united the Kingdom of England and Wales with the Kingdom of Scotland to form the Kingdom of Great Britain.

*Scotland's later history is included in the article on the United Kingdom in Volume 7.* ◆

**Area**
77,174 sq km
(29,797 sq mi)
**Capital**
Edinburgh
**Population**
5,102,400
**Language**
English, Gaelic
**Religion**
Christian

King Malcolm III of Scotland succeeded the ruler Macbeth in 1058. A fictionalized account of this period of Scottish history is Shakespeare's famous play *Macbeth*, written around 1606.

◀ **A view of Edinburgh. In the distance is the Firth of Forth.**

Hadrian's Wall, which the Romans built in the 2nd century A.D. to keep Scotland separate from Britannia, extended across Great Britain for a distance of 118.3 km (73.5 mi). The wall was 1.8 m (6 ft) high and 2.4 m (8 ft) thick. The remains of it can still be seen today. Hadrian's Wall is one of the most famous structures erected by the Romans in Britain.

▼ **See also**
British Isles
Celts
Europe
Industrial Revolution
Protestant Christianity
United Kingdom

**BIOGRAPHY**
Burns, Robert
Mary, Queen of Scots
Scott, Walter
Stevenson, Robert Louis

# Sculpture

Sculptors create works of art in three dimensions. A piece of sculpture may be free-standing, so that you can walk around it and view it from any angle. Other sculptures are made in relief; this means that they bulge out from a flat surface. Occasionally the design is cut into the surface rather than standing out from it.

## Sculpture materials

Sculpture has been made from a huge variety of materials, including plastics, fiberglass, polystyrene, concrete and bricks. Modern sculptors have often used scrap material, including crushed car bodies. However, the traditional materials are wood, clay, stone and metal. Wood has been the principal material for sculpture in many parts of the world, including Africa and Oceania. However, even the

▲ This relief sculpture was made by a member of the Yoruba peoples of southwestern Nigeria. It is wooden, and so cannot be very old or it would have begun to rot, but pottery and brass sculptures in this style have been found from as early as 1100 A.D.

▼ *Pietà* by Michelangelo (1475–1564), in the cathedral in Florence, Italy. Much sculpture of the past carried a religious message, like this famous unfinished work made during the Renaissance in Italy. A Pietà is any image of Mary holding the dead body of Jesus (in this case with Joseph of Arimathea). Pietà means "pity" in Italian.

hardest wood is liable to rot unless it has been carefully preserved, so most of the ancient sculpture that has survived is made of other materials. Stone and metal can be extremely durable. For example, several Greek bronze sculptures have been discovered in remarkably good condition after lying under the sea for more than 2,000 years.

Hardwoods such as oak, walnut, yew, mahogany, ebony, cherry and pear are all good for carving and have a wide range of colors and markings. Clays, too, have different textures and a variety of colors, including gray, reddish-brown, and blue-black.

Stone also has a great range of color, weight, strength and texture. Granite is the hardest and most weatherproof, so it has often been used for large outdoor monuments. It is difficult to carve, but it can be polished to an almost mirror-like smoothness. Marble is a favorite stone for many sculptors because it produces such a beautiful surface. Many sculptors have favored a pure white type called Carrara marble; others have preferred marbles with flecks of color or other markings.

Bronze is the most popular metal for sculpture because, apart from being tough and attractive, it can be worked easily by a variety of methods. It has been used in virtually every civilization, and

▶ *Grand Arabesque*, by Edgar Degas (1834–1917). This bronze dancer defies the heavy nature of clay and metal. Although the human form is weighty and solid, Degas is more interested in the challenge of creating the appearance of light and weightless free movement.

wax and mold it into the shape you want. You can add on bits of material and fuse them together to build up the model. When the model is finished it can be fired in a kiln, like pottery, to make it hard and durable. Or it can be used to make a cast in metal, usually bronze.

Modern sculptors have added a third basic approach. They sometimes put together a sculpture from different materials by some of the most superb examples have been produced in Africa and China. Gold, silver, iron, lead, steel and aluminum are other metals that sculptors use.

In spite of the lovely colors and textures of many of these materials, sculptors have often preferred to paint them rather than leave them in their natural state. Most ancient Greek marble sculpture was originally painted, but the color has almost always faded over the centuries, with only tiny traces remaining.

## Subtracting or adding

Throughout most of the history of sculpture there have been two basic approaches to shaping the materials, involving either subtracting or adding. The first approach is to take a block of stone or wood and carve into it, subtracting the material you do not want and so creating a shape. It is as if the final sculpture were hidden inside, ready to be revealed by the skill of the sculptor. The second way is to start with a lump of soft clay or

▶ *Walk, Don't Walk*, by U.S. sculptor George Segal (1924– ), combines metal, plaster, cement, wood and a flashing electric light to portray pedestrians waiting to cross a city street. Segal makes life-size sculptures of Americans in the midst of ordinary tasks, using plaster casts of actual people that he combines with everyday objects. The figures are usually painted white, making them both anonymous and universal.

▲ This sculpture of a horseman on a temple in Tamil Nadu, India, still provides some structural support, even though a large amount of the stone has been cut away.

of women, small enough to hold in the hand. Archaeologists think that they probably had some religious or magical purpose.

Since then sculpture has had many purposes. The function that we see most often is probably the creation of memorials to the dead (occasionally very famous people have monuments erected to them while they are still alive). Most towns of any size have statues of prominent citizens. Many also have war memorials. The great cities of the world have hundreds of such monuments. Stone and bronze are very appropriate materials for such sculptures because they can last through the centuries, as the fame of the people commemorated is meant to last. On a more modest scale are the memorials found in cemeteries all over the world.

joining, welding, gluing, or simply grouping items together.

Traditionally sculpture has been solid and weighty, but modern artists have often used much lighter materials. Some of the "mobiles" of the American sculptor Alexander Calder are made of thin sheets of metal suspended so that they move even in gentle breezes.

### Forms and functions

Sculpture is a very ancient art. The earliest known examples are thought to be about 25,000 years old. They are little stone figures

◀ *The Venus of Willendorf* is a figure of a woman that was carved out of limestone by prehistoric people. It is 11 cm (4.35 in) high and was made about 25,000 years ago in the Old Stone Age. It was probably a fertility symbol.

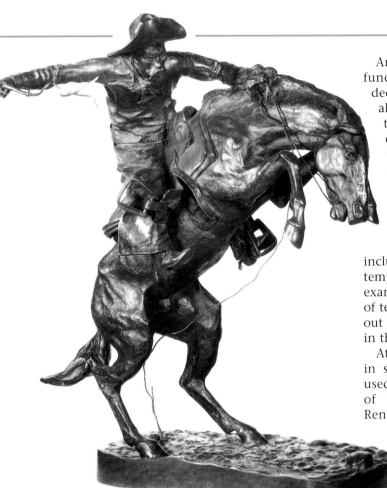

Another highly important function of sculpture is the decoration of buildings. In almost all the great civilizations the most important buildings, especially the churches and temples, have been richly adorned with carvings. Some temples are so richly encrusted that it is virtually impossible to separate the sculpture from the architecture. The most breathtaking examples include some of the great Hindu temples in India. At Ellora, for example, there is a wonderful series of temples that have been sculpted out of rock cliffs rather than built in the normal sense.

At the opposite end of the scale in sheer size, sculpture has been used for portrait medals. Some of the leading artists of the Renaissance made this kind of portrait in bronze. Even smaller are coins, some of which are impressive works of sculpture in miniature.

◀ *The Bronco Buster*, a bronze sculpture by U.S. artist Frederic Remington (1861–1909), captures an American cowboy in action as he struggles to control a bucking horse.

One of the largest sculptures in the world is carved on Mount Rushmore, in South Dakota, and features the heads of four U.S. Presidents. You can see a picture of Mount Rushmore and read more about it in the article on South Dakota in this volume.

▶ Visitors to the Yorkshire Sculpture Park in northern England enjoy the texture and shape of an outdoor sculpture by Henry Moore.

▶ *Pelagos*, by Barbara Hepworth (1903–1975). Often the message of sculpture is simply to show how interesting shapes and features can look together without having to mean anything more than that. This hollowed, curved shape is a beautiful rhythmic form from every angle. The contrasting strings almost suggest a musical instrument.

Apart from these public functions, many artists have used sculpture, like painting, as a vehicle for their own feelings and experiments. Since the birth of abstract art in the early 20th century, some sculptors, such as English artist Barbara Hepworth, have drawn particular attention to the natural beauty of their materials, inviting us to enjoy their shapes and textures. Others have turned to waste material to show us how even junk can be transformed by a lively imagination. ◆

# Sea anemones

**Distribution**
Rock pools everywhere
**Lifespan**
Sea anemones may live for a very long time. One survived in captivity almost 100 years
**Phylum**
Cnidaria
**Class**
Anthozoa
**Order**
Actinaria
**Number of species**
6,000, including corals

Sea anemones live attached to rocks and breakwaters on the seashore and in shallow water. When the tide is out they seem to be just blobs of jelly, but when they are covered with water they look more like flowers. The reason for this is that they have a frill of short tentacles like petals around the top of their jar-like bodies. But sea anemones are not plants; they are animals. They are flesh-eaters, and feed on any small creature that brushes against their tentacles. These are studded with sting cells which paralyze little fish or shrimp; then their tentacles pull them into the anemone's open mouth. Most sea anemones in northern waters do not have sting cells powerful enough to harm a

▲ A sea anemone near Fiji, in the South Pacific Ocean.

human, but there are many tropical species that can do so.

Sea anemones are entirely soft-bodied, but they have some close relatives that are able to use calcium and other minerals from the water to build a hard skeleton for themselves. These are called corals. Some of them form colonies in the warm seas of the world, which become coral reefs and atolls. ◆

▼ The mouth is the anemone's only opening. Food is pulled into the mouth, and waste products are pumped out through it.

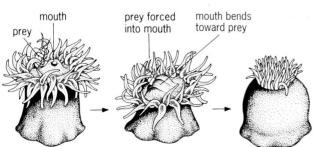

mouth
prey
prey forced into mouth
mouth bends toward prey

# Seals

Seals and their relatives the sea lions and walruses are mammals whose four walking limbs are replaced with flippers, which make them slow and clumsy on dry land. But once they have slipped into the water, they are transformed. Their bodies are streamlined, and far more flexible than those of land mammals, and they propel themselves forward swiftly with their flippers. They can twist and turn with amazing speed and grace as they play or chase after their prey.

Some seals, known as true seals, swim with an up-and-down movement of the rear flippers, combined with side-to-side movements of their bodies. The eared seals use their forelimbs, and the walruses swim by propelling themselves forward with their hindlimbs.

Most seals hunt fish, often those not valued by humans. A few kinds feed on krill, and walruses eat shellfish and sea urchins. Seals can hunt in murky or dark water. The huge whiskers around their faces can detect changes in water pressure as something swims past, and so even blind seals are able to feed.

Seals can remain in the water, even in polar regions, for long periods. Beneath their skin they have a thick coat of special fat called blubber, which helps to keep them warm. When they dive, they are able to close their nostrils and their ears. Some species can stay below the surface for over 30 minutes and can go to depths of over 600 m (2,000 ft). As they

◀ Gray seal cow greeting her pup. The pups have a creamy-white lanugo (birth coat), which they shed after 2–3 weeks. The new coat will resemble that of the adult.

dive, they breathe out and hold their breath, and at the same time they slow their heart rate to 4–15 beats per minute so that the oxygen carried in their blood is used up more slowly.

Seals have to come to land to produce their young. They haul ashore, sometimes in their thousands, on islands or isolated beaches that are traditional breeding places. Only one well-grown baby is produced by each female. Seal's milk is very rich—more than half fat—so the baby's growth is rapid. The females mate again very soon after the birth, and in some cases leave the calf to fend for itself before it is three weeks old. ◆

**Distribution**
Mainly in cold waters of the northern and southern oceans. A few species found in warmer places, and one in Lake Baikal (Siberia).
**Largest**
Elephant seal: males up to 4.9 m (16 ft) in length; weight up to 2,400 kg (5,280 lbs). Females much smaller. (This is a greater difference in size between males and females than in any other mammal.)
**Smallest**
Ringed seal: length 117 cm (3.8 ft), weight up to 45 kg (100 lbs)
**Number of young** 1
**Lifespan**
Up to 40 years in the wild. Enemies include large sharks, killer whales, leopard seals, polar bears, and, most important, humans.
**Subphylum**
Vertebrata
**Class**
Mammalia
**Order**
Pinnipedia
**Number of species**
33

◀ The walrus uses its huge tusks (up to 1 m/3.3 ft long in males) to dislodge clams and other shellfish on the seabed. It then gathers them with its mobile, whiskery lips.

▼ **See also**
Mammals

# Seashore

The world has 312,000 km (193,400 mi) of coastline.

The seashore is where the oceans and seas meet the land. It is the part of the coast between the high-tide mark and the low-tide mark. In some parts of the world, the tide does not go out very far and the seashore is only a few yards wide. In other places the tides go out up to 3 km (2 mi), and the seashore is very wide.

The lower shore is covered in sea water for much of the day, while the upper shore is covered for only a short time. The upper shore dries out between tides, and any remaining pools of water become very salty, but after heavy rain they may contain water that is nearly fresh. The temperature may change rapidly, so the animals and plants that live on the shore must be very adaptable.

## Rocky shores

Rocky shores have many pools, each with its own community of animals. The rocks are often covered with seaweeds. Seaweeds also fringe the rock pools, providing shade from the sun, and a place where small animals can hide from predators such as seagulls. Limpets, periwinkles and barnacles on the upper and middle shore have strong shells to protect them from the waves and the drying effect of wind, and strong muscles to grip the rock. Farther down the shore, mussels fix themselves to the rock with tough threads called byssus. Crabs, sea slaters and shrimps survive by hiding in crevices. The lower shore is wetter, and animals such as sea anemones, starfish and sea urchins live among the wet seaweeds in the rock pools, which are also home to small fish such as blennies.

Most of these animals breathe oxygen from the water using gills, and so they come out to feed when the tide is in. Crabs scavenge for seaweed and animal remains. Barnacles and shrimp filter food from the sea water using fine bristles on their legs. Mussels sieve the water with their gills, and limpets and periwinkles graze on the seaweeds.

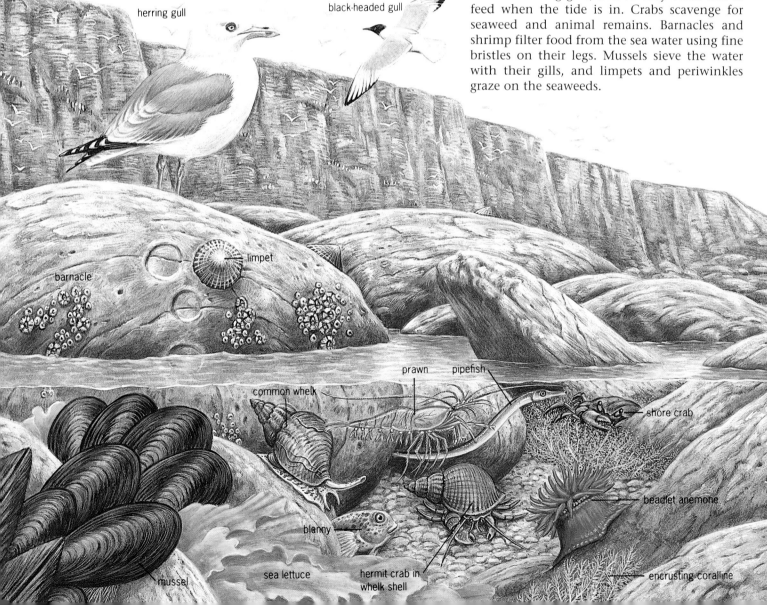

herring gull

black-headed gull

barnacle

limpet

prawn    pipefish

common whelk

shore crab

beadlet anemone

blenny

mussel

sea lettuce

hermit crab in whelk shell

encrusting coralline

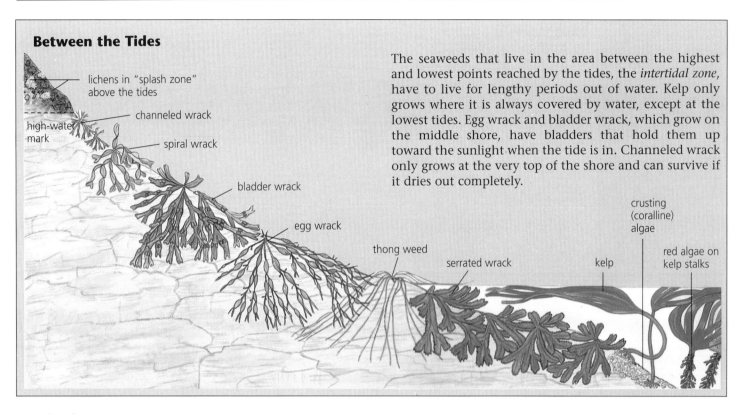

## Between the Tides

lichens in "splash zone" above the tides

channeled wrack

high-water mark

spiral wrack

bladder wrack

egg wrack

thong weed

serrated wrack

kelp

crusting (coralline) algae

red algae on kelp stalks

The seaweeds that live in the area between the highest and lowest points reached by the tides, the *intertidal zone*, have to live for lengthy periods out of water. Kelp only grows where it is always covered by water, except at the lowest tides. Egg wrack and bladder wrack, which grow on the middle shore, have bladders that hold them up toward the sunlight when the tide is in. Channeled wrack only grows at the very top of the shore and can survive if it dries out completely.

## Sandy shores

A sandy shore often appears to have very little life, but if you dig down in the wet sand you will probably find a variety of burrowing animals. In fact there may be as many as 100,000 animals per square yard living in the mud below the sand. They are out of sight of predators and protected from the sun and wind, and emerge to feed only when the tide comes in.

Some live in permanent burrows, drawing in water and sieving out food from it. Burying themselves also prevents them from drying out when their part of the shore is exposed by the tide. The lugworm (sandworm) lives in a U-shaped burrow. It takes in water and food at one end, and pushes out a pile of waste to form a squiggly worm cast at the other end. Cockles and razor shells use siphons to sieve the water. Tube worms surround themselves with tubes made of sand and mud. They put out sticky tentacles to trap food from the water. Small shrimp and crabs venture out to feed at high tide, but burrow in the mud before the tide goes out so they are not swept away.

## Muddy shores

Where rivers meet the sea, there are huge expanses of mud. These shores can support an incredible amount of life. In just a square yard of mud, up to 1,000 ragworms, 42,000 spire-shell snails, or 63,000 mud-burrowing sand-hoppers have been recorded (although not all together).

Muddy shores and estuaries also attract large numbers of seagulls and wading birds (shore birds), which come to feed on the seashore animals. ◆

bladderwrack

starfish

# Seasons

▲ Summer and winter on the same street.

▶ How the Sun's path through the sky, as seen from somewhere in the Northern Hemisphere, changes between the seasons. In summer the Sun gets much higher in the sky at midday than it does in winter.

**See also**
Constellations
Day and night
Equator
Midnight Sun

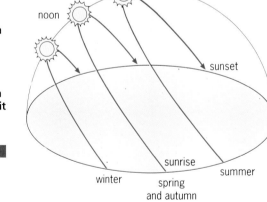

noon

sunset

sunrise

winter    spring
and autumn    summer

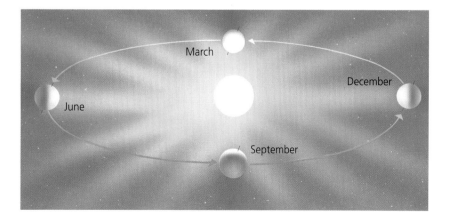

March

December

June

September

As the seasons change through the year, we notice the different things that happen in the world around us. In spring, the days get longer again after the short days of winter, and the Sun climbs higher in the sky each day. Because there is more sunshine and warmer weather, plants start to grow, and it is a good time for sowing seeds. It is also the season when many animals have their young. Summer is the warmest time of the year. The higher the Sun is, the stronger the warming effect of its rays. Then, in autumn, the days shorten again, trees drop their leaves, and the weather gets cooler as winter draws nearer.

In the night sky, the constellations you can see also change day by day, so the stars you see in the summer are quite different from the ones you can see in winter.

The seasonal changes are more extreme the farther you are from the Equator. Near the poles, there are enormous differences between the length of winter and summer days, but it never gets really warm because the Sun is not very high in the sky, even in midsummer. Near the Equator, the number of hours of daylight does not change much through the year, and the Sun always climbs high in the sky.

## Why we have the seasons

Our planet Earth is spinning around its axis, an imaginary line going through the North and South poles. That is why we get day and night. At the same time, the Earth travels around the Sun once each year. There are seasons because the Earth's axis is tilted to its path around the Sun at an angle of $23\frac{1}{2}°$.

This means that the Northern Hemisphere is tipped toward the Sun for half the year. During this time, from about March 21 to September 21, places in the Northern Hemisphere have spring followed by summer. At the same time, the South Pole is facing away from the Sun and the Southern Hemisphere is having autumn and winter.

From September through March, this is reversed. The North Pole tilts away from the Sun and the Northern Hemisphere has autumn and winter while the Southern Hemisphere has spring and summer. The seasons in these hemispheres are always opposite. In July, when it is summer in the U.S., it is winter in South America and Australia. ◆

◀ In June, the North Pole is tilted toward the Sun. It is summer in the Northern Hemisphere. In December, the South Pole is tilted toward the Sun. It is summer in the Southern Hemisphere.

# Seaweeds

Seaweeds are the plants you see growing on seashore rocks or washed up onto beaches after they have been torn off by storms. Most are brown or reddish in color, although there are also green seaweeds that usually grow on mud.

Seaweeds belong to a group of organisms (living things) called *algae*. These can use sunlight to make food (photosynthesize) like higher plants, using the green chemical *chlorophyll* or other pigments, but they do not really belong to the plant kingdom. Most of the 26,900 known species of algae are microscopic and consist of a single cell or clump of cells that float freely in sea or fresh water. Only a few algae are classed as seaweeds.

## Seaweed structure

Seaweeds are larger than most algae and look more like plants. Many have a *holdfast*, which looks like a mass of strong roots. The holdfast attaches them to rocks. Most seaweeds have leafy fronds, but the cells inside these fronds are much simpler than the specialized cells of higher plants. Seaweed cells do not have walls to strengthen them, so they can only stand upright when supported by water. Some seashore species have air-filled bladders at the tips of their fronds. These act as floats to buoy them up when the tide is in, so that they are held near the surface of the water where there is the most sunlight for photosynthesis.

## Reproduction

Some seaweeds spread by breaking off fragments that grow into new plants. However, seaweeds can also reproduce sexually. Male and female sex cells are produced by reproductive organs found in bladder-like sacs near the tip of a frond. The fertile sex cells are squeezed out through pores onto the surface of the frond. They are washed off by currents and mix together. Male and female cells fuse to form a fertilized egg cell. This is spread by sea currents, and if it settles somewhere suitable, it grows into a new plant.

## Zones

There is bright sunlight only in the zone near the surface of the sea. Seaweeds need sunlight for photosynthesis, so they can only grow in this zone, although in the clear waters of tropical seas seaweeds can reach depths of 100 m (330 ft). When we explore the seashore, even at low tide, we therefore see only a few of the range of seaweeds.

◀ The fronds of two common seaweeds, thongweed and serrated wrack, are buoyed up toward the sunlight by the sea at high tide.

Seaweeds living on shores between the tides have to cope with periods out of the water. Large kelp seaweeds grow at the bottom of the shore where they are exposed for only a few minutes at low tide, because they cannot survive if they dry out. At the top of the shore, seaweeds may be out of the water for 11 hours at a time. They can survive drying, and return to life when the tide comes in. Between these two extremes, different seaweeds grow in bands or zones down the shore, according to how long they are able to stay out of the water.

## Uses of seaweeds

Seaweeds gathered from the shore after winter storms are used as organic fertilizers by farmers in many coastal areas. Seaweeds like kelp are a natural source of minerals, such as iodine. Glue-like substances called alginates, made from seaweed extracts, are used in the food industry to help substances like ice cream to "set."

In Ireland a seaweed called carrageen is cooked with milk to make a kind of pudding. Along the south coast of Wales a red seaweed, *Porphyra*, is used to make laver bread. The Chinese and Japanese also cook with this seaweed. It is considered a very healthy food. ◆

▼ See also
Algae
Classification of living
  things
Cliffs
Oceans and seas
Photosynthesis
Plants
Seashore

# Seeds

Seeds of flowering plants develop inside fruits, while those of conifers (cone-bearing evergreens) develop inside cones.

A seed is a structure containing all the material from which a new plant can begin to grow. A seed's main role is to multiply the plant and scatter it to new sites.

### Structure of a bean

If you soak a seed, such as a bean, overnight it absorbs water, softens and swells. You can then open it up and see what is inside. Covering the seed is a protective skin called the testa (seed coat). Make a slit around the outer edge of the bean, avoiding the scar where it was attached by the seed stalk to the inside of the pod. Ease off the testa carefully, without damaging the radicle (root) that fits into a pocket on one side of the scar. The contents will easily separate into two halves called *cotyledons,* or seed leaves. These contain stored food in the form of starch and protein. Sandwiched between the cotyledons is the tiny plant that will grow into a new bean plant. You will see a radicle (root), and a plumule (shoot) with tiny leaves. Food contained in the cotyledons helps this young plant to grow before it can make its own food. ◆

▼ **See also**
Beans
Flowering plants
Fruit
Nuts
Trees

▶ Seeds contain a partly developed plant complete with tiny root, leaves and a supply of food. These are wrapped in a protective seed coat called a *testa.* Seeds enable plants to survive periods like winter or a dry season when normal growth is impossible.

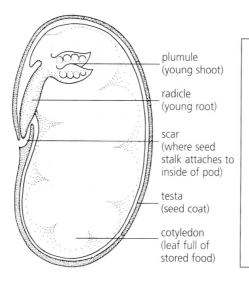

plumule (young shoot)

radicle (young root)

scar (where seed stalk attaches to inside of pod)

testa (seed coat)

cotyledon (leaf full of stored food)

## How to Sprout a Seed

Roll blotting paper into a cylinder and drop it into a glass jar. Put sawdust, loose soil or sand in the jar to hold the blotting paper in place, then slide beans or other seeds in between the paper and the glass. Pour in water to moisten the blotting paper. Watch the seeds sprout roots and leaves. Make drawings of the stages of development.

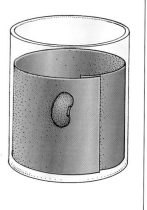

# Senegal

Senegal lies on the Atlantic coast of West Africa. The coast is warm and wet. Inland it is hot and drier.

Most people wear colorful cotton robes called *boubous.* They live in villages, growing food crops and groundnuts (peanuts), which are used to make oil and are exported. Peanut sauce, spicy fried fish and chicken stew are all popular dishes. Phosphate rock, which is used to make fertilizers, and fish are also sold abroad. Senegal's capital, Dakar, is one of West Africa's chief industrial cities. It is a major center of the African film industry.

### LOOKING BACK

France ruled Senegal as a colony from the 17th century, so the country has strong French traditions. It became independent in 1960 under Léopold Senghor, a poet as well as a statesman.

In 1982 Senegal made an agreement to work with Gambia, a country almost enclosed by Senegal. The Senegambia Confederation was set up and cooperated on defense and foreign policy, but in 1989 it collapsed and the countries became independent again. Gambia is a former British colony and its institutions are based on British ones. ◆

▼ **See also**
Africa
Gambia

**Area**
196,720 sq km
(75,954 sq mi)
**Capital**
Dakar
**Population**
8,102,000
**Language**
French, various African languages
**Religion**
Muslim, Christian
**Government**
Parliamentary republic
**Currency**
1 African Financial Community (CFA) franc = 100 centimes
**Major exports**
Groundnut (peanut) oil

# Senses

To survive and be successful, an animal needs to know from second to second what is going on in the world about it. Without this information it could not find its food or a mate, stay in the right habitat, or avoid being caught by hunting animals. This vital information is provided by its senses.

Vision tells an animal what things look like and where they are. Hearing tells it the position of things, and, like the other senses, is important in communication. Smell and taste enable an animal to detect the chemicals in its environment, such as those in its food, so that it can choose the right things to eat. It can also detect smells released by rivals or mates. Touch tells an animal what things feel like. Some of the most important organs of touch are the long whiskers around the snout of many animals. A blind seal can catch fish because its whiskers can feel changes in water pressure as its prey swims by.

## Sense organs and the brain

Eyes see, ears hear, tongues taste and noses smell, and the animal's outer surface is its organ of touch. The sense organs pass information along nerves to the animal's brain. The brain merges all the different messages together to produce its "picture" of the outside world.

## Special senses

Animals also need information about their own bodies in order to function well. They need to know where all the parts of the body are in relation to one another in order to move about. They need a sense of balance to stay the same way up, and they need to know when a part of the body is damaged or sick.

This information is provided by special internal sense organs. In humans and other vertebrates (animals with backbones), for instance, there are sense cells in muscles and joints that help control body movement. There are balancing organs connected with the inner ear, and there are also sense cells for pain. The greatest concentration of nerve endings that tell our brain about the things that we touch and taste are in the tips of our fingers and toes and around our mouth and tongue.

## "Super-senses"

In some animals ordinary sense organs may become super-sensitive and so well developed that they seem like completely new senses. Bats have hearing so good that they can navigate in

▼ This chimpanzee's sense organs—its eyes, ears, nose, tongue and skin—are very much like ours.

▲ Birds of prey, like this hawk, have very good eyesight. Each eye has a special part, called the pecten, which acts like the sight of a gun, so that the bird can line up accurately on its prey.

▼ The moth's feathery antennae are its organs of smell, enabling it to find a mate.

the dark by using the echoes of bursts of ultra-high-pitched sound, like a ship's sonar. Whales use the same sense in finding food and can even tell the difference between a sort of fish that they like to eat and one that they do not, by using sonar. Sharks can hunt for food in the dark by sensing very faint electrical signals given off by prey. A male emperor moth's antennae are so sensitive to the mating smell of the female that it can sense the female's presence well over a mile away. And cockroaches have built-in draft detectors—which is why they are almost impossible to swat. ◆

▼ See also
Bats
Brains
Ears
Eyes
Noses
Radar
Skin

# Serbia

Serbia is part of what remains of the country of Yugoslavia; the other part is Montenegro. The fertile Danube plains in the north and the hills and rich river valleys support a varied agriculture.

In the Middle Ages Serbia was a powerful kingdom, but in 1389 it was defeated by the Ottoman Turks and it did not regain its independence until 1878. Conflict between Serbia and Austria over Bosnia and Herzegovina led to the outbreak of World War I. After the war Serbia became part of the Kingdom of Serbs, Croats and Slovenes, later named Yugoslavia.

The 1991 civil war in Yugoslavia began when Serbia tried to take over parts of Croatia, where many Serbs lived. In 1992 Slovenia, Croatia, Macedonia, and Bosnia and Herzegovina became independent countries, leaving Serbia to dominate a small area at the bottom of Yugoslavia. Serbia then supported Serbs in Bosnia and Herzegovina who wanted their country to unify with Serbia. The bloody war continued for three more years. In 1995 Serbia took part in talks in Dayton, Ohio, and an uneasy peace was established. ♦

▼ **See also**
Bosnia and Herzegovina
Croatia
Ottoman Empire
World War I
Yugoslavia

# Sets

A set is a collection of items that have something in common. For example, you could have a set of four-legged animals or a set of even numbers. {2, 4, 6, 8, 10, ...} is the set of all the even numbers (the dots show that the set goes on forever). Each member of the set is called an element. Like every set, it has a clear rule for deciding whether something belongs or not. Here, the rule is that each element must be a multiple of 2. ♦

▼ **See also**
Arithmetic
Mathematics
Numbers

▼ **Combining sets of numbers.**

Here is a way of showing two sets of numbers.
One is the set of all the multiples of 4 under 31. The other is the set of all the multiples of 6 under 31.

Sets can be combined to make a new set. The *union* of two sets is a new set made up of elements that were in one or the other of the original sets, or both.

The *intersection* of two sets is a new set made up of only those elements that were in both the original sets. Here, the intersection gives all the multiples of 12 under 31.

# Seven Wonders of the World

Various ancient Greek writers compiled lists of the most impressive man-made structures known to them. The authors differed on what marvels (and how many) to include, but the following seven eventually became accepted as the standard list. They are arranged in the order in which they were built.

**The pyramids of Egypt**. There are many ancient pyramids in Egypt, but the greatest—the ones considered to be wonders—are the three at Giza, built as royal tombs. The largest of these is the Pyramid of Cheops, generally known simply as the Great Pyramid, built about 2600 B.C. Although the pyramids are the oldest of the Seven Wonders, they are the only ones that survive virtually intact. The Great Pyramid would certainly get on any list of wonders compiled today. Originally it was about 146 m (479 ft) tall (a few meters are now missing from the top). It was the tallest structure in the world for about 4,000 years, until it was slightly overtaken by the spires of some of the great Gothic cathedrals. In terms of sheer volume of stone it is still probably the largest single building ever constructed.

**The Hanging Gardens of Babylon**. These were spectacular gardens, rising in a series of terraces (rather than "hanging") and ingeniously irrigated by water pumped up from the River Euphrates. They were probably built by Nebuchadnezzar II, who was king of Babylon from 605 to 562 B.C. and was famous for his love of luxury. Nothing remains of them.

**The statue of Zeus at Olympia**. This gold and ivory statue of the king of the gods was made for the temple of Zeus at Olympia in about 430 B.C. It was created by Phidias, who was regarded as the greatest of all Greek sculptors. The statue was destroyed in the 5th century A.D., but we have a reasonable idea of what it looked like because it was described by ancient authors and it was reproduced on coins. It was a majestic seated figure about 12 m (39 ft) high.

**The temple of Artemis (or Diana) at Ephesus**. This was begun in 356 B.C. to replace an earlier temple that was burned down in that year (on the same day on which Alexander the Great was born) by a man called Herostratus. He committed this crime purely to have his name go down in history. The new building was famed for its immense size and the splendor of its decoration. Ephesus was an

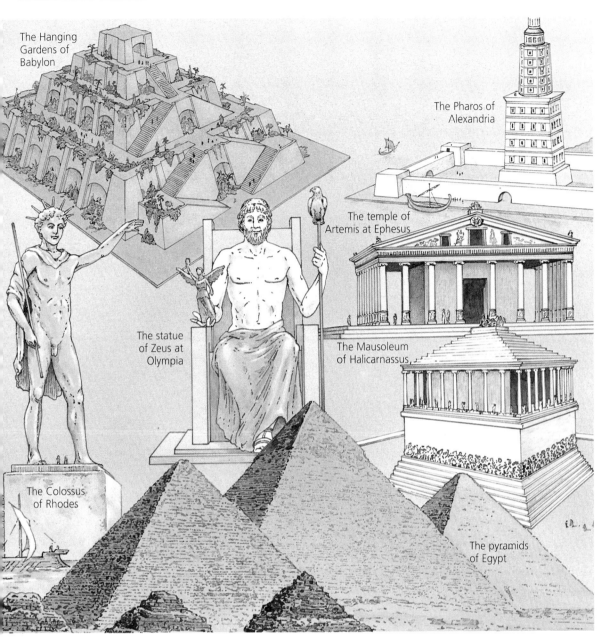

The Hanging Gardens of Babylon

The Pharos of Alexandria

The temple of Artemis at Ephesus

The statue of Zeus at Olympia

The Mausoleum of Halicarnassus

The Colossus of Rhodes

The pyramids of Egypt

**OTHER WONDERS OF THE WORLD**

Since ancient times, people in other historical periods have compiled their own lists of wonders, both natural and man-made. Here are two of the best-known. (Many of them are illustrated elsewhere in this encyclopedia; look them up in the Index in Volume 9.)

**Seven Wonders of the Middle Ages**

1. Colosseum (Rome)
2. Catacombs of Alexandria (Egypt)
3. Great Wall of China
4. Stonehenge (England)
5. Leaning Tower of Pisa
6. Porcelain Tower of Nanking (China)
7. Mosque of Hagia Sophia (Turkey)

**Seven Wonders of the Natural World**

1. Grand Canyon of the Colorado River (Arizona)
2. Mount Everest (China and Nepal; world's highest mountain)
3. Ayers Rock (Australia; largest single rock)
4. The Matterhorn (Italy and Switzerland; pyramid-shaped Alp)
5. Meteor Crater (Arizona)
6. Victoria Falls (Zimbabwe and Zambia)
7. Great Barrier Reef (Australia; longest coral reef)

important city in what is now Turkey. The site of the temple was discovered in 1869, and extensive remains of it have been excavated.

**The Mausoleum of Halicarnassus.** This was the magnificent tomb of Mausolus, a ruler of Caria (now in Turkey), who died in 353 B.C. Halicarnassus, his capital, is now the town of Bodrum. The immense tomb was built of white marble; it had a pyramidal roof topped by a sculpture of a chariot drawn by four horses. The site was excavated in the 19th century, and some of the highly impressive sculpture from the Mausoleum is in the British Museum in London.

**The Colossus of Rhodes.** This was a huge bronze statue, about 30 m (98 ft) high, erected by the people of Rhodes to celebrate the city's successful defense against a siege in 305–304 B.C. (Rhodes was the capital of a Mediterranean island, also called Rhodes.) The statue represented the sun god Helios and stood at the entrance to the harbor. It toppled over during an earthquake about 225 B.C. and was broken up for scrap in the 7th century A.D.

**The Pharos of Alexandria.** This was the largest lighthouse of the ancient world. It was built on the island of Pharos, off Alexandria in Egypt, about 280 B.C. According to ancient authors, it was about 135 m (443 ft) tall and its light could be seen 65 km (40 mi) away. It was destroyed by an earthquake in the 12th century A.D. ◆

▼ **See also**
Ancient world
Pyramids
Temples

# Sewage

**See also**
Pollution
Water supplies

Sewage is waste material from houses and factories. When you flush a toilet, the waste is carried away by drains that empty into sewers. These lead to a sewage works, where the sewage is treated to make it safe. Untreated sewage can cause pollution and disease.

## At the sewage works

When sewage arrives at the sewage works, any large objects like rags or pieces of wood are removed by large metal screens. The sewage then flows slowly through channels where any sand and soil sink to the bottom.

Next the sewage flows into large tanks where the sludge settles to the bottom. It is scraped away by electrical machinery. Sometimes the remaining liquid sewage may be put into large tanks and have air blown through it. It is often sprayed on circular beds of stone or gravel. Either way, special bacteria feed on any waste matter, turning it into harmless gases and water. The water is then clean enough to be pumped straight into a river, lake or the sea.

▼ At a sewage works, sewage is treated to make it clean and safe so that the water can be returned to rivers.

## Sewage sludge

Sewage sludge is pumped to tanks containing bacteria that destroy the unpleasant materials in the sludge and change them into the gas methane. This can be burned. Often it is used to make all the electricity and other power needed by the sewage works. The "digested sludge" is sometimes taken in trucks to be spread on farmland as a fertilizer.

## LOOKING BACK

Sewage has not always been treated. Even today in some places untreated sewage is still poured into the sea. Before the 20th century, sewage flowed down the streets of many villages, towns and cities. It was simply tossed out of the windows of nearby houses. There were a few sewers, but these discharged the sewage straight into the rivers from which drinking water was taken. The sewage polluted the water, and this caused epidemics of diseases such as cholera and typhoid. Gradually, these filthy conditions were overcome. Much work was done to ensure that towns and cities had adequate sewers and that sewage was not allowed to spoil drinking water. ◆

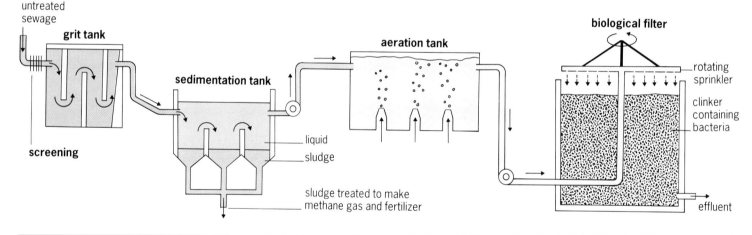

# Sewing

**See also**
Clothing
Embroidery
Textiles

**BIOGRAPHY**
Howe, Elias

Sewing is a way of joining pieces of fabric or leather using a needle and thread. Sewing is used in the making and mending of clothing, curtains and furniture upholstery, in making shoes, bags and other leather goods, in making sails for most sailing boats, and in making saddles and bridles. Different types of needles, and different stitches, are used for different tasks.

The type of needle that you choose depends on what you want to sew. A thick needle, for example, might leave holes in a fine fabric. A thin needle with a round eye and a sharp point

is used for most sewing. A crewel needle has a sharp point and a long eye for thicker, embroidery thread. Special curved needles are made for repairing chairs, tents, lampshades and sails.

## Sewing machines

All sewing was done by hand until the 19th century, when the first practical sewing machine was perfected. Crude sewing machines had been made in England and France in the late 18th century but had never become popular because they were clumsy to use.

In 1844 American inventor Elias Howe succeeded in making a machine with an eye-

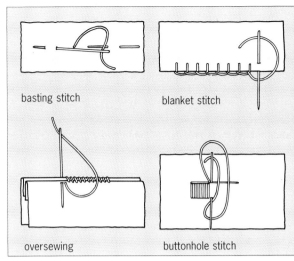

basting stitch

blanket stitch

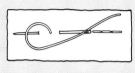

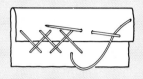

oversewing

buttonhole stitch

backstitch

herringbone stitch

## Types of Stitching

*Basting stitch* is used for temporarily holding seams together. *Backstitch* is used in place of machine stitching. *Blanket stitch* is used for making neat edges. *Buttonhole stitch* is used for strengthening button holes. *Oversewing* (French seam) is used where two folded edges are sewn together. *Herringbone stitch* is used to secure a hem in thick fabric.

pointed needle that stitched on top while a shuttle carried the thread below the fabric. Although he received a U.S. patent for his machine in 1846, other Americans, including Isaac Singer, copied his design and began manufacturing sewing machines. Singer improved upon Howe's design and  became the best-known manufacturer of sewing machines.

These early sewing machines were foot-powered: they were operated by a treadle on the floor. The operator pushed up and down on the treadle, moving the needle. In the early 20th century, electric-powered sewing machines were developed. Modern electric machines use a small treadle that is operated by continuous foot pressure, or a lever that is operated underneath the machine by pressure from the knee. ♦

Quilting is a type of sewing used to make cloth constructions called quilts. Quilts have been made for thousands of years as bedcovers, but they are also created as decorative items. A quilt is made of a layer of insulating material, such as cotton, that is sandwiched between two layers of fabric; the three layers are sewn together with tiny stitches. Quilts are usually ornamented with decorative embroidery or appliqués (cutout pieces of material that have been sewn to the surface).

Quilts were an important part of American households in the 18th and 19th centuries. Most women made quilts for their families. On the American frontier, quilting and sewing "bees"—groups of women who gathered together to sew—provided opportunities to socialize and gossip.

◄ A Baltimore album quilt, sewn by hand in the mid-19th century in Baltimore, Maryland. Album quilts were decorative quilts that were made to preserve memories of special occasions. Often groups of women got together and created an album quilt to honor a friend.

# Sex and sexuality

When you are born, you are either male or female. This is called your sex. Males and females have different sexual parts. They produce different sex cells, both of which are needed to start a new life (reproduce).

Not all living things are divided into males and females. Those that are not are called *asexual*. Many plants, invertebrates (animals without backbones) and fish have both male and female parts (gonads) within them. They are called *hermaphrodite*.

All males have *testes* that produce *sperm*, and all females have *ovaries* that produce eggs (ova). A sperm and an egg must join for a new life to begin. Sexual creatures that live in water, such

as fish and frogs, eject eggs and sperm into the water. The eggs and sperm float around in the water until some sperm and eggs join and start to grow. This is called *external fertilization* because it takes place outside the body.

Insects, birds, mammals and reptiles use *internal fertilization*. The male finds a female and mates. The male releases sperm inside the female's body where the sperm fertilizes the egg.

Eggs and sperm are made up of chromosomes. One of these is called a sex chromosome because it helps decide the sex of the baby. In humans there are two kinds of sex chromosome, X and Y. All the female's eggs have an X chromosome, but half of the male's sperm have X and half have Y chromosomes. If a sperm with an X chromosome joins with an

In many countries women are not allowed the same rights as men, and may not vote or get equal pay.

Sometimes people are prevented from doing something just because of their sex, by laws or out-of-date ideas about the kinds of things men and women can do. We call this sex discrimination. In some countries laws have been passed to try to make sure that women and men have equal rights. This is called sexual equality.

▼ The male and female sex organs.

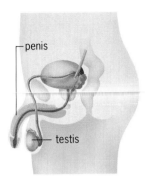

male

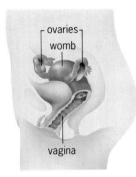

female

Sexually transmitted diseases (STD) are diseases that are spread by sexual intercourse. They include not only AIDS but also syphilis, gonorrhea, chlamydia, herpes, and the human papilloma virus. AIDS is a fatal disease: death can occur months or even years after being infected with the AIDS virus. Other sexually transmitted diseases are usually not fatal if treated promptly with appropriate drugs, but they can permanently damage the reproductive system and other organs. Some sexually transmitted diseases, such as herpes, can be treated but not cured completely.

▼ **See also**

AIDS
Cells
Mating
Parenthood
Pregnancy
Puberty
Reproduction

egg, the baby will be female. If a sperm with a Y chromosome joins with an egg, the baby will be male.

## Human sex differences

Men are usually taller, stronger and hairier than women and have larger and heavier skeletons. They have broader shoulders, coarser skin and, when fully grown, a deeper voice than women. For their size they also have more muscle and less fat.

Women have broader hips than men to allow a baby to pass out of the body at birth. They have breasts that will produce milk when they give birth.

One of the main differences between men and women is their sex organs (*genitals*). A man has a *penis*, which is usually small and soft but becomes larger and harder when he is sexually excited. Below and behind the penis is a bag called the *scrotum* containing two testes. In an adult, these produce several million sperm each day.

A woman's sex organs are mostly inside her body. The outside opening of these organs is called the *vulva*, which consists of two thick folds of skin that protect the *clitoris*, a tiny sensitive area at the front of the vulva. The vulva leads inside the body to the *vagina* and then the womb (*uterus*). Two tubes lead from the womb to the ovaries, which produce eggs.

## Sexual intercourse

Sexual intercourse is often called "having sex." When a man and woman are together and become sexually excited, many changes take place in their bodies. Their muscles become tense, and breathing and heartbeats become faster. The man's penis grows larger and harder so it points upward away from his body. This is called an *erection*.

Sexual intercourse takes place when the man pushes his penis into the woman's vagina; then one or both partners move their hips so the penis slides in and out. The vagina produces fluid, which makes this easier. These movements give both of them pleasurable feelings that eventually reach a peak (an *orgasm*), when strong muscular contractions occur in the sex organs.

Muscular contractions of tubes inside the man's body squirt *semen*, a liquid that contains sperm, from his penis into the woman's vagina. This is called an *ejaculation*.

The sperm swim into the woman's womb and up toward her ovaries. If one of the sperm joins with an egg from the woman (fertilization), the egg and sperm will begin developing into a baby

and the woman will be pregnant.

## Sexuality

Sexuality is the word used to describe sexual feelings and behavior. When people are emotionally and physically attracted to members of the opposite sex, they are called *heterosexuals*. Some people are not heterosexual but *homosexual*. This means that they are attracted to people of their own sex. Homosexual men are often called "gay," and homosexual women are called lesbians.

Because most societies have traditionally been based on heterosexual behavior, homosexuals have often been discriminated against, and in some countries homosexual relationships are illegal. However, homosexuality is now generally regarded as a normal kind of human sexuality.

## Sexual responsibility

Sexual intercourse is also called "making love," because it can give a lot of pleasure and a feeling of being very special to the other partner. Ideally, sexual intercourse and caring for the other partner should always go together. Responsible sexual behavior is also important because of the danger of diseases (including AIDS) that can be spread during sexual intercourse.

## Birth control (contraception)

Birth control includes various ways of preventing the woman from becoming pregnant. One method is a *condom*, which is put onto the man's penis and collects semen as it is ejaculated. A woman can fit a rubber disk called a *diaphragm* over the opening of her womb, or she can choose to take pills that keep her ovaries from releasing eggs. Contraception allows couples to decide when to have children, and how big a family they will have. However, no method of contraception yet developed is 100-percent effective in preventing a baby from developing after intercourse.

## Sex roles

In many societies men and women are expected to do different jobs. What someone is expected to do by society is called his or her role, like a part in a play. In the past men used to go out to work to earn money. Women stayed at home to look after the home and the children. Today women work alongside men and often share the care of the home and children. We are coming to realize that all people should be able to develop their talents without restrictions. ◆

# Shakers

Shakers belong to a Christian religious group whose official name is the United Society of Believers in Christ's Second Appearing. The group originated in the 1740s in England, and their members soon acquired the nickname "Shakers" because they often shook with emotion during worship.

The Shakers believed that people should live separately from the world and form their own communities in order to lead a proper Christian life without sin. Members had to give up sexual relations and share all their possessions with the community.

In 1758 a woman named Ann Lee became the leader of the Shakers, who were being increasingly persecuted for their beliefs. In 1774, Mother Lee, as she was called, and eight followers migrated to the American colonies. They eventually established Shaker communities in New England as well as New York, Ohio and Kentucky. Shaker communities gradually died out by the 20th century. Today there is one remaining Shaker community in America, at Sabbathday Lake, Maine. ◆

▲ The Shakers became well-known for their simple furniture and other home furnishings, which they made for their own communities. Some of the best-known Shaker designs can be seen in this museum exhibit of a Shaker retiring room (bedroom). Today original Shaker furniture like the items shown here is quite valuable and highly sought after. Several U.S. furniture companies make less costly but still expensive reproductions of Shaker designs.

▼ See also
Furniture
Protestant
Christianity

# Shapes

▲ A circle has an edge that is the same distance from the center all the way around.

▲ A triangle has three sides.

▲ A square has four sides, all the same length.

▲ A rectangle has corners like a square, but one pair of sides is longer than the other.

▲ A pentagon has five sides.

▼ See also
Arches
Geometry
Mosaics
Symmetry

Everything you look at has a shape, whether it is a box, a ball, a bottle or a house. If you tried to describe the shape of a house, you might have to use lots of words. However, some shapes are much simpler and have their own special words to describe them.

## 3-D shapes

Shapes like squares and triangles are easy to draw on a piece of paper because they are flat. But some shapes are not flat; they are solid. A cube is a solid shape. It has length, width and height. Mathematicians say that it has three dimensions (3-D for short). Spheres, cones and pyramids are all 3-D shapes. ◆

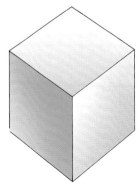

▲ A cube has six faces. Each of these is a square.

▲ A sphere has the outline of a circle from wherever you look at it.

▲ A cone has a point at one end and a circle at the other.

# Sharks

Many species of shark have attacked human beings. The great white shark, which grows to a length of 6 m (20 ft), is the most feared. About 50 attacks a year are officially reported, but less than half of them are fatal. Perhaps as many as 1,000 attacks a year go unreported. Many thousands of sharks are killed each year for vitamin-rich oil from their livers, as well as food.

There are many different types of shark. Some, like the bullhead sharks, are sluggish and feed on shellfish and sea urchins on the seabed. Others, like the whale shark and basking shark, filter the sea water for plankton. The best-known sharks are fast-swimming predators such as the mako and the great white. They feed mainly on fish, and the larger species also eat seals and dolphins.

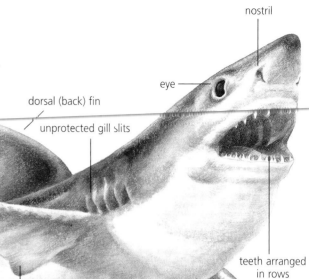

nostril

eye

dorsal (back) fin

unprotected gill slits

teeth arranged in rows

tail fin

fins that cannot fold up

claspers (male only)

Sharks, together with rays and skates, are different from other fish. Their skeleton is made of cartilage rather than bone, and their skin is protected not with thin scales but with thousands of tooth-like structures. These are covered with enamel, just like teeth. They are called placoid scales, or dermal denticles, which means "skin teeth." Small denticles make the shark's skin like sandpaper. Large ones provide a very strong armor.

Sharks' teeth have developed from their body armor. When a flesh-eating shark opens its mouth, you can see the triangular, pointed teeth that fringe the jaws. But a shark may have up to 3,000 teeth at any time. Most of them cannot be seen for they are behind the front teeth. When one of these is damaged, it drops out and the next tooth moves forward to replace it. Most sharks replace a single tooth about every 8 days, though a few shed and renew all the front row at once.

Some sharks sleep on the seabed, but most seem to swim without rest. This is because, unlike other fish, they have no swim bladder to make them buoyant. Instead, they have huge and very oily livers, which help to support them.

Sharks lay very few eggs, which are usually protected by horny egg cases. The "mermaid's

**Distribution**
In oceans throughout the world but more common in warmer water
**Largest**
Whale shark, grows to a length of 15 m (49 ft).
**Smallest**
Dwarf shark, 15 cm (6 in) long
**Subphylum**
Vertebrata
**Class**
Chondrichthyes (cartilaginous fishes)
**Number of species**
370

 **See also**
Fish
Teeth
Vertebrates

▼ A zebra horn shark, one of the smaller shark species. It feeds mainly on shellfish and sea urchins.

purse" you may find on the seashore is the empty egg case of a small shark. It contained only one baby shark, which took several months to develop and was over 10 cm (4 in) long when it hatched. Other species, like the blue shark, give birth to live young, which have been protected and nourished inside their mother's body.

Sharks' eyesight and hearing are not very good, but they have a keen sense of smell, which they use to find their prey. They can also sense vibrations produced by an injured or struggling fish. Besides this they can detect electric currents in the water. This means they can trace prey by the electricity made in its body. ◆

# Sheep

Wild sheep live in mountainous areas. They are good climbers, but are less agile than their cousins the goats, so they are generally found at lower and less rocky levels. Both males and females have horns, which are usually curled into a flat spiral. The horns of the males are larger and are used particularly in fighting for mates. Like goats, wild sheep are wary, tough animals, with dense hairy coats. In the winter-time they grow a thick undercoat (fleece) of fine wool, which helps to keep them warm and dry in even the harshest weather. It is molted (shed) completely in the summer.

A wild ewe about to give birth to her lamb leaves the small group with which she normally lives and finds a safe ledge. The lamb remains there with her for several days after birth. At this time its main enemies are eagles, but later it may have many enemies. Of these, humans are the most dangerous, and, largely because of over-hunting, most kinds of wild sheep are now very rare.

## Domestication

The value of the winter wooly coat for making warm clothing and carpets led people to keep sheep, and breed them to retain their wool until the summer time. Today, most domestic breeds have lost their dense, hairy coats and have only the wooly fleece, which has to be sheared once a year.

There are now more than 800 breeds and over 680 million domestic sheep. Humans have taken them to many parts of the world and millions are reared every year in New Zealand, Australia, and North and South America.

The mouflon, a wild sheep from southwest Asia, was domesticated about 9,000 years ago. Today it is an endangered species. A form of mouflon that is found in Europe may be a descendant of the first domestic sheep that were taken to the Mediterranean region by early farmers. Some escaped in remote areas and a few survived in Corsica and Sardinia. They are now strictly protected and their numbers are increasing. Mouflon have even been taken to mountainous parts of Europe, where they thrive on the Alpine pastures. ◆

◄ The mouflon, smallest of the wild sheep, is the ancestor of today's domestic sheep.

**Distribution of wild sheep**
Mountains of Asia and North America
**Size**
Up to 180 cm (5.9 ft) head-and-body length
**Weight**
Up to 200 kg (440 lbs)
**Number of young**
In the wild 1 lamb, weaned in 4–6 months; domestic sheep often have twins or triplets
**Lifespan**
Up to 24 years
**Subphylum**
Vertebrata
**Class**
Mammalia
**Order**
Artiodactyla (cloven-hoofed animals)
**Family**
Bovidae (cattle family)
**Number of species** 8

**V**arious breeds of sheep are reared all over the world for wool, meat, milk and cheese.

◄ Sheep are sheared once a year at the beginning of summer, when the winter coat is attached to the skin by fewer hairs.

▼ **See also**
Domestication
Goats

# Shintoism

Shinto is the name for the folk religion of Japan. It is so old that there is no known date for its beginning and no founder figure. Shinto is often translated as "the *kami* (spirit) way." The most important kami is Amaterasu, the Sun goddess. Japan is often called the "land of the rising Sun," and Shinto has been the state religion at certain times in history. There are public Shinto shrines (places of worship) with priests, and also small home shrines. All Shinto shrines have a *torii*, a special gateway marking the entrance to the sacred area. People pray there when they have personal problems, to offer their thanks, and to meditate on the harmony there should be among the kami, nature and people. ◆

▼ **See also**
Japan
Religions

# Ships

When people talk about ships, they usually mean seagoing vessels with engines driving an underwater propeller. Ships used to carry sails and to rely on the wind, but there are very few large sailing ships in use today.

Most ships have one propeller (also called a screw), but some have two or even three. Usually, the propeller is driven by a diesel engine, but a gas turbine or a steam turbine may be used instead. For a steam turbine, the steam comes from a boiler using the heat from burning oil or from a nuclear reactor.

▶ This catamaran ferry is one of a new breed of large, double-hulled ships.

### First Modern Ship
The *Great Britain*, designed by Isambard Kingdom Brunel and launched in 1845, was built of iron and had a screw propeller.

### World's Largest Ship
The oil tanker *Seawise Giant* (564,000 tons) was 458 m (1,503 ft) long and 69 m (226 ft) wide. It was completed in 1976, but destroyed in a rocket attack in 1988.

**O**il tankers are so massive that it can take them over 10 km (6 mi) to stop, even with their engines in full reverse.

## Cargo ships

At one time, a cargo ship would carry many different cargoes, depending on what needed to be transported from port to port. Today, most cargo ships are specially designed to carry one type of goods only. The cargo might be several hundred cars, containers packed with washing machines, or grain pumped aboard through a pipe.

## Passenger ships

Nowadays, passenger ships are either ferries or luxury liners taking people on holiday cruises. However, before air travel became popular, huge passenger liners provided regular services between all the major ports of the world. When people had to travel long distances around the world, they went by sea.

▶ Different types of ship carry passengers, cargo, vehicles and aircraft. (Drawing not to scale.)

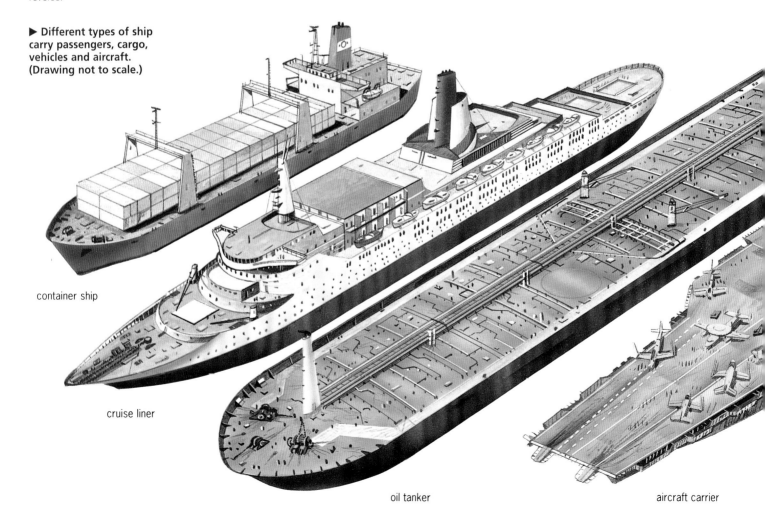

container ship

cruise liner

oil tanker

aircraft carrier

## Naval ships

Naval ships are used in time of war to hunt and destroy enemy ships, submarines and aircraft, and for launching missiles against targets on land. Aircraft carriers are the largest naval vessels of all; the biggest can carry over 90 aircraft. Frigates and destroyers are used for escorting and protecting other vessels. Minesweepers hunt for explosive mines that might sink other ships. They have plastic or aluminum hulls that do not set off magnetic mines. Most naval vessels are packed with radar and other electronic equipment that can detect and track missiles or torpedoes launched against them.

## Building a ship

Modern ships are built of steel and other metals, and not of wood as the early ships were. Traditionally, building starts with the laying of the keel, the "backbone" of the ship; then the frame is added. The body of the hull, with

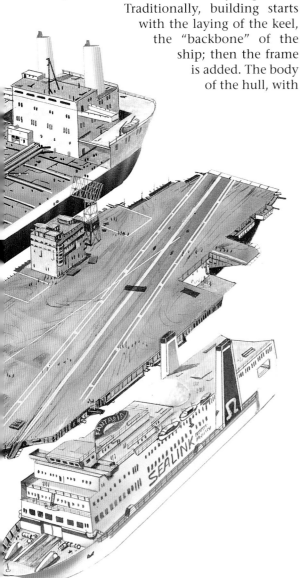

roll-on roll-off car ferry

the stern and stem, is welded on, and the engines and boilers installed. Most modern ships are built of large prefabricated sections that are welded together. The ship is normally built on a gently sloping slipway. When it is ready to be launched, it is allowed to slide slowly down the slipway into the water. It is then floated to a quay where the remaining parts are added.

As ships have become longer, it has become more important to strengthen them lengthwise, to keep their long hulls from bending and cracking in heavy seas. Many are fitted with stabilizers (small, movable underwater "wings") to keep them from rolling too much.

### LOOKING BACK

Ships driven by steam engines started to replace sailing ships at the beginning of the 19th century. At first, steamships were propelled by large paddle wheels at the sides, but more efficient screw propellers were used from about 1840. Steamships needed huge supplies of coal as fuel, so they became much bigger. Iron, and later steel, rather than wood became the main building material. By the end of the 19th century, the engine room of one of the biggest liners was almost as big as a cathedral.

From about 1900, steam turbines began to replace steam engines in the largest ships. Steam turbines are still used in some large ships, using a nuclear reactor or oil to heat the boiler, rather than coal. Today, most ships are propelled by diesel engines, though some fast naval vessels use gas turbines similar to those in aircraft. ◆

▶ Ships have become larger over the years. The largest ships of all were the supertankers built to carry oil in the 1970s.

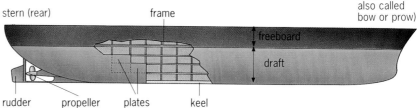

stem (front; also called bow or prow)

stern (rear)     frame

freeboard

draft

rudder    propeller    plates    keel

▲ The hull of a ship.

▼ See also
Boats
Docks
Navies
Nuclear power
Ports and harbors
Sailing ships
Steam engines
Submarines
Turbines
Vikings
Yachts

1590 galleon

1850 sailing clipper

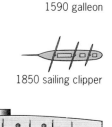
1858 iron steamship

1907 ocean liner

1952 ocean liner

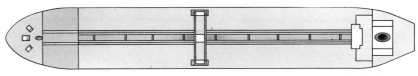
1976 oil tanker

# Shoes

**See also**
Clothing
Factories

New England used to have a major shoemaking industry, but it declined in the 20th century. Most shoes sold in the U.S. are now made in Asia and South America, where labor costs are cheaper.

Many shoes made today have leather uppers and synthetic soles. More expensive shoes are lined with leather, and cheaper shoes have plastic uppers. Some shoes, such as sports shoes, have fabric uppers and rubber soles.

In a shoe factory the shape of the upper is cut out by a worker. The upper is "closed" (stitched) and set on a "last" (mold). It is usually attached to the sole with adhesive, although on some more expensive shoes sole and upper are stitched together. The sole and heel are usually premolded in one piece.

### LOOKING BACK

Shoes from the Roman and medieval periods have been found near the River Thames in London, because the type of mud there preserves leather well. Shoemaking used to be a highly skilled craft. Cobblers would make strong shoes to last for years, as well as fashionable shoes in exaggerated shapes. Pointed toes and high heels have often been fashionable. In the 1470s in England, pointed toes became so long that laws had to be passed to restrict their length. The points were stuffed to keep them firm.

Shoes with silk uppers were popular among fashionable ladies in the 17th and 18th centuries. They wore shoes with a raised sole that were called pattens or clogs. Very poor people could only afford wooden clogs. ◆

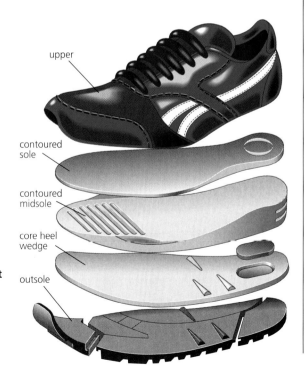

upper

contoured sole

contoured midsole

core heel wedge

outsole

▶ Training shoes are made to support and protect the feet. Outer soles should be strong and hard-wearing. The tread molded into the bottom grips the ground. Inner wedges and insoles provide support and flexibility, and they cushion the feet from impact against the ground. The upper provides support and stability and, ideally, should both allow the foot to breathe and be water-resistant.

# Show-jumping

▲ Horse and rider rear up to clear a jump at the 1992 Volvo World Cup.

Show-jumping is the most popular equestrian sport. Riders take their horses around a constructed course of obstacles, which they try to jump without incurring faults.

Young riders can get their first taste of show-jumping at mounted games, or *gymkhanas*, where they jump their ponies over simple, low obstacles. At the other end of the scale come the big international competitions, including the Olympic Games. The best riders in the world negotiate testing courses with high jumps of 1.3 to 1.6 m (4–5 ft). Often they have spent years training their horses for these events.

### Obstacle course

Competitions are held in both indoor and outdoor arenas. A course might have about 12 to 15 obstacles, which are jumped in a set order. They are constructed to look like fences, gates or walls, and horses must jump them cleanly, without dislodging a rail or a brick.

If two or more riders are level at the end of a competition, they usually take part in a jump-off against the clock over a shorter course. ◆

**See also**
Horses
Sports

# Shrews

▲ The shrew is one of the smallest of all mammals. Most species are less than 12 cm (5 in) long, and many are very tiny.

**Distribution**
Almost worldwide
**Number of young**
About 6 in a litter; a female may produce 5 or more litters in her life
**Lifespan**
Most shrews do not survive much over a year
**Subphylum**
Vertebrata
**Class**
Mammalia
**Order**
Insectivora
**Family**
Soricidae
**Number of species**
265

▼ See also
Hedgehogs
Moles

Shrews are sometimes called "shrew mice," but they are related to moles and hedgehogs, not to rodents. They are among the most active of all mammals, hunting small prey day and night. Their tiny bodies burn energy at such a rate that many species need to eat their own weight of insects or grubs every day of their lives. Some can starve to death if they go more than four hours without a meal. Their eyesight is poor, but they give an impression of busyness, as they rush about, whiskers twitching, searching for food.

Shrews have the reputation of being deadly animals. While this is not so, it has been discovered that some shrews have saliva that acts as a poison on their prey. Fortunately, most shrews have teeth too small to pierce the skin of large animals, or even a human hand.

Shrews are defended against larger predators by stink glands on their sides. These make them very unattractive food for mammals such as weasels and cats. Birds, which have a poor sense of smell, have no objection to eating shrews, and shrew remains are often found in the pellets of owls and birds of prey. ◆

# Shrimp

Shrimp are shellfish and are relatives of crabs and lobsters. Most of them live at the edge of the sea. Usually their bodies are flattened from side to side, which helps to make them streamlined for swimming. Unlike their heavyweight cousins, they have only a light exoskeleton (shell). They may have pincers on their first pair of legs, but no powerful crushing or tearing claws. They have stalked eyes, and two pairs of delicate feelers for exploring scent and shape. Many of them are scavengers, eating the remains of dead sea creatures.

Pistol shrimp live in rocky areas. Unlike most of their relatives, they have a claw. When a suitable prey animal, such as a little fish, swims near to their lair, they snap this claw. It makes such a noise that the prey is stunned and can be caught easily by the shrimp.

Some shrimp clean parasites from fish. Some do the same for other sea creatures, and actually live on their bodies. These associates include sea anemones, sea whips and at least one very poisonous sea urchin. ◆

▼ See also
Crabs
Crustaceans
Lobsters

**Distribution**
Throughout the world
**Size**
2.5–30 cm (1–12 in)
**Phylum**
Arthropoda
**Class**
Crustacea

Shrimp are a valuable seafood in the U.S. and other parts of the world. In Europe, most edible shrimp are referred to as prawns; in the U.S., the word "prawn" is sometimes used to describe very large shrimp.

▼ Shrimp are swimmers, rather than crawlers like crabs and lobsters. Many live shrimp are nearly transparent; after they are cooked they usually turn a bright pink.

# Shrubbery

Any plant that has a woody stem is a shrub. The that is made from a mass of tube-shaped cells which transport water and food up and down the shrub's stem. Some of the tubes become thickened with a material called *lignin*, and it is this that gives wood its strength.

## Shrubbery or trees?

The term "shrub" or "shrubbery" is used for smaller plants, which often have a number of shoots that give them a bushy appearance. Any shrub taller than 7.5 m (25 ft) is usually called a tree. Foresters know that plants above this height are likely to yield good timber.

However, there is no real difference in nature between shrubs and trees. Some species, such as hawthorn and hazel, can stay at shrub size in a hedge, especially if they are cut regularly or grazed by animals. If they are protected from this, they will eventually grow into a tree. Similarly, high in the mountains or on exposed coasts, even pine or oak trees will grow in a low, shrubby form that helps to protect them from the wind.

In the lowlands, if a forest is felled, shrubs will quickly move back in, forming a dense thicket called *scrub*. Many of these shrubs, such as gorse, hawthorn and blackthorn, have thorns or spines as protection against grazing animals. In among these, more typical tree species will begin to grow, until, in time, the trees grow clear of the scrub. Some of the shrubs will not be able to grow in the shade cast by the trees and will die out. Others, such as holly, may go on growing beneath the trees, forming the *shrub layer* of the forest.

In many Mediterranean countries, large areas are covered by bushes of cistus shrubs, which have beautiful, showy white or pink flowers. These are naturally the main vegetation (plant cover) near coasts, but in many other areas they took over when the Romans felled the trees that once grew there.

## Heathers

Above the highest level at which trees can survive in mountains, there is a zone of short shrubs, including ling heather, bell heather and bilberry. Mountain birds feed on the leaves and fruits of these dwarf shrubs or on the insects that live among them. These shrubs in the heather family are the main vegetation where the soil is very poor and peaty, and this type of vegetation is called *heathland*. The same heathers also grow naturally beneath pine forest, and in some

countries of Northern Europe, the pine trees have been felled to leave open areas of heather. These are burned regularly to produce the best crop of heather and encourage grouse, which feed on the heather, for people to shoot as sport.

## Ornamental shrubs

Gardeners grow a wide variety of colorful, low-growing shrubs. Among the most commonly grown are rhododendrons, many of which originally came from the Himalayas. Other attractive garden shrubs include laburnum and buddleia, which is valuable for attracting butterflies to the garden.

Raspberries, currants and gooseberries are shrubs grown in gardens for their crop of fruit. Tea and coffee are important crops gathered from shrubs grown by farmers in tropical countries.

## Hedges

People grow shrubs in a tight mass to produce hedges. These act as a living green fence to protect property from intruders or to mark boundary lines of property. The hedges are valuable wildlife habitats; several pairs of birds may nest in a hedge.

There were once more than half a million miles of hedges in the English countryside. They were known as *hedgerows*, and were used to contain animals on farm property. However, they are expensive to look after, and because farmers want larger fields, hedges are now disappearing rapidly. ◆

▼ **See also**
Coffee
Flowering plants
Fruit
Photosynthesis
Plants
Tea
Trees
Wood

There is more on how wood is formed in the article on Trees.

In gardens, privet is the shrub most often planted to make a hedge.

▼ Hedging is the ancient skill of producing a dense hedge. Shrubs were planted by hand. When they were tall enough, the stems were partially cut through, bent down and woven into the base of the hedge to make it bushy enough to block farm animals.

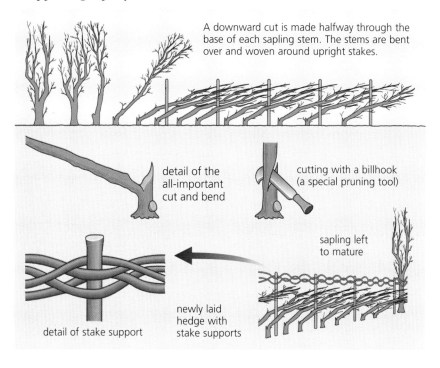

A downward cut is made halfway through the base of each sapling stem. The stems are bent over and woven around upright stakes.

detail of the all-important cut and bend

cutting with a billhook (a special pruning tool)

sapling left to mature

newly laid hedge with stake supports

detail of stake support

# Sierra Leone

Sierra Leone, which means "lion mountains," possibly got its name from the shape of a mountain near the coast. But it may have been named after the roaring sound of thunder often heard during rainstorms. This hot, wet country has broad, swampy plains along the coast, north and south of the mountain. Inland are plains and uplands.

Rice is the main food crop, and it is grown in the swampy plains. Farther inland are small plantations where coffee, cocoa and oil palms are grown for export.

But diamonds are by far the country's leading export.

## LOOKING BACK

In 1787, a British society for freed slaves founded a settlement on the coast of Sierra Leone. It was named Freetown because it was a home for slaves who had escaped or gained freedom. The descendants of these slaves now make up much of Freetown's population. They speak Krio, which is a dialect of English. Great Britain ruled Sierra Leone from 1808 until 1961, when it became independent. ◆

**Area**
71,740 sq km
(27,699 sq mi)
**Capital** Freetown
**Population**
4,402,000
**Language**
English, Krio, others
**Religion**
Traditional, Muslim, Christian
**Government**
Parliamentary republic
**Currency**
1 leone = 100 cents
**Major exports**
Diamonds, iron ore, coffee, cocoa, palm oil

▼ **See also**
Africa

# Sign language

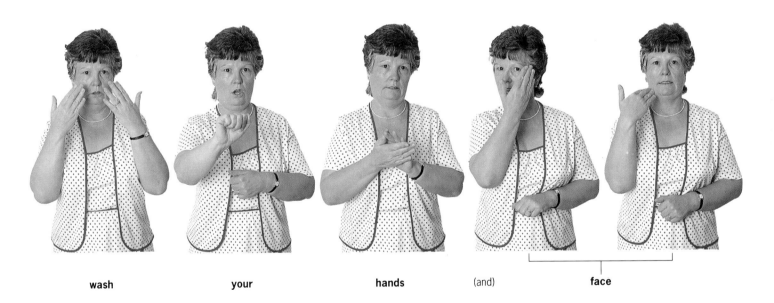

wash          your          hands          (and)          face

The various tribes of North American Plains Indians had different spoken languages, but they all used the same sign language, such as two fingers astride the index finger of the other hand for "horseback rider."

▼ **See also**
Deafness

People who are deaf or who cannot speak learn to talk to one another in a language that uses the hands, the face, and the upper part of the body. This is called sign language.

The signs they use with their hands do not just mean words on their own: their meaning depends on the person's movements and on the expression on her or his face. The difference between saying "I gave you a hat" and "Did you give me a hat?" is shown by the hand signs for these words and the direction in which they are made: from me to you or from you to me, raising your eyebrows to show that it is a question.

There are as many sign languages in the world as there are spoken ones. American Sign Language (ASL) is used by more than half a million deaf people, and is the fourth most common language in the U.S. ◆

▲ These signs are used by deaf people in the Signs Supporting English method. This sequence of signs means "Wash your hands and face." The sign for the word "and" is not used in sentences like this. The meanings of the signs vary with the facial expressions used. Lip patterns are used as well as hand signs.

# Sikhism

The Sikh religion began in the Punjab in northern India where most Sikhs still live. Sikhs also live in many other countries, particularly North America and Great Britain.

The most important thing for a Sikh is learning about God. In the Punjabi language the word *sikh* means "learner" and the word *guru* means "teacher." God is the "True Teacher" and is described by Sikhs as the "Eternal Being" beyond male or female. The title "Guru" is also given to ten important human beings in the history of Sikhism.

All the Gurus teach Sikhs three main things. Firstly, they should remember God frequently by saying or singing his name. Secondly, Sikhs should work hard to earn an honest living. They usually marry and have families, feeling that this is the way God wants them to live. All Sikh men and women are equal and can perform any of the religious ceremonies. There are no monks or priests in Sikhism.

Thirdly, Sikhs should share their earnings and serve others, whatever their nationality, religion or social status. If you visit a gurdwara (Sikh temple), you will see boys and girls, as well as adults, helping to prepare and serve food and drink from the *langar*, the Guru's kitchen. Guests are welcome to stay and eat at any time, but especially after a service.

**LOOKING BACK**

The first of the ten Gurus was Nanak, who lived in the Punjab from 1469 to 1539. His background was Hindu, and Sikhs share the Hindu belief in a final liberation from many reincarnations. They also share some of the same festivals, such as Diwali.

In 1604, the fifth Guru, Arjan, collected teachings from earlier Gurus into a book which became the sacred scripture of the Sikhs. It is called the *Guru Granth Sahib,* and passages from it are read aloud at all Sikh ceremonies. ◆

**See also**
Festivals and holidays
Hinduism
Pilgrimages

# Silicon

Silicon is a brittle, non-metallic element. It is one of the most common elements in the Earth's crust. In nature it is only found joined with other substances as a compound. These compounds are known as *silicates*. Most rocks contain silicates, and so do sand and clay, so silicon can be found in glass, pottery and bricks. Pure silicon is a hard, shiny, brown-black chemical made up of crystals.

Silicon is a semiconductor suited to carrying tiny electric currents. Purified silicon is used in making micro-processors or silicon chips. These tiny wafer-thin slices of silicon contain many complicated electrical circuits. Without silicon chips there would be no computers, pocket calculators or digital watches.

*Silicones* are chemicals made from silicon. They are widely used as polishes and lubricants. Quartz crystals, which contain silicon, are also used in many watches. ◆

**See also**
Bricks
Computers
Crystals
Electronics
Elements
Glass
Materials
Minerals
Pottery
Rocks

# Silk

Silk is a material made from thread from the cocoon of the silkworm. It is so fine that a very large number of threads are required for every inch of woven fabric. Silk is very strong and long-lasting. It is even used in the nose cone of the supersonic Concorde aircraft.

The silkworms hatch from the 400–500 tiny eggs laid in spring by the moth *Bombyx mori.* This moth feeds exclusively on mulberry leaves and so do the silkworms. The silkworms are 2 mm ((0.08 in) long at birth and spend the first four or five weeks of their lives eating. During this time they grow to about 8 cm (3 in). They shed their skin about four times as they grow out of it. When they reach their maximum size, they start the next stage in their lives and produce cocoons. The silkworm produces threads from two glands in its head.

The threads mix with a gummy material that helps to form the cocoon by sticking the threads together. When the cocoon is formed, it is about 3 cm (1.2 in) in length. The silkworm then changes inside the cocoon, first into a pupa and then into a moth.

In order to have complete cocoons from which to unwind the silk threads, the pupa must be killed. If it grew into a moth, it would break the cocoon as it emerged, which would ruin it. Hot air or steam is used to kill the pupa. The cocoon is put into hot water to soften the sticky gum. It is brushed to find the end of the two threads that form the cocoon. These are joined to the threads of another cocoon to form silk thread. This thread is then used to create fabric. ◆

**See also**
Fibers
Moths
Pupae
Spinning
Weaving

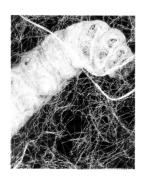

▲ A silkworm beginning to spin its cocoon.

Silk was first produced in the Far East over 4,000 years ago.

# Silver

Some silver is found in a pure state, particularly in Mexico and Argentina. In Australia, parts of South America, the U.S., Canada and some other countries, silver is found combined with other substances.

Silver is a brilliant white shining metal. Along with gold and platinum, it is one of the so-called precious metals.

Silver is widely used to make jewelry, tableware and ornaments. It is also used to coat other cheaper metals in what is called silverplating. Silver can easily be shaped or given a highly polished surface. Because nothing else reflects light as well as silver, it is used to coat mirrors. Silver is also a good conductor of electricity. It is used in electrical switches in telephones, computers and other electronic equipment. One big drawback of silver, however, is that it quickly tarnishes (turns black) in polluted city air and has to be repolished.

Many nations have, at various times, used silver coins. Today alloys of other metals are often used instead, except for coins to celebrate special events.

## Silver in photography

When silver is combined with certain other substances, such as chlorine and iodine, it forms salts that are sensitive to light. If a light shines on them, they turn black. Because of this, large quantities of silver are used to make film and light-sensitive papers used in photography. ◆

▼ A silver bowl made in 1768 in Boston by Paul Revere (1735–1818). Revere, renowned for his patriotism during the American Revolution, was also colonial America's leading silversmith (a person who makes silver objects). This classic shape, first created by Revere, is known as a Revere bowl and has been copied by many silver manufacturers. Revere bowls are often given to commemorate special occasions and are engraved with a message, like the bowl shown here.

▲ For centuries, silversmiths have marked the objects they make with their initials or unique designs to identify them as their own work. This mark is usually found on the base of an object. This is Paul Revere's mark (greatly enlarged) and appears on all silver made by him.

▼ **See also**

Alloys
Coins
Illuminated manuscripts
Metals

**BIOGRAPHY**
Revere, Paul

# Singapore

**Area**
618 sq km (239 sq mi)
**Capital**
Singapore City
**Population**
2,818,000
**Language**
Chinese, Malay, Tamil, English
**Religion**
Buddhist, Muslim, Christian, Taoist, Hindu
**Government**
Republic
**Currency**
1 Singapore dollar = 100 cents
**Major exports**
Oil, electronics

Singapore is one of the smallest countries in the world. It is densely populated, but rich. It includes a main island, also called Singapore, and 60 smaller islands. The weather is hot and humid and rainstorms are common.

Singapore City is a mass of skyscrapers. At the center are offices, banks, hotels and government buildings. Farther out are apartment buildings. The government encourages builders to build upward to save land.

Outside the city there are a few villages left, and farmland with neat vegetable plots and orchards. But there is not enough land to grow food, and most is imported. Marshy land is being gradually reclaimed to provide more space for homes and industry. People earn their living by working in banking, manufacturing and trade. Singapore has a modern system of roads and highways. It has one of the most advanced systems of telecommunications in the world. The island is joined to Malaysia by a road on a causeway. Both the port and airport are among the busiest in the world.

## LOOKING BACK

In 1819 a British officer, Sir Stamford Raffles, rented Singapore island from the Sultan of Johore. It soon became a British colony. In the 20th century it became a busy port and an important British naval base. In World War II the Japanese attacked overland and captured the colony in 1942. Singapore became an independent state in 1959. It joined the Federation of Malaysia in 1963, but left in 1965 to become an independent republic. ◆

▼ **See also**

Asia
Commonwealth of Nations
Malaysia

# Singing and songs

▲ To communicate their feelings to the audience, opera singers must express themselves through their gestures as well as their voice.

**A** *castrato* was an adult male soprano who was castrated in youth so that his voice did not break and remained high. Some of the greatest singers of the 18th century were *castrati*, but nowadays this cruel practice has been abandoned.

**S**inging has always been associated with religion and magic. Priests and sorcerers have used singing or chanting to give power to their prayers or spells. Christians sing hymns.

▶ Salif Keita, from Mali, is one of Africa's best-known singers.

Singing is making music with the human voice. A song is a poem set to music that expresses different emotions and different experiences—like love or despair, going to war, having a night out, playing a game or lulling a child to sleep. Most songs are accompanied by instruments such as the guitar or piano, but some of the most effective songs stand alone, without accompaniment.

## How we sing

The human voice is often compared to a wind instrument. We breathe a column of air up from the lungs. The air passes across the vocal cords, which are tiny folds of muscle in the larynx, so that they vibrate to produce sound waves in the same way that a wind instrument does. These vibrations are then amplified in the cavities of the throat, the mouth and the sinuses on either side of the nose and above the eyes. Finally the tongue and the lips alter the shape of the sound to produce vowels and consonants that make up words.

The special quality of a voice depends on the size and shape of the larynx and the resonating cavities of the throat, mouth and head, as well as how the sound is produced. Training a person to be a singer can take many

years, and pop and jazz singers are now realizing the importance of using their voice in the right kind of way to create their music.

## Breathing

The basis of singing is how we use our breath. This means being able to take in air into all parts of the lungs, and letting it out steadily with the support of the rib muscles and the diaphragm, which is a sheet of muscle beneath the lungs. Most people pick up bad breathing habits very early, and a good voice teacher will spend a lot of time establishing a steady breathing technique.

## Pitch

Pitch is the degree of highness or lowness of a note. We do not have direct control over the pitch of the sounds we sing. Our minds first imagine the pitch of the note we want, and then the brain sends out a message through the motor nerves to the vocal cords, which causes them to shorten or lengthen as they vibrate and so produce a higher or a lower note.

## Resonance

Many singing teachers talk about a "head" or a "chest" voice. Someone who sings in a head voice will feel vibrations in the mouth and head cavities, while in a chest voice the singer will feel vibrations in the chest area. For a note like A above middle C, a classical singer will normally use a head voice, which gives a much purer sound than that of a jazz or pop singer, who will use the chest register for a note of exactly the same pitch.

## Type and range of voice

Most children have high voices. As they grow older, boys' voices change. Around the ages of 13 to 16 they "break" and get lower in pitch. Girls' voices also change very slightly, though they do not break in the same way. Men generally have longer and thicker vocal cords than women, and their vocal range is about an octave lower.

Overall, voices are grouped into the following categories (from highest to lowest): soprano, mezzo-soprano, contralto ("alto") or counter-tenor (highest male voice), tenor, baritone and bass. Some counter-tenors are also able to sing in an upper register using a falsetto voice.

There are a number of sub-groups within the main voice groupings. For instance, a coloratura soprano, or a jazz singer who can "scat," can sing very high notes, while a dramatic soprano is able to give weight and substance to the long, sustained emotional phrases of an aria from an opera.

## Styles of singing

As singing is very much to do with expressing emotions, singers combine the techniques they have learned with the best way of putting over a particular song. Classically trained singers base their interpretation of a song on the notation written by the composer, but all singers bring their personality to performance.

Jazz, rock and pop singers are much more ready and able to use a song as a basis from which to develop their own individual performance. They may swing and syncopate the rhythm (make strong beats weak and weak beats strong), improvise on the chord changes,

move into different keys and create their own endings. A "standard" may be sung up-tempo and with a Latin rhythm by one artist and in a slow blues style by another.

## Cultural differences

Singers in different parts of the world have also developed singing styles that are most suited to their music. Arabic singers, whether in North Africa or the Middle East, have a high nasal quality. Many folk musicians, especially country and western singers, often use a nasal twang to gain a different effect. Soul singers have voices with a range and resonance that are almost a cross between blues and opera. ◆

▲ Gospel singing can be highly emotive and is an expression of religious faith.

◀ A group of Kenyan women singing. African languages have an innate musical quality, and speech and song overlap more than in most other cultures.

▼ **See also**

African music
Blues
Breathing
Choirs and choruses
Country and western
  music
Folk music
Gospel music
Indian music
Jazz
Music
Operas
Rock music
Sound
Spirituals
Voice

# Skeletons

▶ Frogs, like other backboned animals, have their skeletons inside their bodies. A frog has very large back legs for leaping out of danger and to catch its prey.

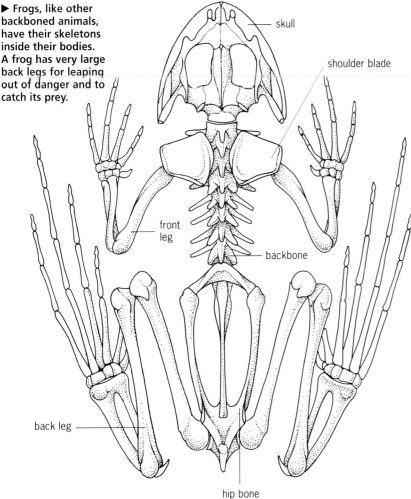

skull

shoulder blade

front leg

backbone

back leg

hip bone

▶ Hinge and ball-and-socket joints are the main joints in backboned animals. Hinge joints allow movement in two directions (experiment with your elbow). Ball-and-socket joints allow movement in many directions (experiment with your hip). Crayfish, crabs, insects and spiders have an outside skeleton. It is made of a stiff, often hard substance called cuticle. There is thin, flexible cuticle at the joints to allow movement.

▼ See also
Bones
Fractures
Human body
Invertebrates
Vertebrates

humerus

**Elbow**

forearm

ulna    radius

hip bone

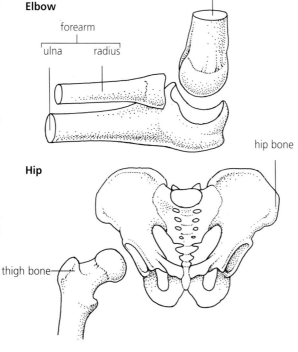

**Hip**

thigh bone

A skeleton is a stiff scaffolding that supports the soft parts of an animal. Without skeletons most animals would be sagging, floppy objects with no distinct shape. Skeletons enable animals to have a wide range of body shapes, with distinct parts to move and carry out separate functions. Without skeletons, swimming, running, picking things up and chewing would be virtually impossible.

Fish, amphibians, reptiles, birds and mammals (the vertebrates) have skeletons of bone and cartilage inside their bodies (inner skeleton). All vertebrates have a backbone made up of a chain of vertebrae, and a skull. Most also have four limbs—legs, arms, wings or fins.

The skull and backbone support and protect the central parts of the nervous system, the brain and the spinal cord. In fish, reptiles, birds and mammals the ribs curve around to form the rib cage that protects the heart, digestive tract and lungs. The shoulder and hip are bony connections between the backbone and the limbs. In different land animals the basic five-toed end of the limb has been adapted in many ways. In the horse, for instance, each leg has only a single functional toe, with a hoof (the toenail) at its tip.

## Joints

Muscles and joints enable bony skeletons to make complicated movements. Joints are the bending and sliding places where bones touch. Muscles are joined to bones by tendons, and where muscles contract they move the bones in relation to each other. Different types of joint allow different sorts of movement. The ends of bones that touch at joints are usually covered in smooth, lubricated cartilage so they move over each other easily.

## Other skeletons

Animals without backbones (invertebrates) do not have bony skeletons. Worms, snails and shellfish, for instance, have taut, fluid-filled bags inside their bodies to support them—just as a balloon becomes firm when it is filled with water.

Other invertebrates such as crabs, lobsters, spiders and insects have a surface skeleton. Their soft inner bodies are supported by a stiff, jointed skin (a cuticle) on the outside, which gives them their shape. The cuticle is hard, so it does not allow growth. As the animal grows, it must shed its cuticle. Underneath is a new, soft cuticle that allows growth until it hardens. The animal will have to shed its cuticle a number of times before it is fully grown. ◆

# Skiing

▲ In slalom racing, skiers weave between sets of poles, or "gates." As long as both feet pass through the gate, the skier is allowed to nudge or even knock over the gate poles. The hips are angled in order to give better control in the turn.

Skiing is traveling over snow on skis, which are flat, narrow runners that curve up at the front. It is a leisure activity in specialized ski resorts, and a popular sport.

Ski equipment consists of skis, made of metal and plastic, and ski poles, used for balance and for leverage. Stiff plastic boots with a comfortable lining support the feet and ankles. Special clamps called "bindings" secure the boots to the skis and have a safety release in the event of a fall. Sunglasses or goggles protect eyes from the glare of the sun on the snow.

The first skiers were the peoples of Northern Europe in prehistoric times, who used skiing as a method of transport. Skiing first developed as a sport around 1850 in Norway.

The chief skiing competitions are held in the Winter Olympics. There are also World Championships and World Cups (over a series of events) in both Alpine and Nordic ski racing.

## Ski racing

The two main branches of the sport are Alpine and Nordic skiing.

In Alpine ski racing, competitors ski down mountain slopes, starting at intervals. Winners are determined on time. In downhill, they find the fastest way down the course. In the slalom events, they have to ski through a series of "gates." In freestyle skiing, a relatively new set of events, skiers perform routines on snow bumps (moguls), in the air off ramps (aerials) and down smooth slopes to music (ballet).

Nordic skiing includes cross-country racing (langlauf) and ski-jumping. Nordic racers use lightweight skis and long ski poles. They start at intervals. Ski jumpers ski down a steep ramp before jumping. They are awarded points for style as well as distance. ♦

▼ See also
Olympic Games
Winter sports

# Skin

Skin is the protective outer surface that covers the whole of the human body. The outer layer is called the *epidermis*. This upper skin is made up of dead skin cells and is used as a protective layer. It is kept supple by an oily substance made by the skin. Its cells are constantly being worn away and replaced from below. The lower layer that makes the epidermis is called the *dermis*. It contains blood vessels, nerves, hair roots, and sweat and oil glands.

The skin also helps to control our body temperature. It secretes sweat to cool the body down, and it makes hair to keep us warm. It is also important as an organ for the sense of touch.

Some skin cells contain a dark pigment called *melanin*. People with dark skins have more of these than people with light skins. These dark cells protect us from skin cancer, by blocking the dangerous ultraviolet rays in sunlight. ♦

▼ See also
Fur
Hair
Radiation

Moles and freckles are made up of clusters of cells containing melanin.

▼ A small piece of skin (magnified). The upper dead layer of skin wears away every time you touch anything. But a layer of live dividing cells replaces it as fast as it is removed. It also repairs cuts and other damage.

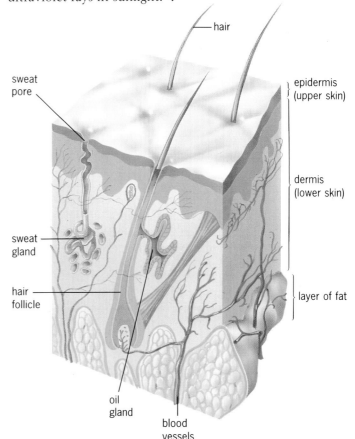

hair

sweat pore

sweat gland

hair follicle

oil gland

blood vessels

epidermis (upper skin)

dermis (lower skin)

layer of fat

# Skunks

| | |
|---|---|
| **Size** Length up to 68 cm (2.2 ft) | |
| **Weight** Up to 3 kg (6.6 lbs) | |
| **Number of young** 2–9 | |
| **Lifespan** About 7 years | |
| **Subphylum** Vertebrata | |
| **Class** Mammalia | |
| **Order** Carnivora | |
| **Family** Mustelidae | |
| **Number of species** 9 | |

▼ See also
Badgers
Mammals
Otters
Weasels

Skunks are members of the weasel family and live in North America. Most species are active at night. They eat small rodents, insects, eggs, birds and plants. Their fur is black with white stripes or spots; this coloring acts as a warning to predators. If a skunk is attacked, it defends itself by banging its front feet loudly on the ground and then doing a handstand and squirting a foul-smelling fluid from stink glands just beneath its tail. Most animals leave skunks alone for this reason. ◆

▶ The striped skunk is the most common species of skunk in the U.S. Its stripes act as a warning.

# Sky

Polaris (the Pole Star) always appears to keep the same position in the northern sky. It is almost exactly at the North Celestial Pole. There is no star bright enough to be seen at the South Celestial Pole.

If you live in a city, there is probably so much artificial light at night that you will only be able to see the brighter stars.

▶ Star trails near an observatory in Australia. The camera was kept still with its shutter open for several hours. The stars seem to move around the sky as the Earth spins.

▼ See also
Constellations
Planets
Seasons
Stars

If you stand outside on a clear, dark night you can see lots of stars. Some are bright and some are faint but you cannot tell how far away they are. You could imagine that they are all on a big dome a very long way away. Centuries ago, people thought that the stars were on a huge crystal sphere around the Earth. They called this the "celestial sphere." We now know that the stars are really scattered through space at different distances, but the best way to make a map of what the star patterns look like is on a globe.

## The dome of the sky

If you traveled out into space until the Earth

looked as small as the Moon, you would see stars all around and above and below you. From the Earth, you can see only half the stars that you would see from space. People who live south of the Equator—in Australia, for instance—can see stars that are quite different from the ones people in Europe and North America can see.

## How the sky changes

We all notice that the Sun rises and sets. It is not so obvious that stars rise and set. Rising and setting happen because the Earth spins around once a day. One way to track the stars as they move across the sky is to take a photograph with the camera shutter left open for several hours. The stars make trails of light across the film. Some stars never set below the horizon but trace out complete circles in the sky. They are called *circumpolar stars*.

Another thing you might notice is that the stars you can see on a winter evening are not the same as the ones in the summer sky. The constellations change with the seasons. In fact, each star rises four minutes earlier every day.

Sometimes you can see bright planets or the Moon. They seem to move through the patterns of stars from night to night because they are very much closer to us than the stars. ◆

### Follow a Star Trail
See if you can follow a star across the sky. Look through a window for a bright star and notice where it is over a building or trees. You could make a sketch and note the time. Stand in the same place an hour later and see how far that star has moved. Try again a few days later.

# Skydiving

Skydiving is the popular name for parachuting sports. Skydivers make their jumps from specially prepared aircraft. They perform maneuvers in the air either before or after they open their parachutes, or they might aim to land on a ground target.

The part of a jump before the parachute, or "canopy," is opened is called "freefall." Any object falling to Earth reaches a certain speed limit called its "terminal velocity." For the average person this is nearly 200 km (124 mi) per hour, and is reached in about 10 seconds. Skydivers can vary their speed of fall and perform aerial maneuvers by changing their body position. In modern "ram-air" canopies it is possible to control both speed and direction of movement.

## Competition jumping

There are individual skydiving competitions for both style and accuracy. In style events, competitors are awarded points for routines that include loops, rolls, turns and other moves. Accuracy jumping might involve landing on or as close as possible to a disk that is 5 cm (2 in) in diameter.

When teams of skydivers link up in special formations during freefall, it is called "relative work." There are competitions for teams of various sizes. Canopy relative work (CRW) involves linking up in the air with parachutes opened. When skydivers link one above the other, this is known as "stacking" and is attempted only by experts. ◆

The first sport-parachuting world championships took place in 1951, with women's events added in 1956. Team events were introduced in 1954. The most successful teams have come from the former Soviet Union.

A U.S. relative work team joined up in a record 144-person formation over Illinois in 1988.

▼ **See also**

Flight
Parachutes
Sports

◄ Skydivers perform maneuvers and link up in the air. The smallest movements of body, arms, legs or head affect a skydiver's position while freefalling.

# Skyscrapers

In the 1890s, architects in Chicago and New York began to design what were at the time very tall buildings, of 10 stories or more. Americans called these tall buildings "skyscrapers."

The first skyscrapers were built of brick and stone. They had very thick walls to carry the load of so many floors, and they looked weighty and massive. Then architects began to use steel or steel-reinforced concrete frames as the skeleton of their buildings to carry the floors, walls and roof, just as the human skeleton supports the rest of the body. The frame could be virtually as high as they wished. Such skyscrapers still had heavy stone cladding to hide their steel frames. Many of them had eye-catching tops, such as the Chrysler Building in New York City, and it is these that make the skyline of New York so memorable.

Soon architects realized that they could use walls of lightweight glass panels instead of stone and brick, and skyscrapers became sleek and transparent. But these sleek buildings all looked rather similar, so in the 1980s architects decided to make skyscrapers more interesting by using colored and decorated cladding. ◆

### The World's Tallest Buildings

Today there are many skyscrapers in the world, but which is the tallest? According to many experts, it is still the **Sears Tower**, which was built in Chicago in 1974. The Sears Tower, an office building, is 443 m (1,450 ft) high and has 110 stories. But in 1997 the title of "world's tallest" was claimed by the **Petronas Towers**, two side-by-side identical structures that were completed that year in Kuala Lumpur, Malaysia. While the Petronas Towers are each 452 m (1,483 ft) high, this distance includes spires—decorative structures at their tops that are not occupied. The occupied space in each Petronas Tower ends at its top story—the 88th, which is  378 m (1,241 ft) above the ground.

The U.S. was the birthplace of tall buildings. Here are some other famous American skyscrapers, all of them in New York City (the dates they were built are in parentheses):

**Chrysler Building** (1930): 319.4 m (1,046 ft)
**Empire State Building** (1931): 381 m (1,250 ft)
**World Trade Center** (1972): 417 m (1,368 ft)

▼ **See also**

Architecture
Building
Illinois
New York
United States of America

**BIOGRAPHY**
Sullivan, Louis

In the 1980s some architects and engineers began to build new kinds of skyscrapers, using a very strong central "core" that supports the floors and light outer walls.

▼ Skyscrapers at the lower end of Manhattan, in New York City. The twin towers of the World Trade Center are at the center of the photo.

# Slavery

The ancient Egyptians used people they had conquered as slaves, just as the Greeks and the Romans did. Slavery continued in Egypt until the late 19th century.

Slaves are men and women who are somebody else's property. Their owner can buy and sell them just like any object. There have been slaves in many different parts of the world, and in many different times in history. There are still slaves today in parts of northern Africa.

## Slaves in ancient Greece and Rome

In ancient Greece, slaves often worked in rich people's houses. Women slaves cooked and cleaned, and served the lady of the house. They entertained guests at feasts as flute girls and dancers. Male slaves in Athens sometimes kept order in the streets like policemen. In Sparta the slaves were Helots, the people who had lived in the area before the Spartans arrived and took their land. Helots were forced to do all the hard, heavy work, so that Spartan men could become highly trained fighters.

The Romans also used slaves to run their homes, and to do hard and sometimes dangerous jobs. Slaves were farm laborers and miners. They trained as gladiators who fought each other, or wild animals, to entertain huge crowds in Roman theaters. Slaves built the aqueduct that supplied Rome with water. Some Roman slaves were well-educated. They ran stores, and became secretaries and important government servants. Slaves won their freedom sometimes, but these "freedmen" did not have as many rights as people who were born free.

There were harsh punishments such as whipping for disobedient slaves. If owners caught escaped slaves, they often branded them on the forehead, and the mark stayed for life. For bad crimes like murder, slaves were thrown to wild animals.

Spartacus was a gladiator who led a rebellion of gladiators and slaves in the 1st century B.C. When he was defeated, over 6,000 of the slaves who had joined him were crucified along the Appian Way, the main road into Rome.

## The Middle Ages

When the Roman Empire broke up, slaves began to gradually disappear in Northern Europe. Instead of keeping slaves in their castles, powerful barons gave the people who worked for them a little land to live on. In return, these *serfs* had to work for their lord for fixed times, and could not leave their land. They were not bought and sold, but otherwise they were like slaves.

Slavery did not disappear in the Mediterranean. Slaves there were often black Africans or Slavs from the Balkans and farther east. The word "slave," in fact, comes from "Slav." Many became human engines in huge warships, called galleys, that were driven by long rows of heavy oars. A slave was chained to an oar for the entire voyage.

## Slavery in Africa

Through the centuries, there have been slaves on the huge continent of Africa. In East Africa, Arab traders sent slaves to Arabia and Asia, probably from the 12th century. In North Africa, from the 15th century, Muslims used white European Christians as slaves.

Some of the peoples of West Africa lived in villages, others in well-organized towns like Benin. Many were skilled craftsmen and farmers, so prisoners taken in wars between different tribes made useful slaves. In the 15th century, European explorers reached West Africa. They discovered they could buy African slaves easily, and in the following century they began selling them across the Atlantic, in the Caribbean, Brazil and North America.

## The Caribbean and the Americas

When Europeans discovered the Americas, they soon found they could make a lot of money growing sugar in the West Indies and Brazil. But the wars and diseases they brought with them had killed off most of the native peoples there, so they needed workers. Growing sugar was hard, hot work, and Europeans were not prepared to do it themselves. Slaves from Africa solved their

▼ A Mediterranean galley in the 17th century. Five slaves are working each oar, and overseers with sticks are supervising them from a central plank.

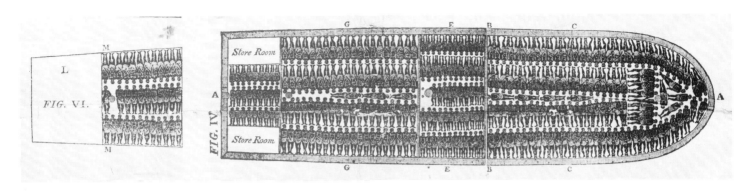

▲ An 18th-century plan of an African slave ship. One observer described it as follows: "The slaves lie in two rows close to each other like books in a shelf. . . . the poor creatures are in irons . . . which makes it difficult for them to turn or move . . . without hurting themselves or each other."

problem. Africans worked long hours cutting tough sugarcanes under the blazing Sun, and in the hot sugar-boiling sheds. From the late 17th century, slaves were also working in tobacco and cotton plantations in North America.

### The slave trade

Africans transported across the Atlantic were sold in auctions. Shipowners from several European countries made huge profits out of this cruel trade. By the 18th century the British were making the biggest profits of all.

The route of the British slave trade was like a triangle. On the first stage, ships from Liverpool and Bristol sailed to West Africa, carrying cheap iron goods, beads and guns. The ship captains exchanged these goods for Africans who had been captured by local slave traders.

The second stage was the terrible "middle passage" across the Atlantic. The ships were packed with slaves. They lay chained together on the dark, stuffy lower decks in horrible conditions, for a journey which could last six weeks. Many died on the way. The slaves who survived were sold by auction.

The empty ships then took on a new cargo for the third side of the triangle: the voyage back to England. They carried the sugar, tobacco and raw cotton

produced on the slave plantations to sell back home.

The slave trade began to end as people started to realize the misery it was causing, and also when it became less profitable. It began to make less money as the sugar trade became less important. Denmark abolished the trade first. England followed with a law passed in 1807, and the U.S. banned the trade in 1808. Gradually the Atlantic slave trade stopped, but slaves were still bought and sold by American and Caribbean owners until slavery itself was made unlawful.

### The practice of slavery

The owners' comfortable lifestyle depended on the slaves. Slaves worked in their houses, cooking, cleaning and caring for their children. Slaves looked after their horses and carriages and tended their gardens. Since slaves were so useful, owners sometimes treated them quite well, but often they were harsh and cruel to them.

Slaves did not accept their lives easily. Their gospel songs (spirituals) remind us how they longed for Africa and hated their captivity. Sometimes they rebelled against their owners.

One such rebellion was led in Southampton County, Virginia, in 1831 by a slave named Nat Turner. Turner, a leader of the slaves on their owner's plantation, plotted the rebellion with 60 of his followers. They killed the owner and his family, and then killed other white people who lived nearby—55 in all. Their revolt was crushed, however, and Turner was later captured and hanged. Turner's Rebellion, as it was called, led to even harsher treatment of blacks throughout the South.

In the Caribbean, many slaves escaped from plantations and successfully hid from their owners. Sometimes they succeeded in fighting off troops sent to find them. In Haiti, for example, an army made up mainly of former slaves defeated French and British

▼ An advertisement for a slave auction held in a British colony in the West Indies in 1829.

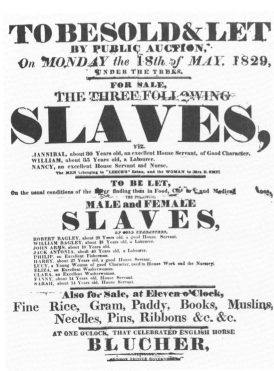

TO BE SOLD & LET
BY PUBLIC AUCTION,
On MONDAY the 18th of MAY, 1829,
UNDER THE TREES.

FOR SALE,
THE THREE FOLLOWING
SLAVES,
VIZ.
HANNIBAL, about 30 Years old, an excellent House Servant, of Good Character.
WILLIAM, about 35 Years old, a Labourer.
NANCY, an excellent House Servant and Nurse.
The MEN belonging to "LEECH'S" Estate, and the WOMAN to Mrs. D. SMIT

TO BE LET,
On the usual conditions of the Hirer finding them in Food, Clothes and Medical
THE FOLLOWING
MALE and FEMALE
SLAVES,
OF GOOD CHARACTERS.
ROBERT BAGLEY, about 20 Years old, a good House Servant.
WILLIAM BAGLEY, about 18 Years old, a Labourer.
JOHN ARMS, about 18 Years old.
JACK ANTONIA, about 40 Years old, a Labourer.
PHILIP, an Excellent Fisherman.
HARRY, about 27 Years old, a good House Servant.
LUCY, a Young Woman of good Character, used to House Work and the Nursery.
ELIZA, an Excellent Washerwoman.
CLARA, an Excellent Washerwoman.
FANNY, about 14 Years old, House Servant.
SARAH, about 14 Years old, House Servant.

Also for Sale, at Eleven o'Clock,
Fine Rice, Gram, Paddy, Books, Muslins,
Needles, Pins, Ribbons &c. &c.
AT ONE O'CLOCK, THAT CELEBRATED ENGLISH HORSE
BLUCHER,
ADDISON PRINTER GOVERNMENT

▲ The symbol of the campaign in England in the late 18th and early 19th century to abolish slavery.

**Abolition of Slavery**

| | |
|---|---|
| United Kingdom | 1834 |
| French colonies | 1848 |
| United States | 1865 |
| Puerto Rico | 1873 |
| Cuba | 1886 |
| Brazil | 1888 |

▼ **See also**

Africa
Civil War, U.S.
Caribbean
Feudal system
Greece
United Kingdom
Spirituals
United States of America

**BIOGRAPHY**
Douglass, Frederick
Lincoln, Abraham
Stowe, Harriet Beecher
Toussaint L'Ouverture,
　François Dominique
Truth, Sojourner
Tubman, Harriet
Washington, Booker T.

▲ This photograph of slaves was taken in 1862 on a plantation in South Carolina.

soldiers and set up an independent country there in 1804.

### Abolishing slavery

Following the end of the slave trade, efforts increased to ban slavery altogether. The British Parliament passed a law abolishing slavery throughout the empire in 1833. It came into effect the following year, but some slaves in British colonies were not completely free until 1838.

In the U.S. there were few slaves in the northern states by this time, but Americans in the southern states fought for the right to own slaves. In 1863, during the Civil War, President Abraham Lincoln issued a proclamation for the emancipation of slaves. Two years later, after the war ended, the U.S. Congress abolished slavery throughout the nation. ◆

The word "slave" comes from "Slav," because these people were often enslaved, first by German knights in the early Middle Ages and later by Ottoman Turks.

▼ **See also**

Bulgaria
Czech Republic
Poland
Russia and the Russian
　Federation
Slavery
Slovak Republic
Soviet Union
Yugoslavia

# Slavs

Slavs are people who live mainly in Eastern and Central Europe. Russians, Bulgarians, Poles, Czechs, Slovaks and Serbs are all Slavonic people. They speak languages that are similar to one another and have developed from the same root language. The first Slavonic tribes moved into Eastern Europe from Asia about 4,000 years ago. These were tribes of peaceful and hospitable farmers who reared sheep and cattle and worshipped nature gods.

In the 19th century many Slavs wanted to unite together to form one country. This movement was known as Pan-Slavism (meaning "all Slavs"). The movement succeeded only among southern Slavs; in 1918 the country of Yugoslavia was created to include the Serbs and five other nationalities. Czechoslovakia was formed at the same time out of Czech and Slovak lands that had been ruled as part of the Austro-Hungarian Empire. But the differences among the Slavs were stronger than the wish for unity. In 1993 Czechoslovakia split into the Czech Republic and Slovakia. By 1996, after nearly five years of bitter civil war, the countries of Croatia, Slovenia, Macedonia and Bosnia-Herzegovina had broken away from Yugoslavia. ◆

# Sleep

Newborn babies do not have a night/day sleep pattern. They wake up at regular intervals during night and day. They sleep for about 16 hours in all. Adults need to sleep for between 7 and 8 hours a night.

Sleep-walking is quite common in children. It usually happens early in the night, during deep sleep. About one in seven children between the ages of 5 and 12 will sleep-walk at least once.

We do not really understand why we sleep. It may be that the body needs sleep to recover and repair damage, and the mind needs it to absorb the day's events and impressions. We tend to sleep during the night and wake during the day. Some animals are *nocturnal*—they sleep during the day and are active at night.

During sleep, heart and breathing rates slow down and muscles relax. Our senses fade. Sight goes first, then hearing and last touch. Our hearing is selective when we are sleeping. A loud noise may not wake someone, but whispering her own name may; parents will often wake at their baby's cry when other people sleep undisturbed. No one yet understands how our brain selects in this way.

## Stages of sleep

Scientists study sleep by measuring the pattern of electrical currents in the brain. They have found that there are different levels of sleep that alternate through the night. Periods of deep sleep alternate with light sleep, during which we make rapid eye movements (REM). ◆

**▼ See also**
Dreams
Hibernation

# Sloths

Sloths are upside-down animals, hanging by their huge, curved claws from the branches of tropical trees. They can eat, sleep, mate and give birth in this position and very rarely descend to the ground, where they are nearly helpless. There are two groups of sloths; those with two toes on their front feet, and those with three. They look similar, but it is thought that they are not closely related.

Sloths have long coarse hair that is grooved lengthwise. Tiny plants (algae) live in the grooves. They give it a greenish tinge, which acts as a camouflage. Specialized insects feed on these plants. ◆

**▼ See also**
Anteaters
Armadillos
Mammals

The word "sloth" also means laziness and comes from an early English word meaning slow-moving. Sloths are so-called because they move very slowly.

◀ This three-toed sloth and its young will probably move less than 40 m (130 ft) in a day. The young will be carried by its mother for 9 months.

**Distribution**
Tropical forests of Central and South America
**Size**
Head-and-body length about 70 cm (2.3 ft)
**Weight**
Up to 8 kg (18 lbs)
**Number of young**
1
**Lifespan**
12 years in the wild, but at least 31 in captivity
**Subphylum**
Vertebrata
**Class**
Mammalia
**Order**
Edentata
**Number of species**
5

# Slovak Republic

The Slovak Republic, also called Slovakia, is in Central Europe, lying west of the Carpathian Mountains. Part of its southern frontier with Hungary is the River Danube, whose fertile plains produce grains, wine, fruit and tobacco. In its mountains are coal, gas and iron ore, and there is a growing timber and paper industry from its forests. The Slovak language is closely related to Czech. The capital, Bratislava, where Austria, Slovakia and Hungary meet, was once the capital of Hungary. Slovakia's important industries include textiles, oil, chemicals and engineering.

## LOOKING BACK

Slovakia was conquered by the Magyars in the 10th century and was ruled by Hungary until the collapse of the Austro-Hungarian Empire in 1918. Many Slovaks resisted its incorporation into Czechoslovakia, and in 1938 it won the support of Germany. In March 1939 Germany occupied Bohemia and Moravia, while Slovakia was declared an independent state "under German protection." After World War II it was re-incorporated into Czechoslovakia. In 1992 the Slovaks voted to set up a separate republic, which came into being on January 1, 1993. ◆

**Area**
49,035 sq km (18,932 sq mi)
**Capital**
Bratislava
**Population**
5,333,000
**Language**
Slovak
**Religion**
Christian
**Government**
Democratic republic
**Currency**
Koruna = 100 halura
**Major exports**
Minerals, agricultural products

**▼ See also**
Czech Republic

# Slovenia

Slovenia is a small country in Southern Europe with a tiny bit of coastline on the Adriatic Sea. The Alps form the mountainous northern part of the country, which gives way to forested hills in the south and east and a rugged limestone plateau known as the Kras. This beautiful region of waterfalls and underground rivers has some famous cave systems near the town of Postojna. You can visit these caves on an underground electric railway 2 km (1.2 mi) long. The highlight is a cavern known as the Concert Hall. It is the size of 20 tennis courts, and the Italian conductor Arturo Toscanini once held a full orchestral concert there.

Coal, lead, zinc and mercury are all mined in Slovenia. Many of the towns are major centers for iron, steel and other heavy industries, and for textile factories. They lie in the fertile valleys of the rivers Sava and Drava, where grain, sugar beets, fruit and potatoes are grown, and cattle and pigs are kept.

## LOOKING BACK

Slovenia was part of the Austro-Hungarian Empire until 1918. From 1919 Slovenia was part of the Kingdom of Serbs, Croats and Slovenes, which became Yugoslavia in 1929. Slovenia gained its independence from Yugoslavia in 1991. It is now one of the richest ex-Communist countries because of its natural resources and important trade and transport links with other countries in Southern Europe. ◆

**See also**
Austria
Europe
Yugoslavia

**Area**
20,251 sq km (7,817 sq mi)
**Capital**
Ljubljana
**Population**
1,942,000
**Language**
Slovene
**Religion**
Christian
**Government**
Parliamentary republic
**Currency**
1 tolar = 100 paras
**Major exports**
Minerals, agricultural products

# Slugs and snails

▶ A Roman snail and its eggs. Land snails are all hermaphrodites (they have both male and female sex organs), so they all produce eggs.

The great difference between snails and slugs is that in times of danger the snail can pull its soft body into a shell, which is usually coiled. Sea snails usually have heavy shells, which are supported by the water. An exception is sea butterflies, which live in the surface waters of the oceans and have shells as fragile as fine glass. Slugs may have a small shell, or an internal shell, but they cannot pull themselves into it for protection.

In most other ways, snails and slugs are very similar. Both glide along on a large, muscular foot. Slugs and land snails ease their way with slime, which you can see after the animal has passed. Both snails and slugs have simple eyes, which are sometimes on tentacles. They may also have other tentacles that help them to feel and smell. Both slugs and snails have a mouth on the underside of the head. This contains very many tiny teeth. A garden snail may have about 14,000 teeth in its mouth. They are arranged in rows on a ribbon-like tongue, which is called a *radula*. This works like a file, to rasp away at food.

Garden snails and slugs eat mostly decaying plants. This is why you rarely notice the damage they do in the countryside, or in an untidy garden, where there is plenty of waste. It is only when all the dead and dying material has been cleared away that they eat tender seedlings and young leaves.

Some snails and slugs feed on other animals and have fewer, but stronger, teeth on their radulae. The cone shells, which are tropical sea snails, even feed on fish. The snails immobilize the fish with a nerve poison injected by a single tooth, a bit like a hypodermic needle, at the end of the radula. ◆

Unlike land slugs, sea slugs are almost all brightly colored. Many are also strange shapes, with feathery gills on their backs. Almost all of them are carnivores that can attack well-protected creatures such as jellyfish and the Portuguese man-of-war. Sea slugs are able to use the powerful sting cells of their prey in their own defense.

**Distribution**
Most live in the sea, but some live in fresh water and some on land, even in deserts.
**Largest sea snail**
The baler shell, from the Australian Barrier Reef, 60 cm (2 ft) long
**Largest land snail**
Giant land snail, *Achatina fulica*, originally from Africa, now found in many parts of the tropics, up to 30 cm (1 ft) long
**Phylum**
Mollusca
**Class**
Gastropoda
**Number of species**
More than 35,000

**See also**
Invertebrates
Jellyfish
Mollusks
Sex and sexuality

# Smoking

People smoke tobacco either as cigarettes or cigars or in a pipe, and they smoke for a variety of reasons. But there is now clear proof from studies comparing the health of smokers with that of non-smokers that smoking causes ill health and early death.

Tobacco smoke contains tar with chemicals that cause cancers of the lungs, mouth, gullet and bladder. Tar also damages microscopic hairs (cilia) that filter air going into the lungs, and irritates air passages, making them sore and causing bronchitis. It contains nicotine, which raises blood pressure and makes blood vessels contract. This can cause heart disease. Nicotine is also an addictive drug, which makes it hard for people to give up smoking.

## Passive smoking

Tobacco smoke can also harm non-smokers. When people do not smoke themselves but must live or work with people who do, we say they are passive smokers. Passive smokers may suffer higher rates of lung cancer and heart disease than non-smokers who live and work with other non-smokers.

## LOOKING BACK

Native Americans smoked for pleasure but also for ceremonial reasons and in religious rituals. The Aztec king Montezuma used to smoke a pipe of scented tobacco after feasts. The Spaniards introduced tobacco to Europe in the 16th century. The habit spread rapidly. At the time many people believed smoking was good for them. Others thought it was a vice.

At first people in Western Europe smoked tobacco in clay pipes. They did not start smoking cigarettes till after the Crimean War in the mid-19th century, having adopted the idea from the Russians. It was not until the 20th century that it became acceptable for women to smoke in public. ♦

**See also**
Addiction
Drugs
Tobacco

# Smugglers

Smugglers are criminals who avoid paying taxes when moving goods from one country to another. These taxes are called *customs duties*. To avoid paying duties, and to get around the restrictions on the movement of goods, smugglers use all sorts of tricks. Mostly these involve concealing things in unlikely places. Modern smugglers use cases with false bottoms, cars and trucks that contain secret compartments, and even the insides of their own bodies. It is forbidden for individuals to bring drugs or guns into most countries, so these are often smuggled.

In 1993 the European Community (now Union) removed all customs barriers between its member states. All citizens of these states were now able to move goods freely from one Community country to another. The main aim of this change was to encourage trade between the countries of the Community, but it has also helped to reduce the amount of smuggling between them.

## LOOKING BACK

Smuggling was particularly common in England in the 18th century. At that time tea, spirits, spices and silks carried high duties. Coffee and tobacco were also smuggled. In villages close to the English Channel, smuggling was often a major occupation. In the U.S., liquor smuggling was common during Prohibition (1920–1933) when alcohol was officially banned. ♦

**See also**
Drugs
European Union
Prohibition
Taxes
Trade

◄ This illustration, from about 1820, shows a violent clash in England between smugglers and the "excise men" (government agents) sent to catch them.

# Snakes

▲ A green python, native to northeast Australia and New Guinea.

**Distribution**
In all habitats, including the sea, in warm parts of the world
**Largest**
Anaconda, may grow up to 10 m (33 ft) in length
**Smallest**
Thread snake, less than 12 cm (5 in) in length
**Most poisonous**
Australian tiger snakes, taipans and kraits
**Fastest-moving**
The black mamba is thought to be able to travel at 16–19 kmph (10–12 mph) in short bursts over level ground.
**Lifespan**
An Indian python survived for over 34 years in a zoo. Lifespan in the wild is unknown.
**Subphylum**
Vertebrata
**Class**
Reptilia
**Order**
Squamata
**Number of species**
Over 2,000

▼ **See also**
Reptiles
Venom

Snakes are reptiles that have no legs. Scientists think that their ancient ancestors were four-legged creatures that began living underground, where a long thin body with very small legs was more useful than one with strong legs for running. This theory is based on the fact that many burrowing lizards have tiny legs, or often none at all. A number of snakes are still burrowers, but most live on the surface of the ground and some even climb into trees, or spend their lives swimming in the sea. There are few snakes on islands.

Most snakes move by throwing their bodies into curves that push against any unevenness of the ground. Such snakes are helpless on smooth surfaces. Snakes are so long and thin that their bodies are not wide enough for all the internal organs that other vertebrates have, so snakes have only one very long lung, instead of the usual two.

In cool parts of the world snakes hibernate during winter. In spring they look for mates. Males often compete with each other or put on displays for females. After mating, most female snakes lay eggs, although some give birth to live young.

Snakes are not slimy creatures. Their skin is dry and scaly. Every now and then, the outer part of the skin is molted, or shed. Unlike us, and most other creatures, snakes shed their skin whole. Starting at the head, the snake wriggles out of its old skin, which is often turned inside out, like a rubber glove when it is pulled off.

All snakes are flesh-eaters. They track their prey using their long, forked tongues, which flicker over the ground, covering a wider area than a single-pointed tongue could do. The tongue picks up tiny traces of scent left by animals such as mice. Some snakes, like grass snakes, catch their food by grabbing and swallowing it. Others, like pythons, which are called constrictors, loop their powerful bodies around their prey and suffocate it.

## Poisonous snakes

About one-third of all kinds of snakes use poison. This usually affects the nervous system and paralyzes the prey. It also helps to break down the food, so poisonous snakes digest their meals much more quickly than non-poisonous snakes. The poison glands are at the back of the upper jaw. In most cases the poison is carried by a duct to hollow or grooved teeth called fangs, which are in the front of the jaws.

▶ Back-fanged snakes, like the boomslang, have small fangs toward the back of the mouth.

hinged fang

poison gland

▶ Vipers are front-fanged snakes. They have long hollow fangs at the front of the mouth that fold back when not in use.

In the vipers and their relatives, the poison is injected into the prey, for the fangs are like hypodermic syringes. Each fang is on a movable bone, which enables it to be folded away; otherwise the snake could not close its mouth.

Snakes' teeth are like needles, so they cannot cut or chew their food. Instead, they swallow it whole. A snake that has just eaten a large meal will have a distinct bulge in its body. To take such a mouthful they must unhinge their lower jaws, at the center and the sides. They can move each part of the jaw independently and so "walk" their prey into their throats.

Snakes also use their poison to defend themselves, and can injure and sometimes kill large animals, including humans. Many people fear and dislike snakes, killing them whenever possible. This is usually unnecessary: most snakes are shy creatures that try to avoid humans. ◆

# Snow

Have you ever caught a snowflake on a woolen glove and looked at it through a magnifying lens? You would have seen that the flake is made up of tiny ice crystals stuck together. Each crystal has a beautiful shape that is hexagonal and symmetrical.

A thick layer of snow does not allow heat to escape from the ground beneath it. It works like a blanket to save plants and animals from the damage caused by freezing temperatures.

Snow is often a source of water, especially in hot, dry countries. Deep layers of snow on high mountains form a reservoir of water. These snows do not melt until warmer weather comes. Rivers like the Nile in Africa, and the Indus in India, would dry up in hot weather without supplies of melting snow. ♦

▲ There are thousands of different shapes of snow crystals, but each of them has six points.

Ice is transparent, yet snow looks white. This is because the ice crystals in snow reflect daylight in all directions. Daylight is white, so the snow appears white.

# Soap

All types of washing soap are made by adding plant oil or animal fat to a strong alkali at a high temperature and pressure. (An alkali is a dissolvable substance made from plant ashes.) Soap and a substance known as glycerol or glycerine are produced. The glycerine is removed and then the molten soap is poured into mixing machines. Perfumes, preservatives and whiteners or colorings are added to it. The molten soap is cooled and cut or molded to size.

## Soap flakes and soap powder

Soap flakes are made by spreading molten soap over water-cooled drums. This makes ribbons of soap, which are rolled thinner and then broken into flakes. Soap powders are made by adding substances known as silicates and phosphates to soap. The mixture is then heated and sprayed into the top of a tower. As the droplets fall, they turn into a powder.

## The disadvantages of soaps

Soaps have a number of disadvantages. They do not work in even slightly acid water and, more important, they do not work well in "hard" water—water that contains lots of calcium and magnesium salts that dissolve from rocks in the ground. The soap reacts with the calcium and magnesium salts to form a "scum." This leaves rings on baths or a whitish film on glassware. Synthetic detergents have neither of these disadvantages, which is why they have replaced soaps for many cleaning purposes. ♦

Rather surprisingly, water is not very good at wetting things. This is because water often behaves as if it had a skin on it. It runs off a greasy surface or stays there in blobs and droplets. Only when soap or a synthetic detergent is added to water can it spread out and clean things by breaking up grease.

Soap was probably first made by Egyptians in the Nile Valley several thousand years ago.

▶ A magazine advertisement from the 1950s for Ivory soap.

You can have That Ivory Look in just 7 days

Very young beauties have it—so can you! Yes, the *milder* your soap, the more your skin will look like hers. A simple change to regular care with her pure, mild Ivory leaves your skin deliciously *clean*, so soft and healthy-looking. That Ivory Look becomes you, too!

Wash your face with pure, mild Ivory ... mild enough for baby's skin an

# Soccer

**F**IFA is the abbreviation of the French title Fédération Internationale de Football Association (the international federation of association football), the organization that regulates professional soccer.

**S**occer is a popular children's game in the U.S. for both boys and girls. Many of them play in competitions organized by the United States Youth Soccer Association. This organization is part of U.S. Soccer, a national group that oversees adult soccer competitions in the United States.

Soccer, which is known as "football" outside the U.S., is the most popular game in the world, and also one of the simplest. A full-sized game has two teams of 11 players, two goals, and a full-sized ball.

## Rules and how to play

A professional soccer match lasts for 90 minutes, played in two halves. In some competitions, two 15-minute periods of extra time are played if the scores are level after 90 minutes. If there is still no result, there may be a "penalty shoot-out," in which five players from each side take it in turn against the opposition goalkeeper. Teams are usually allowed to bring on up to three new players, or substitutes, during the match.

Players may use any part of their body, except hands and arms, to play the ball. Only the goalkeepers are allowed to handle the ball, as long as they are in their own penalty area and the ball is not deliberately passed back to them by a teammate (a headed pass is allowed).

The object of the game is to score goals by kicking or heading the ball into the opponents'

goal. Players move up the field by passing or running with the ball (dribbling). A certain amount of physical contact is allowed, but tackling must be directed at the ball. Fouls include tripping, kicking, pushing and holding an opponent.

## Controlling the game

A referee has full control of the game, helped by two assistant referees ("linesmen"), who patrol the two touchlines. A fourth official serves as an off-field assistant, helping, for instance, when substitutions are made. This official may also report to appropriate authorities any incidents missed by the referee during the match. The referee may caution, or "book," a player for certain offenses (displaying a yellow card), and send players off for the rest of the game (red card) for more serious offenses or for a second bookable offense.

## The World Cup

The World Cup is the most important international competition in soccer. It takes place every four years. Over 170 countries enter the regional qualifying rounds, with 32 going on to the finals in a particular host country.

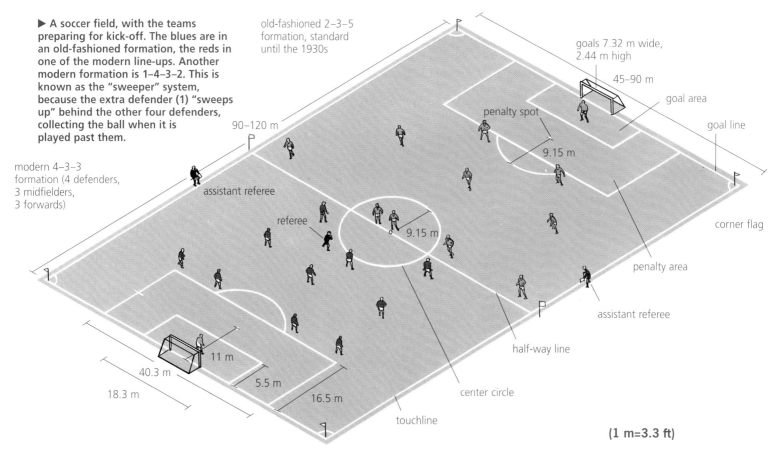

▶ A soccer field, with the teams preparing for kick-off. The blues are in an old-fashioned formation, the reds in one of the modern line-ups. Another modern formation is 1–4–3–2. This is known as the "sweeper" system, because the extra defender (1) "sweeps up" behind the other four defenders, collecting the ball when it is played past them.

modern 4–3–3 formation (4 defenders, 3 midfielders, 3 forwards)

old-fashioned 2–3–5 formation, standard until the 1930s

goals 7.32 m wide, 2.44 m high

45–90 m

goal area

penalty spot

goal line

9.15 m

90–120 m

assistant referee

referee

9.15 m

corner flag

penalty area

assistant referee

11 m

40.3 m

18.3 m

5.5 m

16.5 m

half-way line

center circle

touchline

**(1 m=3.3 ft)**

The competition has been dominated by European and South American countries, but African and Asian teams are growing stronger and have made great progress in recent tournaments. In the 1994 finals in the U.S., Brazil won a record fourth title.

The first Women's World Cup was held in China in 1991 and was won by the U.S.

## Other major competitions

Other major international tournaments are the European Cup-Winner's Cup and the South American Libertadores de América Cup. Famous club competitions include the European Champions' Cup (for the champion clubs of each country) and the English Football League and FA (Football Association) Cup, which were the first ever competitions of this kind, starting in the late 19th century.

Over 500 clubs enter the FA Cup. It is an elimination competition, with the first preliminary-round games taking place in August and the top League clubs entering the competition in January. The final, which is televised to countries all over the world, is played at Wembley, in London, in May.

## Great players and teams

The story of soccer is the story of great players, great teams and great games. Many experts believe that the greatest soccer player of all was Pelé, who played for Brazil, possibly the greatest

▲ The Brazilian team celebrate their record fourth World Cup title, in 1994, following victory over Italy in a dramatic penalty shoot-out.

team of all, in three successful World Cups. He scored more than 1,000 goals for his club (Santos) and country, and starred in the 1958 World Cup final as a 17-year-old. He appeared again in 1962 and then in 1970, having missed the 1968 final through injury.

Another outstanding player was Alfredo di Stefano. He played for Argentina, Spain and Real Madrid (perhaps the finest club side of all time), helping them to win five consecutive European Cups (1956–1960) and scoring a record 49 goals in the competition.

## Fans

Soccer is the most popular spectator sport in the world. Many people also follow the game on television and in the newspapers.

Fans have occasionally been involved in major tragedies. For instance, in 1985 over 40 people were killed in a riot at the Heysel Stadium, Brussels, at a European Cup final.

### LOOKING BACK

A game similar to soccer was recorded in China 2,500 years ago, and there are references to the game throughout the Middle Ages in Europe. The modern game as we know it began in boys' schools in England in the 19th century. The game grew in popularity and spread to other countries, where it was played by both professional and college teams. In 1904 FIFA, the international organizing body, was set up. The first World Cup was held in 1930. ◆

The 1950 World Cup was the only one that did not have a final. The top placings were decided by a final pool of four countries. In the very last match Uruguay surprisingly beat Brazil 2–1.

In order to avoid replays, some competitions are decided by penalties after extra time has been played. Each side has five penalties, taken alternately by different players against the other team's goalkeeper. If the scores are equal after five penalties each, they keep having one each until a winner emerges.

▼ **See also**
Football
Sports

◀ Michelle Akers of the U.S. in action against Norway in the semi-finals of the 1995 Women's World Cup.

The United States has several political parties based on socialist principles. The biggest is the Socialist Party, founded in the 19th century. One of its early leaders was social activist Eugene V. Debs, who was its U.S. presidential candidate several times in the early 20th century. He was succeeded by Norman Thomas, who ran for President on the Socialist Party ticket in every election from 1928 through 1948.

▼ **See also**
Communism
Economics
Utopias

**BIOGRAPHY**
Marx, Karl

# Socialism

The word "socialism" refers to various economic and political theories that oppose the ownership of private property. Under socialism, property is either owned in common by everyone, or it is owned by the government. Communism is based on the principles of socialism, but most people who call themselves socialists are strongly opposed to modern Communism because of its totalitarian nature.

A number of countries in the world have socialist political parties, including the U.S. In addition to supporting government ownership of property, socialists believe that social welfare services such as medical care should be provided free of charge by the government to everyone and that everyone should have a guaranteed income.

No country today has an entirely socialist government, although socialist parties have been in power in nations in Asia, the Middle East and Africa in the past. However, many nations have adopted social welfare programs supported by socialists, such as free medical care and child daycare.

**LOOKING BACK**
Socialism developed in Europe in the early 19th century, in response to the often terrible social conditions created by the Industrial Revolution. One of the century's leading socialists was Karl Marx, the founder of Communism with his associate Friedrich Engels. ◆

# Social workers

Social workers are people who are specially trained to help those who for some reason are not coping well with the problems of everyday life.

Most social workers are employed by local governments or charitable organizations. Some work with families who find it difficult to care for their children on their own. Occasionally, children may have to be taken into foster care, but most social workers prefer to keep families together whenever they can. Other social workers work with schools, ensuring that children attend regularly and dealing with any educational problems that might arise. There are also social workers who specialize in helping people with specific disabilities, such as blindness or deafness. Others organize services for elderly people so that they can continue to live in their own homes. These services might include home aids who assist with the household chores, and centers where people can meet each other and maintain a social life.

Voluntary workers still play an important part in social work. For instance, many "meals-on-wheels" services, which deliver meals to elderly and housebound people, rely on volunteer drivers to help with the distribution of meals. Hospitals, too, use volunteers to provide additional services for their patients. In many cases the work of these volunteers is organized by trained social workers.

The money for social work comes from taxes when social workers are employed by the state. However, private charities have to rely on donations from the general public. Social workers usually have a college degree, and some have a graduate degree known as an MSW (master of social work). ◆

# Softball

▼ **See also**
Baseball
Games

Softball is a ballgame that resembles baseball, but it is played on a smaller field and uses a larger ball. In softball, the ball must be pitched underhand rather than overhand, and from 43 ft (13 m), as compared with 60.5 ft (18 m) in baseball.

Softball was invented in Chicago by George Hancock, who developed it as an indoor game in 1887. A few years later it was adapted to outdoor play. At various times the game was called indoor baseball, playground ball, mush ball, kitten ball, and even ladies' baseball, since it was played by women as well as men.

There are two types of softball: slow-pitch and fast-pitch. In slow-pitch the ball must be pitched slowly enough so that it arches on the way to the batter. In fast-pitch the ball can be pitched at speeds up to 100 mph (62 kmph). Most of the softball played in the U.S. is slow-pitch.

The Amateur Softball Association was founded in 1933 to govern and promote the game in the U.S. The set of rules it established is now accepted in most parts of the world. The International Softball Federation, founded in 1952, governs international play and sponsors regional, national and world championships. Today it has more than 70 member countries. ◆

# Soil

Soil is a combination of rock particles and decayed plant and animal matter. It is formed when rocks are slowly broken down by weathering (the actions of wind, rain and other weather changes). Plants take root among the rock particles. The roots help to bind the particles together, and protect them from rain and wind. When the plants die, they decay and produce a dark sticky substance called *humus*. The humus sticks the rock particles together and absorbs water.

## The soil environment

Soil is made up of a mixture of rock particles of various sizes, with air spaces between them. The particles are coated with humus and a thin film of water. The larger the soil particles, the bigger the air spaces between them and the faster water drains out of the soil.

The air in the soil is important for plants because their roots need oxygen to breathe. The humus supplies minerals to the plants as it decays. In some parts of the world wind-blown dust accumulates to form a soil called *loess*. In parts of China the loess is as much as 300 m (1,000 ft) thick.

## Soil animals

Millions of animals live in the soil. One square yard of fertile soil contains over a billion animals. Many of them are too tiny to see with the naked eye. Fungi and bacteria break down plant and animal remains, releasing minerals that are then absorbed by plant roots. These tiny living things, or micro-organisms, also affect the way that soil looks and feels, how wet or dry it is, and the amount of water in it. Earthworms tunnel through the soil, letting air in, helping water to drain through, and mixing the different layers. Earthworms can move thousands of pounds of soil each year. Ants, beetles, centipedes, millipedes and spiders hunt in the soil, and larger animals like foxes, rabbits and mice make their burrows there.

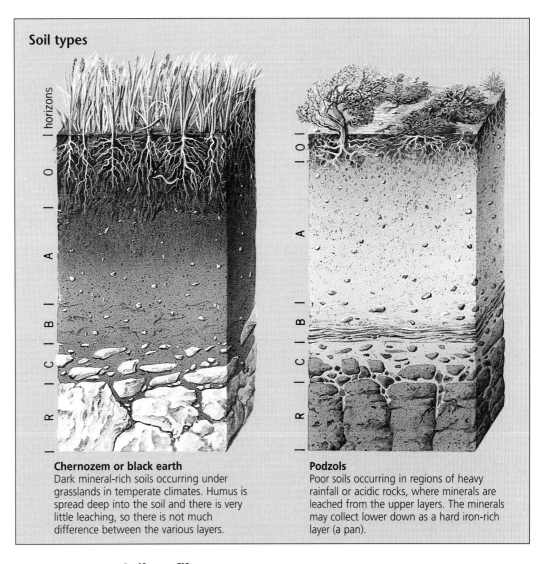

**Soil types**

**Chernozem or black earth**
Dark mineral-rich soils occurring under grasslands in temperate climates. Humus is spread deep into the soil and there is very little leaching, so there is not much difference between the various layers.

**Podzols**
Poor soils occurring in regions of heavy rainfall or acidic rocks, where minerals are leached from the upper layers. The minerals may collect lower down as a hard iron-rich layer (a pan).

## Soil profiles

Different kinds of parent (original) rock and different climates produce different kinds of soils. You can see this by looking at soil profiles. A soil profile is a sample taken from the surface down through the soil. Each profile is divided into a series of layers called *horizons*.

*O horizon*, the surface layer, contains many plant roots and soil animals. It is rich in dark-colored humus.

*A horizon* still has a lot of humus, but is a paler, grayish color because many of the minerals have been washed out by rainwater. This process is called *leaching*.

*B horizon* contains much less humus, but has some of the minerals washed out of the A horizon. Any iron left here may oxidize, producing a yellow or reddish-brown color.

*C horizon* is where weathering is taking place, and the parent rock is being broken down.

*R horizon* is the parent rock. ◆

▼ **See also**
Earthworms
Erosion
Grasslands

# Solar power

Light and heat from the Sun pour down on the Earth all the time. When we turn this energy into electricity or use it as heat, we call it solar power. On a sunny day, a square patch of Earth facing the Sun with sides a yard long gets up to 1,000 watts of power from the Sun. The Sun could supply all the power we need for the whole world if we could collect it and use it efficiently. The equipment needed to turn the Sun's energy into useful power is expensive but the costs of running and maintaining that equipment are less than those of ordinary power stations.

## Electricity from sunlight

Electricity is probably the most convenient type of power we use every day, and solar cells can turn sunlight directly into electricity. Solar cells are made from thin slices of pure silicon, a material that can be extracted from sand. The top of the slice is a slightly different kind of silicon from the bottom, and when light shines on it, an electric current will flow along a wire connecting the top to the bottom. A single solar cell produces only a tiny current, but an array of cells connected together makes a useful amount of power.

Solar cells are expensive to make, so we use them only where there is no convenient electricity supply. Satellites in space have huge panels of solar cells to supply their electricity. In remote parts of some developing countries, solar cells provide electricity to pump water for drinking and growing crops and to power refrigerators storing medicines.

## Using the Sun's heat

If you have ever been in a greenhouse, you will know that the Sun's energy can be trapped as heat. Solar panels on the roofs of buildings can also trap this heat, providing us with hot water. In the solar panel, under a sheet of glass, are pipes fixed to a black plate. The Sun heats up a liquid in the pipes, and this liquid heats up a tank of water.

Huge solar furnaces use the Sun's heat to make electricity. A field of mirrors collects sunlight and concentrates it onto a furnace, where the heat boils water to make steam. This drives a turbine making electricity in the same way as an ordinary power station. While the Sun is shining, any extra hot water or electricity is stored to be used at night when the Sun's energy is not available.

## LOOKING BACK

Energy from the Sun has always been important to people. Over 2,000 years ago the Greeks and Romans were building their houses to face the Sun. In 1714 Antoine Lavoisier, a French scientist, made a solar furnace that could melt metals.

The first steam engine to work on solar power ran a printing press in Paris in 1880. By 1900 many houses in the hotter parts of the U.S. had solar water heaters. All these inventions used the heat from the Sun. It was not until 1954 that the first practical solar cells, capable of turning sunlight directly into electricity, were produced. ◆

▼ A solar power system used to heat water for a house. The solar panel in the roof collects heat from the Sun.

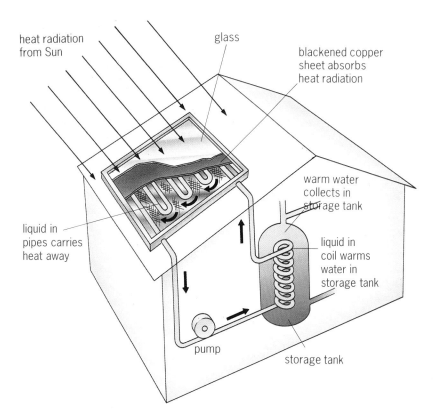

heat radiation from Sun

glass

blackened copper sheet absorbs heat radiation

warm water collects in storage tank

liquid in coil warms water in storage tank

liquid in pipes carries heat away

pump

storage tank

▶ Solar thermal power stations have large dish-shaped mirrors. This one is in the Pyrenees. These so-called heliostats reflect the Sun's rays onto a large parabolic reflector, which then reflects all the light it receives onto a special collector. Temperatures of up to 3,000 °C (5,432°F) can be reached, generating 1 megawatt (1 million watts) of power.

# Solar System

A family of planets travels around our Sun. Many of these planets have moons, and lots of other smaller objects such as asteroids (minor planets), comets and smaller particles called meteoroids. The Sun and all the things in orbit around it make up the Solar System.

The largest bodies in the Solar System, apart from the Sun, are the nine planets: Mercury, Venus, Earth, Mars, Jupiter, Saturn, Uranus, Neptune and Pluto. Seven of them have moons, and more than 60 moons are known altogether. The diameter of Jupiter, the largest planet, is about one-tenth of the Sun's diameter. The Sun could contain a thousand bodies the size of Jupiter.

Most of the known asteroids are small rocky bodies that travel around the Sun between the orbits of Mars and Jupiter. Astronomers have recently discovered a number of icy asteroids beyond the orbits of Neptune and Pluto. These objects are probably part of a huge ring of icy bodies called the Kuiper Belt.

A comet is a lump of ice, dust and rock that travels around the Sun, usually in a very stretched-out orbit. Each time it comes near to the Sun, some of its ice turns to gas and forms a tail. Some of the comets come from the Kuiper Belt. Astronomers think that others come from a huge cloud of icy bodies, called the Oort cloud, which surrounds the Solar System and stretches out to a distance of about one light-year (9.5 trillion km/5.8 trillion mi).

## Birth of the Solar System

Most astronomers believe that the Solar System was formed when a huge cloud of gas and dust fell together, pulled by its own gravity, just under 5 billion years ago. The cloud was spinning very slowly at first, but as it fell inward, it began to spin faster and faster until it formed a central ball surrounded by a flattened sheet of gas and dust. As it continued to fall together, the central ball became hotter. Eventually it became hot enough to shine like a star and became our Sun.

In the surrounding sheet of gas and dust, tiny particles of dust collided and stuck together to form small rocky or icy bodies. These then collided with each other to form complete planets like the Earth, and the cores (central parts) of the four giant planets (Jupiter, Saturn, Uranus and Neptune). Huge amounts of gas fell in to surround the core of each of the giant planets. Many of the remaining lumps of material collided with the newly formed planets and moons and blasted out craters on their surfaces. The lumps that were left over are the asteroids and comets that we see today.

## The paths of the planets

The orbits of the planets round the Sun are not circles but have a squashed oval shape called an ellipse. A planet's distance from the Sun changes as it moves along its elliptical orbit. Most of the planets vary only slightly in distance, but Pluto's distance varies from about 30 to about 50 times the Earth's distance.

The word "solar" means "related to the Sun." It comes from *sol*, the Latin word for Sun.

▼ The sizes of the major planets compared with the Sun and a plan of their orbits around the Sun. Mercury, Venus, Earth and Mars are small rocky planets that together make up the inner Solar System. Jupiter, Saturn, Uranus and Neptune are giant planets made mainly of gas. Pluto is a tiny planet made of rock and ice. All of the planets except Pluto have been visited or passed by spacecraft carrying cameras and scientific equipment.

The distance of each planet from the Sun, and the time it takes to orbit the Sun, are listed below. (1 km=0.62 mi)

| Planet | Million km | Days |
|---|---|---|
| Mercury | 58 | 88 |
| Venus | 108 | 224.7 |
| Earth | 150 | 365.3 |
| Mars | 228 | 687.0 |

| Planet | Million km | Years |
|---|---|---|
| Jupiter | 778 | 11.86 |
| Saturn | 1,427 | 29.46 |
| Uranus | 2,870 | 84.01 |
| Neptune | 4,497 | 164.8 |
| Pluto | 5,900 | 247.7 |

Although Pluto is farther away than Neptune most of the time, a small part of its orbit crosses just inside Neptune's.

Apart from Pluto's, none of the planetary orbits is tilted by much, so the Solar System is like a flat disk. Pluto's orbit is tilted by 17° so that when it crosses Neptune's orbit it passes above Neptune, and there is no danger of a collision. The way gravity acts means that the farther a planet is from the Sun, the longer the period of time it takes to complete an orbit. The Earth takes one year, Mercury 88 days and Pluto nearly 248 years. The spaces between the planets are huge compared to their sizes. If the Sun were the size of a football, the Earth would be the size of this spot ● and would be 30 m (about 100 ft) away. ◆

### Make a Solar System Model

The Solar System is bigger than you think. Find out for yourself by making this scale model. First, collect 10 Popsicle sticks (wide ones) or pointed garden markers. Then go to a park or playground with your friends, or to a very large backyard.

Near the end of one stick, draw a circle 9 millimeters (0.35 in) across. This is the Sun. Draw a planet on each of the other sticks. Jupiter is a tiny circle 1 millimeter across. Saturn is a little smaller. The other planets are tiny dots like this: . . . . . . .

Place the stick with the Sun on it upright in the ground. Then place the planets at these distances from the Sun:

| | |
|---|---|
| Mercury 20 cm (8 in) | Saturn 6 m (20 ft) |
| Venus 46 cm (18 in) | Uranus 12 m (40 ft) |
| Earth 60 cm (2 ft) | Neptune 18 m (60 ft) |
| Mars 90 cm (3 ft) | Pluto 24 m (80 ft) |
| Jupiter 3 m (10 ft) | |

**See also**
Asteroids
Astronomers
Comets
Gravity
Meteors and meteorites
Moon
Planets
Sun

# Somalia

Somalia is a big country. It dominates what is called the Horn of Africa, the northeastern tip of the continent. Somalia has coastlines facing both north to Arabia and east to the Indian Ocean. The weather is hot and dry for most of the year, and the land is largely desert or semi-desert. Most of the population, who are extremely poor, work on the land, either growing fruit along the coast and in the fertile valleys, or living as nomads, grazing animals farther inland.

Over the centuries, trading with Arabian and Indian ports has been part of the way of life. The country's main port is at Mogadishu, with a second one at Berbera. Somalia was a federation of two distinct areas—British Somaliland in the north and the Italian colony of Somalia to the south. The federation was never strong, and by 1990 its Communist government had lost control. The federation broke up and southern Somalia dissolved into civil war. A large UN force was unable to end the fighting. ◆

**Area**
637,660 sq km (246,201 sq mi)
**Capital**
Mogadishu
**Population**
9,077,000
**Language**
Somali, Arabic, English, Italian
**Religion**
Muslim
**Government**
Republic
**Currency**
1 Somali shilling = 100 cents

▲ Once nomadic, the people in this picture have settled down as farmers. They are threshing the rice they have managed to grow on this barren land.

**See also**
Africa
Arabs
Islam

# Sound

Everything that can be heard is a sound. The sounds that we hear are made when something makes the air vibrate (shake backward and forward very quickly). Twang a rubber band and you can see it vibrating and hear a sound. Place a finger on the band to stop the vibrations and there is nothing to hear. When the rubber band is plucked, its vibrations make the air next to it vibrate. Then the air next to that is forced backward and forward, and so the sound moves outward away from the band. When the vibrating air reaches your ear, it makes the eardrum move in and out, and you hear a sound.

## Making sounds

Anything that vibrates makes a sound. A bee's wing moves backward and forward very quickly and we hear a buzz. Put a hand firmly on your throat and sing "Aaaaah." Sing it low and high. You can feel the vibrations that produce your voice. Speak a few words with the palm of your hand just in front of your mouth and you can feel the air being pushed through your voice box and out of your mouth. You cannot feel all the tiny vibrations in the air. Only your ear is sensitive enough to detect them.

## How sound travels

All sound that we hear has traveled through the air around us. If you took the air out of the room you are in, you would hear nothing. There is no sound out in space where there is no air.

But sound does not travel only through air. Vibrations can travel through water, glass, wood, brick, concrete and other substances. Vibrations move particularly easily and fast through water. Whales and porpoises make sounds that can travel through hundreds of miles of oceans.

Sound can travel through buildings, too. A heavy truck passing outside your home can make the whole building feel as if it is shaking and produce a low rumbling noise. Vibrations from traffic have damaged some old buildings that are close to busy truck routes.

## Loudness of sound

The loudness of a sound is measured in decibels (dB). The closer you are to whatever is producing the sound, the louder it is. If you are close to a very loud sound, like an explosion, your hearing can be damaged. But loud sounds, even if they do not affect your hearing immediately, can produce serious damage if your ear receives them for a long time. Pop groups and their fans often get hearing damage from standing too close to the loudspeakers. Listening with headphones to loud music can also produce deafness.

## Speed of sound

In air, sound travels at a speed of about 332 m (1,088 ft) every second. That is about four times as fast as a racing car but only half the speed of the Concorde jet. Sound travels slightly faster on a hot day than it does on a cold day. Sound travels much faster through solids and through water than it does through air.

### High and low sounds

When a sound is made, the number of vibrations every second is called the *frequency*. Frequency is measured in hertz (Hz): 1 hertz means one vibration every second.

The highest note a human ear can hear has a frequency of about 20,000 vibrations every second (20,000 Hz). This corresponds to a note more than two octaves above the top note on the piano.

The lowest note the ear can hear has a frequency of about 20 vibrations every second (20 Hz). This corresponds to a note even lower than the bottom note of a piano.

## Acoustics

Acoustics is the study of the way sound behaves and is important in a room such as a concert hall. The hard, bare walls of any empty room will bounce sound around and make the room echo. Having materials that absorb sounds on the walls and ceiling will help prevent this echo effect in a small room. Heavy curtains and a thick carpet will also help. But in a large room like a concert hall you need smooth, hard surfaces behind the players or singers to help to send out the sound to the audience, and then materials that will absorb the sound at the back of the hall to prevent echoes. ◆

Ernst Mach (1838–1916) was an Austrian physicist who studied sound. His name is used to describe the ratio of the speed of a jet plane or rocket to the speed of sound. An aircraft moving at the speed of sound (332 m/1,088 ft per second) is said to be flying at Mach 1. When it moves at a *supersonic* speed—a speed faster than sound—its Mach increases accordingly. For example, an aircraft flying at twice the speed of sound would be flying at Mach 2.

◄ When a plane starts to travel faster than sound, it breaks the sound barrier. This creates a loud, explosive noise, called a sonic boom, which is caused by a shock wave set off as the aircraft squashes the air in front of it.

The pitch of a sound (that is, its *frequency*—how high or low it is) coming from any moving object, such as a train or a police car siren, gets higher and higher as it comes toward you and decreases as it moves away from you. This is known as the Doppler effect. This happens because the sound waves in front of a moving object are short and bunched together, producing a high frequency, while waves behind a moving object are stretched out and have a lower frequency.

▶ The city of Cape Town lies at the foot of Table Mountain.

**Area**
1,219,916 sq km
(470,566 sq mi)
**Capital**
Pretoria (administrative)
Cape Town (legislative)
Bloemfontein (judiciary)
**Population**
40,555,000
**Language**
Afrikaans, English,
Ndebele, North Sotho,
South Sotho, Swazi,
Tsonga, Tswana, Venda,
Xhosa, Zulu
**Government**
Parliamentary republic
**Religion**
Christian, Hindu, Muslim
**Currency**
1 rand = 100 cents
**Major exports**
Gold, diamonds,
agricultural products

# South Africa

South Africa is a country at the southern tip of the African continent. Parts of its boundaries are formed by the Limpopo and Orange rivers. At the center is a huge grassy plateau called the highveld. To the northeast of the highveld lies Kruger National Park, where elephants, lions, zebras and other animals roam free. The western parts of the plateau merge into the Kalahari and Namib deserts. The eastern highveld is bounded by the steep slopes of the Drakensberg Mountains. To the south are plains and lower mountain ranges.

South Africa has a pleasant climate, although the nights can be cold on the highveld in winter. The country is the richest in Africa, with huge reserves of gold, diamonds and other valuable minerals that it exports. It also exports maize (corn), fruit, wine and other agricultural products. It has busy, modern cities with skyscrapers.

## LOOKING BACK

The first people in southern Africa thousands of years ago were hunter-gatherers. Their descendants are known as Bushmen (San) and Hottentots (Khoikhoi); together they are known as Khoisan. Today the majority of the population are Bantus. Their ancestors lived in southern Africa at least 1,600 years ago. They hunted, kept cattle and grew crops. They lived mostly in the north and east of the region, which had the best farmland.

In 1652 the Dutch established the first European settlement at the Cape of Good Hope, on Africa's southern tip. They brought in slaves, and inland they forced Khoisan to work for them.

England captured the Cape during the Napoleonic wars in the early 19th century. English-speaking colonists began arriving in the 1820s. A decade later, Dutch farmers in the region, called Boers, traveled north, fighting the Zulus of Natal and founding the republics of the Orange Free State and the Transvaal.

In 1877 England tried unsuccessfully to take over the Transvaal. Later, in the Boer War (1899–1902), the British defeated the Boers and took over their territory. South Africa became a self-governing British Dominion in 1910 and an independent republic in 1961.

By that time, a rigid system of racial segregation had been imposed on South Africa's non-white population, comprising blacks, Asians, and people of mixed races,

called "coloreds." Although non-whites were an overwhelming majority—nearly 90 percent of the population—they were denied the most basic rights: the government controlled where they lived, the schools they could attend, whom they could marry, the sports they could play, and the public facilities they could use.

These restrictions had become even greater in 1948, when *apartheid* ("apartness") laws were passed. Under apartheid, the travel of black South Africans was severely limited, and all Bantu-speaking blacks were forced to live either in rural districts called "homelands" or in overcrowded townships on the edges of cities.

Apartheid was condemned throughout the world, and a political group called the African National Congress (ANC) began an anti-apartheid campaign. Following acts of sabotage organized by the ANC, its leader Nelson Mandela was imprisoned in 1962. Meanwhile, the government secretly stirred up trouble between the ANC and the Zulus.

As the situation grew worse, increasing numbers of nations refused to trade with South Africa. The government relented somewhat by giving seats in parliament to coloreds and Asians, but still denied them to black Africans. The situation began to ease in 1989 after F. W. de Klerk was elected president. In 1990 he released Mandela from prison and began discussions on sharing political power with all South Africans. In 1994, South Africa had its first democratic elections, which ANC candidates won overwhelmingly. Mandela was elected president, and De Klerk became vice president. Apartheid ended, the "homelands" were abolished, and people began learning to live and work together. ◆

# South America

South America, the fourth largest continent, includes the land south of Central America. The phrase "Latin America" includes Central America, too, as well as the Caribbean, but both Central America and the Caribbean are considered part of the North American continent. (Central America and the Caribbean are shown on a map in Volume 2, p. 13.)

South America contains the places that Spanish and Portuguese people began

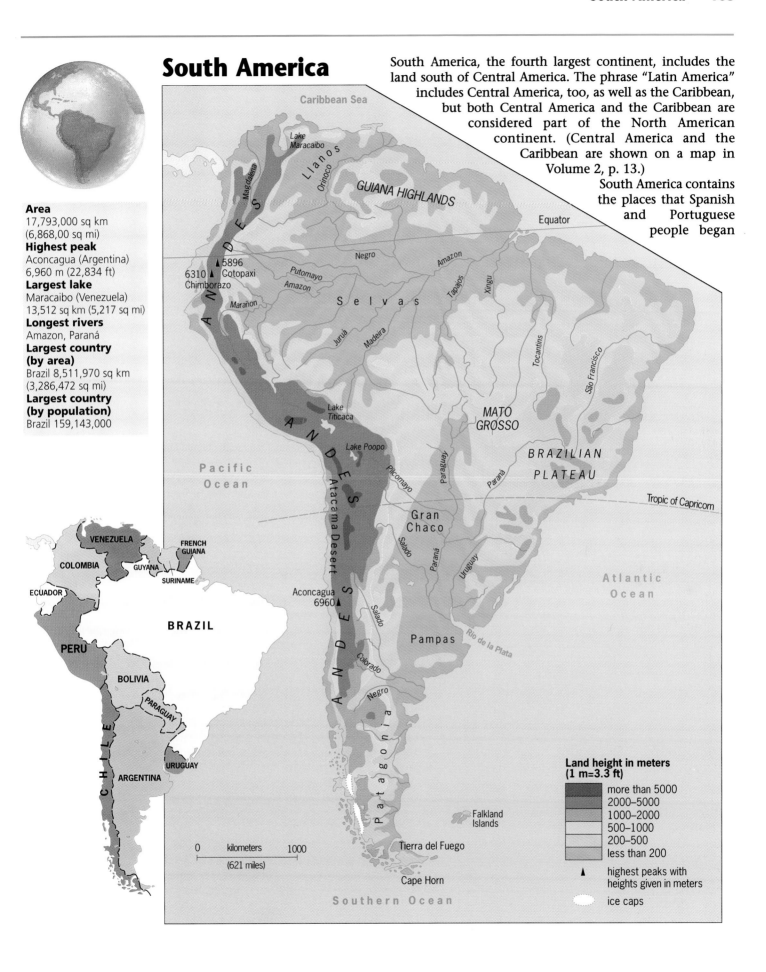

**Area**
17,793,000 sq km
(6,868,00 sq mi)
**Highest peak**
Aconcagua (Argentina)
6,960 m (22,834 ft)
**Largest lake**
Maracaibo (Venezuela)
13,512 sq km (5,217 sq mi)
**Longest rivers**
Amazon, Paraná
**Largest country
(by area)**
Brazil 8,511,970 sq km
(3,286,472 sq mi)
**Largest country
(by population)**
Brazil 159,143,000

Caribbean Sea

Lake Maracaibo

Llanos

Orinoco

Magdalena

GUIANA HIGHLANDS

Equator

ANDES

▲5896
6310▲ Cotopaxi
Chimborazo

Marañon

Negro

Putomayo

Amazon

Amazon

Selvas

Tapajós

Xingu

Tocantins

São Francisco

Juruá

Madeira

ANDES

Lake
Titicaca

Lake Poopo

MATO
GROSSO

BRAZILIAN
PLATEAU

Pacific
Ocean

Pilcomayo

Paraguay

Paraná

Tropic of Capricorn

Atacama Desert

Gran
Chaco

Salado

Paraná

Uruguay

Atlantic
Ocean

Aconcagua
6960▲

Salado

Pampas

Rio de la Plata

ANDES

Colorado

Negro

Patagonia

Falkland
Islands

**Land height in meters
(1 m=3.3 ft)**

| | |
|---|---|
| | more than 5000 |
| | 2000–5000 |
| | 1000–2000 |
| | 500–1000 |
| | 200–500 |
| | less than 200 |
| ▲ | highest peaks with heights given in meters |
| | ice caps |

0  kilometers  1000
(621 miles)

Tierra del Fuego

Cape Horn

Southern Ocean

VENEZUELA

FRENCH
GUIANA

COLOMBIA

GUYANA

SURINAME

ECUADOR

BRAZIL

PERU

BOLIVIA

PARAGUAY

CHILE

URUGUAY

ARGENTINA

exploring and settling in the 16th century. It has been called Latin America because the Spanish and Portuguese languages still spoken there grew out of Latin.

## Landscapes

The Andes are the world's longest mountain range and, after the Himalayas, the second highest. They extend for over 7,100 km (4,400 mi) along the continent's western edge, from the Caribbean Sea in the north to Tierra del Fuego in the south. Snow-capped volcanoes such as Chimborazo and Cotopaxi rise among the mountain peaks. Cotopaxi is still very active. Earthquakes are common in the Andes and have caused much damage in southern Chile.

The western slopes of the Andes are very steep. Between the Andes and the Pacific coast there is an area of desert that stretches for 1,600 km (1,000 mi) from southern Ecuador to northern Chile. The Atacama Desert is the driest place on Earth. Rain has never been recorded in some places.

There are three plateau areas in South America. The Guiana Highlands in the north are rugged, with deep, narrow, forested valleys. They are uninhabited. The Brazilian Plateau in the east is where most Brazilians live. Its western part forms the savannah grasslands of the Mato Grosso. In the south lies the dry plateau of Patagonia.

## The Amazon

The Amazon River, the second longest river in the world, winds through the northern part of South America, from high in the Andes Mountains to the Atlantic Ocean off the coast of Brazil. The Amazon is 6,450 km (4,010 mi) long and contains more than 2,000 different kinds of fish. The lowlands of the Amazon basin are covered with dense rain forest, with a great variety of species of trees, insects, monkeys and parrots. Away from the Amazon the forest becomes more open, changing to wooded grassland (the Gran Chaco) and more fertile grasslands (the pampas) in the Paraná-Paraguay basin farther south, and to the savannah lands (llanos) of the Orinoco basin in the north.

Huge deposits of metals and minerals, including gold, are found in the Amazon region. The area's countries want to exploit these resources and also provide farmland for their growing populations. As a result, a lot of forest is being lost to pasture and farmland, and being submerged beneath dammed lakes. Native Americans and people who make their living from harvesting forest products such as rubber are being pushed aside in this race for development. Scientists are also concerned that much of the region's vast and largely unrecorded diversity of species will be lost.

## Climate

The Amazon and other equatorial regions are hot all year and very wet. In the Brazilian Highlands the climate is much less extreme. Farther south, on the Gran Chaco, there are distinct wet and dry seasons. Cold climates only occur in the extreme south of Argentina and Chile, and high up in the Andes. In northeast Brazil frequent drought has created a landscape of low trees, thorny bushes and cacti, known as caatinga.

## Countries

Brazil is by far the largest country in South America and contains half the population. Bolivia is the "roof" of South America: one-third of Bolivia is over 1.5 km (1 mi) high. Argentina and Uruguay share the estuary of Río de la Plata, a great trading route to and from the continent's interior. South America exports many agricultural and mineral products. Chile is the world's leading producer of copper. Brazil produces the most coffee and is a leading exporter of sugar, cocoa, tin and fruit. Peru exports copper, lead and zinc.

Most South American countries became independent from Spanish or Portuguese rule in the first 30 years of the 19th century.

## People

Brazilians speak Portuguese. Most other South Americans speak Spanish. Many Native American languages are spoken, especially in the northern Andes and the Amazon. Native Americans in the Andes trace their ancestors back to the Inca Empire, a great civilization that existed for centuries before being conquered by Spain in the 16th century. Portuguese people settled in Brazil, and in 1494 a treaty was made, dividing the lands of South America between Spain and Portugal. The Portuguese brought slaves from Africa to work on the plantations. Modern-day Brazilians are descended from Europeans, Africans and Native Americans. Roman Catholicism is the most important religion in South America.

In the last 100 years other Europeans have settled in the continent—for example, Italians in Argentina and Welsh in Patagonia. Japanese have settled on the west coast, especially in Peru. Most South Americans live near the coast and the majority live in cities such as Rio de Janeiro, São Paulo, Buenos Aires and Lima. ◆

South America stretches much farther south than any other continent. The tip of the continent is only about 1,000 km (600 mi) from Antarctica. The far south of South America is therefore cool for much of the year.

Suriname was ruled by the Netherlands until 1975, when it became independent. French Guiana is a department of France. Guyana became independent from Britain in 1966.

**Area**
80,779 sq km
(31,189 sq mi)
**Capital**
Columbia
**Population**
3,673,000
**Entered Union**
1788
**Places to visit**
Charleston: Fort Sumter National
Monument, Charleston Museum,
various gardens; Myrtle Beach; Hilton
Head Island
**Famous South Carolinians**
John C. Calhoun, Jesse Jackson

# South Carolina (U.S.A.)

South Carolina was the first state to leave the Union after Abraham Lincoln's election as President in 1860. It was also the site of the first shots fired in the Civil War. The state is renowned for its beautiful seaport city of Charleston. Off the coast, the Sea Islands, stretching from South Carolina down to northern Florida, were once the site of vast cotton plantations; they are now major wildlife refuges and vacation resorts.

## History

Cherokee and Catawba Indians greeted the first Europeans to explore the region: adventurers from Spain who arrived in the 1520s. In the early 17th century, England claimed the region, and it was included in an enormous parcel of land that King Charles I granted to a friend, Sir Robert Heath. The region was later named Province of Carolina in honor of Charles. (Carolina is a variation of the Latin name for *Charles*.) However, no attempt was made to establish settlements there.

In 1663 King Charles II of England awarded land in Carolina to eight of his friends, who became the managers, or *proprietors*, of a colony established there in 1670. Early settlements were made in what later became the city of Charleston. The colony was divided in the early 18th century, and South Carolina became a

crown colony with its own royal governor.

South Carolina grew and prospered as wealthy settlers created plantations that were worked by indentured servants and slaves, both African and Native American. Smaller plots were farmed by settlers who were given free land to encourage them to migrate. Corn (maize), cotton and tobacco became major crops, and huge rice plantations were created in the southern marshes. South Carolina's lush forests provided timber for building homes and ships. Fur trading with Indians was also a major source of revenue.

By the 1760s, however, South Carolina had grown resentful of England's restrictive trade policies. In March 1776 it declared its independence and chose John Rutledge as its president. Two years later, as the Revolutionary War raged, South Carolina approved the Articles of Confederation, forerunner of the U.S. Constitution. During the war, British forces attacked in various parts of South Carolina; they besieged Charleston in 1780 and held the city for two years.

In the early 19th century, South Carolina senator John C. Calhoun emerged as a leading champion of slavery and states' rights as the national debate grew over that issue. The Civil War began on April 12, 1861, when Confederate artillery opened fire on Union-held Fort Sumter, in the Charleston harbor. Although Union naval forces pounded Charleston during most of the war, the city was able to withstand the bombardment. Most of South Carolina was spared the horrors of war until early 1865, when General William T. Sherman led Union forces through the state, destroying everything in their path.

South Carolina was readmitted to the Union in 1868, but its great plantation system had been ruined. During the following decades, the growth of a textile industry helped improve the state's economy, though progress was complicated by bitter struggles over racial segregation. Since the 1970s, South Carolina has benefited from the general growth of business and population throughout the South.

## Geography

South Carolina's Atlantic coastline features beautiful beaches in the north

▼ An aerial view of the Charleston waterfront, known as the Battery.

### ▼ See also

American Revolution
Civil Rights Movement
Civil War, U.S.
Constitution, U.S.
North Carolina
Thirteen Colonies
United States of America

**BIOGRAPHY**
Calhoun, John C.

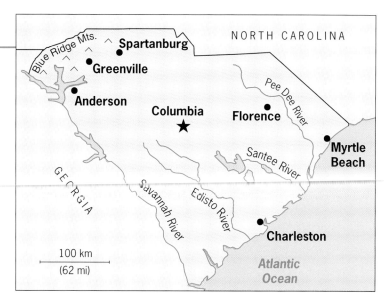

and marshland in the south, where rivers and creeks form networks of inlets and islands. The humid, subtropical climate on the coast provides long, hot summers and brief, mild winters. The coast is also subject to violent storms, including highly destructive hurricanes.

The state's inland climate is temperate and grows progressively cooler as the altitude increases. The coastal plain gives way to rolling upland terrain, and the land continues to rise toward the Blue Ridge Mountains in the northwest.

Several large rivers—the Savannah, Edisto, Santee and Pee Dee—flow southeastward to the ocean, creating many rapids and waterfalls. Many dams have been built along these rivers to provide the state with hydroelectric power, one of South Carolina's most important resources. This water power fuels many new industries that have transformed the state's economy from agriculture to manufacturing.

### What people do

Today South Carolina's main products are chemicals, machinery, wood, pulp, asbestos, steel products and textiles. Farms have decreased in number but increased in size; they grow tobacco, corn, peaches, oats, peanuts, cotton, sweet potatoes and soybeans. Dairy products and poultry are also important sources of income.

Charleston is a major tourist attraction, with many restored homes dating from before the Civil War. The Charleston Museum, founded in 1773, is among the nation's oldest. Nearby is the Fort Sumter National Monument, commemorating the opening battle of the Civil War. South Carolina is noted for its beautiful flower and shrubbery gardens, many of them in the Charleston area; Middletown Place Gardens, first planted in the mid-18th century, are the oldest landscaped gardens in the U.S. Myrtle Beach and Hilton Head Island are beach resort areas that attract many vacationers throughout the year. ◆

# South Dakota (U.S.A.)

South Dakota is famous as the site of Mount Rushmore, which includes one of the largest sculptures in the world. The state is also the home of the Black Hills, a mountainous area sacred to the Sioux and the scene of a famous gold rush in the 1870s. Two noted Native Americans came from the region: Crazy Horse and Sitting Bull.

### History

Many Plains Indians once roamed what are now the states of North and South Dakota, but it is the Sioux who gave the Dakotas their name: these Native Americans were also known as the Lakota or Dakota.

French explorers in the mid-18th century were the first Europeans to visit the Dakota region, which became part of France's large holdings in the New World. Half a century later, when it became a U.S. possession as part of the Louisiana Purchase, Lewis and Clark passed through it as they traveled on their famous expedition up the Missouri River, en route to Oregon. The first permanent settlement in what is now South Dakota was Fort Pierre, a U.S. Army post established in 1817. (It is now the city of Pierre, the state capital.)

In 1861, Congress created Dakota Territory, which then also included parts of what later became Montana and Wyoming. Settlement was slow, however, until a railroad line was completed in the early 1870s. Soon many European immigrants came surging in to farm the land. The discovery of gold in the Black Hills in 1875 drew hordes of prospectors.

The Sioux were not pleased to find so many newcomers invading their lands, and, led by Crazy Horse and Sitting Bull,

**Area**
199,744 sq km
(77,121 sq mi)
**Capital** Pierre
**Population** 729,000
**Entered Union** 1889
**Places to visit**
Deadwood and the Black Hills; Mount Rushmore; Badlands
**Famous South Dakotans**
Crazy Horse, Sitting Bull

they resisted settlement. The force of U.S. troops proved too powerful, however, and the Sioux were finally put down permanently at the Battle of Wounded Knee in 1890, in what was now South Dakota: the year before, Congress had divided the territory into two states, North and South.

The population grew quickly in the following decades and had reached more than half a million by the early 20th century. The state's farming economy was hit hard during the

1930s by the Great Depression, drought and dust storms, and locust plagues that devoured the few crops that were grown. Farmers recovered during the 1940s, but by mid-century much of the farmwork was being done by machine. As a result, many young people left to seek jobs elsewhere, and the state began attracting industry to boost the economy and maintain its population.

## Geography

The Missouri River cuts a wide path as it flows southward through South Dakota; smaller rivers flow into the Missouri throughout the state. South Dakota has distinct geographical regions: in the east are prairies, while the Great Plains cover much of the rest of the state. The plains include an area known as the Badlands, a hilly region with deep gullies where wind and water have created unusual rock formations. West of the Badlands are the Black Hills, a picturesque region of low mountains and canyons.

The Black Hills contain the state's leading mineral resource, gold. Other resources include petroleum, coal, granite, limestone, sand and gravel. The state has

hot and very dry summers, followed by cold winters with massive snowfalls.

## What people do

South Dakota is an agricultural state, and its farms raise wheat, corn, hogs and cattle. Many South Dakotans also work in mining. Service industries such as insurance, finance and real estate have become of major importance in the state's economy, and the city of Sioux Falls is a major financial center.

The most famous tourist attraction in the state is Mount Rushmore, located in the Black Hills, where the faces of Presidents George Washington, Thomas Jefferson, Theodore Roosevelt and Abraham Lincoln are carved on the mountainside. On a nearby mountain, visitors can see an even more massive sculpture, an image of Crazy Horse, in the process of being carved.

The Black Hills also draw visitors, especially to the restored mining town of Deadwood. Several colorful figures from the Old West are buried in the local Mount Moriah Cemetery, including "Wild Bill" Hickok and his friend Calamity Jane (1852–1903), one of the few women to work as a frontier scout, marksman and Pony Express rider. ◆

▼ **See also**
Native Americans
North Dakota
United States of America

**BIOGRAPHY**
Crazy Horse
Lewis, Meriwether, and
 Clark, William
Sitting Bull

▼ Mount Rushmore, in the Black Hills, bears the faces of four U.S. Presidents: Washington, Jefferson, Theodore Roosevelt and Lincoln. The faces, each about 18 m (60 ft) high, were carved into the granite mountainside between 1927 and 1941 by sculptor Gutzon Borglum. The carvings are so large that they can be seen from nearly 100 km (60 mi) away.

# South Korea

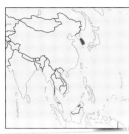

**Area**
99,020 sq km
(38,232 sq mi)
**Capital** Seoul
**Population**
45,563,000
**Language** Korean
**Religion** Buddhist,
Christian, Confucian
**Government** Republic
**Currency** 1 South
Korean won = 100 chon
**Major exports**
Transportation equipment,
electronic products

South Korea's unique
written script, called
han'gul, has 28 letters. It
was invented in 1443 to
replace the thousands of
characters of Chinese they
had previously used.

South Korea was divided from the rest of Korea, now known as North Korea, at the end of World War II. Since the Korean War (1950–1953), the country has depended for its security on a large military force from the U.S. and a heavily defended border with North Korea.

Much of the land in South Korea is mountainous. Lowland areas make up only about a third of the total area of the country. Large numbers of people live in the lowlands, because rice can be farmed there. South Korea's climate is moderate, but occasional typhoons in late summer and cyclones in the spring can bring heavy rains and cause terrible damage to crops.

Separation from North Korea has left the south with few natural resources. Despite this, the country achieved remarkable economic growth and is now one of the leading industrial nations in shipbuilding, electronics, cars and banking. Success was gained by strong state direction, under military rule until 1987, and the hard work of a well-educated population.

In spite of the country's success, many South Koreans with relatives in North Korea hope that the two countries will one day be reunified. ◆

▲ Seoul, the capital city
of South Korea. The
Taebaek mountain
range is in the distance.

▼ **See also**
Asia
Korean War
North Korea

---

# Soviet Union

▼ **See also**
Armenia
Azerbaijan
Belarus
Cold war
Commonwealth of
  Independent States
Estonia
Georgia (C.I.S.)
Kazakhstan
Kyrgyzstan
Latvia
Lithuania
Moldova
Russia and the Russian
  Federation
Tajikistan
Turkmenistan
Ukraine
Uzbekistan
World War II

**BIOGRAPHY**
Gorbachev, Mikhail
Lenin
Stalin, Joseph
Trotsky, Leon
Yeltsin, Boris

▲ The republics of the Soviet Union
as they were in 1990.

After the Russian Revolution in 1917, the Bolshevik Communist government divided the Russian Empire into a number of republics. In 1922 the new state was named the Union of Soviet Socialist Republics (U.S.S.R.), or the Soviet Union. *Soviet* is Russian for "council."

Under the harsh rule of Stalin, from 1924 to 1953, millions of people starved because the state-owned farms on which they were forced to work did not provide enough food. Anyone who opposed Stalin was either imprisoned or killed.

During World War II Germany invaded and 27 million Soviet people were killed. In 1945 an army from the Soviet Union liberated Poland and Czechoslovakia from the Nazis. The army also occupied Hungary, Romania and eastern parts of Germany.

Under the leaderships of Khrushchev from 1953 and Brezhnev from 1964, Communist rule remained strong. In 1985 Gorbachev became leader and tried to reform the Soviet Union. But in 1991 the Communist Party was disbanded and the republics became independent. A Commonwealth of Independent States was formed by most of the republics. ◆

# Space exploration

On Earth, we are surrounded by air, but this gradually gets thinner as it gets farther from the ground. Beyond the air there is almost empty space stretching out between the Sun, the Moon, the planets and the stars. So far, astronauts have visited only our nearest neighbor, the Moon. Robot spacecraft have explored all of the planets in our Solar System, apart from Pluto, but it would take them many thousands of years to get to the next nearest star after the Sun.

## Into Earth orbit

The Space Age began on October 4, 1957, when the Soviet Union launched the first artificial satellite, *Sputnik 1*, into orbit round the Earth. One month later, *Sputnik 2* carried the first living creature into space—the dog Laika.

The first person to fly in space was Yuri Gagarin, a Russian. On April 12, 1961, he made one complete orbit around the Earth in the spacecraft *Vostok 1*. The first American to orbit the Earth was John Glenn, in February 1962. Valentina Tereshkova, on *Vostok 6*, became the first woman in space, in June 1963. Two years later, Alexei Leonov became the first man to

step outside an orbiting spacecraft and float in space while attached by a cable to his spacecraft. A series of American *Gemini* spacecraft, each carrying two astronauts, tried out in orbit around the Earth many of the techniques that would be needed when men flew to the Moon. These included the first docking (joining together) of two orbiting spacecraft in March 1966.

## Exploring the Moon

The exploration of the Moon began with the unmanned Soviet spacecraft *Luna 1*, which flew past the Moon in January 1959. Nine months later, *Luna 2* crashed onto the Moon's surface. Then, in October 1959, *Luna 3* passed behind the Moon and sent back the first pictures of its far side, which is always hidden from Earth. Between 1959 and 1976 the Soviet Union launched 28 unmanned probes toward the Moon and achieved many space "firsts," including the first soft landing on its surface by *Luna 9* in 1966.

After many setbacks, the U.S. program had great success with its last few *Ranger* crash-landers, the soft-landing *Surveyors* and the *Orbiters*. Tens of thousands of pictures of the Moon's surface were sent back, and these were

***Apollo* Missions to the Moon**
*Apollo 8*, December 1968, first men to orbit the Moon
*Apollo 10*, May 1969, second orbital mission
*Apollo 11*, July 1969, first men on the Moon
*Apollo 12*, November 1969, 32 hours on the Moon
*Apollo 13*, April 1970, no landing because of explosion on spacecraft; astronauts returned safely to Earth
*Apollo 14*, February 1971, visited lunar highlands
*Apollo 15*, July 1971, first use of Lunar Rover
*Apollo 16*, April 1972, drove 26 km (16 mi) on Moon
*Apollo 17*, December 1972, last visit to the Moon

The most recent spacecraft to study the Moon from orbit was the U.S. robot probe *Clementine*. In 1994 it spent two months mapping the Moon and looking at areas around the Moon's poles that had not been seen before.

◄ The liftoff of the U.S. space shuttle *Discovery* in April 1990, which carried the Hubble Space Telescope into orbit. The first U.S. space shuttle was *Columbia*, which made its first flight in 1981. Several space shuttles have been built since then, and all but one have continued to fly in space. The space shuttle *Challenger* disintegrated shortly after being launched on its 10th flight in January 1986; all aboard were killed, including six crew members and Christa McAuliffe, a grade-school teacher from New Hampshire.

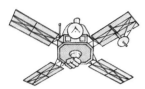

▲ A *Viking* orbiter.

▲ The *Mariner 10* space probe.

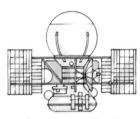

▲ The *Venera 12* lander. *Venera 12* was one of two Soviet probes that investigated the surface of Venus.

▲ The *Luna 16*, launched in 1970, was the first automatic spacecraft to voyage to the Moon, collect samples of rock and soil by remote control, and return successfully to Earth.

**Space Stations**
*Salyut 1*, in use 1971
*Skylab*, in use 1973–1974
*Salyut 3*, in use 1974
*Salyut 4*, in use 1975
*Salyut 5*, in use 1976–1977
*Salyut 6*, in use 1977–1981
*Salyut 7*, in use 1982–1986
*Mir*, launched 1986

used to choose landing sites for astronauts when they went to the Moon.

## Man on the Moon

In July 1969, the giant *Saturn 5* rocket launched three astronauts toward the Moon on the *Apollo 11* mission. For three days they traveled in a small spacecraft called the command module. While Michael Collins remained aboard the command module orbiting the Moon, Neil Armstrong and Edwin Aldrin landed on the Moon in the lunar module. After spending almost a day on the surface, they took off and met the command module, which took them all back to Earth. Five more visits followed. The astronauts explored different parts of the surface, collected Moon rocks and set up scientific equipment. On the last three missions they used a battery-powered car called the Lunar Rover to explore further afield.

## Space stations

A space station is a home in space where astronauts can live and work. It contains everything that they need, including water, food and air, which must all be brought up from Earth.

The first space station was *Salyut 1*, launched by the Soviet Union in 1971. The most recent space station is the Russian *Mir*. It has been in orbit since 1986 and has been extended over the years by adding on extra sections (modules) sent up from Earth. Some astronauts have spent more than a year on board *Mir*. The U.S., Russia, Canada, Europe and Japan are building an International Space Station (called *Alpha*) to be launched in the 21st century.

## Exploring the planets

The first spacecraft to send back information from another planet was *Mariner 2*, an American probe that bypassed Venus in 1962. *Venera 7* made the first soft landing on that planet in 1970. These, and other craft, showed that Venus is extremely hot and has a thick, heavy atmosphere. Although Venus is covered in thick clouds, spacecraft such as *Pioneer Venus* (1978) and *Magellan* (1990) have been able to map its surface by using radar. Mercury, the innermost planet, has been visited by only one spacecraft, *Mariner 10*.

*Mariner 5* flew past Mars in 1965 and sent back the first close-up photographs. Later on, Mars was mapped by *Mariner 9* (1971), the first orbiter, and by *Viking 1* and *2* (1976) which also landed two probes on the planet. In 1997, the U.S. spacecraft *Pathfinder* landed on Mars, took pictures, and explored the Martian terrain.

Jupiter, the largest planet, was bypassed first by *Pioneer 10* in 1973 after a journey lasting nearly two years. *Pioneer 11*, which flew past Jupiter in 1974, made the first pass of Saturn in 1979. *Voyager 1* flew past Jupiter in 1979, sending back detailed pictures of the planet's cloud belts and moons. Most surprising was its discovery of active volcanoes on the moon Io. *Voyager 1* carried on to Saturn, which it passed in 1980, returning amazing pictures of the planet's rings. It also took a close look at several of Saturn's moons. *Voyager 2* flew past Jupiter

▲ A photograph of the planet Mars, one of many relayed back to Earth in July 1997 by the U.S. spacecraft *Pathfinder*, which landed there. *Pathfinder* carried a small (10-kg/22-lb) roving vehicle called *Sojourner*, which rolled down a ramp (seen at the left of this photograph) from the spacecraft. *Sojourner*, seen in the middle of this photo, explored the nearby Martian terrain and relayed data back to Earth about the climate, geology and atmosphere of the planet. (The arrows in the large photo and small inset photo point to different examples of Martian rocks.) The data are still being analyzed. In September 1997 another unmanned spacecraft, *Surveyor*, went into orbit around Mars and sent back additional data about the planet.

and Saturn, then went on to Uranus in 1986 and Neptune in 1989. This four-planet mission was possible because the planets were lined up in a special way that happens only once every 180 years. All four of these spacecraft are now heading out toward the stars.

The most recent probe to Jupiter was *Galileo*, which arrived there in December 1995. The spacecraft consisted of two parts—a probe that plunged into the atmosphere and an orbiter.

▶ *Mir* orbiting space station.
 1 Mir station
 2 Spaceship *Soyuz 7*
 3 Passage
 4 Socket
 5 Six docking ports
 6 Approach system
 7 Working unit
 8 Entrance to working unit
 9 Central control unit
10 Hand rail
11 Shelves
12 Solar batteries
13 Solid state bicycle
14 Table
15 Personal unit
16 Toilet
17 Wash-basin
18 Antenna for connection with Earth
19 Main docking system
20 Training unit— running strip
21 Intermediate chamber
22 Engine with cover
23 Docking target
24 Assembly model
25 Hatch cover
26 Window
27 Window blind

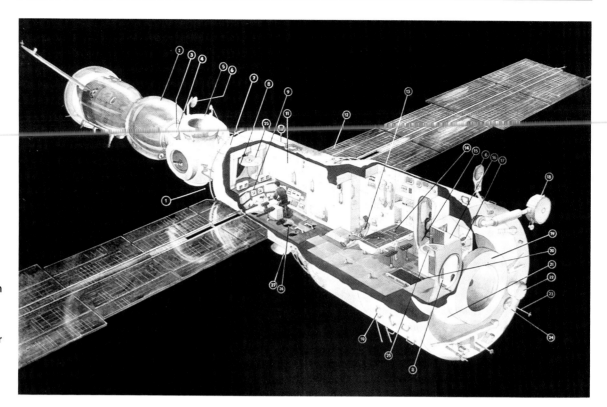

Spacelab is a portable laboratory built by the European Space Agency that has been sent on U.S. space shuttle flights. Scientists aboard the shuttle use instruments in the laboratory to conduct a wide range of scientific experiments in space.

▼ **See also**
Astronauts
Moon
Observatories
Planets
Rockets
Satellites
Solar System
Telescopes

**BIOGRAPHY**
Armstrong, Neil
Gagarin, Yuri
Glenn, John
Tereshkova, Valentina

## Going into space

To explore space we have to overcome the pull of gravity, which holds us on the Earth. We can do this by traveling very fast. You need a speed of at least 40,000 kmph (25,000 mph), about 20 times as fast as the Concorde jet, to escape completely. This is called the Earth's *escape velocity*. Satellites that go into orbit round the Earth do not need to go quite so fast. Close to the Earth, their speeds need to be about 28,000 kmph (17,000 mph).

Only powerful rockets can launch astronauts or satellites into space, because they can reach these speeds and a rocket engine will work in space, unlike aircraft engines (which need air). Most rockets can be used only once. The space shuttle is the first space plane that can fly into space many times. The only part that is new for each flight is the huge fuel tank. The two booster rockets that help lift the shuttle orbiter into space fall back into the sea when their fuel runs out; the rockets are then recovered by ships. The shuttle takes off upward like a rocket, but when it returns to Earth it lands like a glider on a runway.

## Living and working in space

In an orbiting spacecraft or space station, everything floats around, including the astronauts. We call this weightlessness. If astronauts want to stay in one place, they must fix themselves to something. They sleep strapped into sleeping bags. Food is made sticky so that it sticks to a spoon, and drinks are sucked from containers through straws to keep them from floating around as balls of liquid. Weightlessness also affects their bodies, so astronauts have to exercise hard while they are in space to keep fit.

Orbiting astronauts study the Earth below, the distant stars and galaxies, and the space around them. They measure the effects of weightlessness on themselves, on growing plants and on small creatures such as spiders and bees. In space, astronauts can make crystals, alloys (mixtures of metals), and some medicines that are difficult to make on Earth. Shuttle astronauts are kept busy launching satellites from the orbiter's cargo bay and occasionally recapturing them for return to Earth. They have also carried out repairs to satellites and to the Hubble Space Telescope.

## Returning to Earth

The most dangerous parts of any spaceflight are the launch and return to Earth. A returning spacecraft meets the blanket of air surrounding the Earth at very high speed. It rubs against the air, getting so hot that the outside of the craft glows red. This would melt the spacecraft and kill the crew if they were not protected. Early spacecraft had a thick outer layer that melted away, but the space shuttle has special reusable heat-proof tiles. ◆

# Spain

Spain is one of the most mountainous countries in Europe. Madrid, at 646 m (2,100 ft) above sea level, is Europe's highest capital city. It is near the center of a high plateau called the Meseta. Rivers such as the Tagus and Duoro have cut deep valleys into this plateau. The Meseta is surrounded by high mountains that keep out the winds from the sea. This is "dry Spain," with little rain, very cold winters and very hot summers.

## Wet Spain

Mountains called the Pyrenees separate Spain from France. At the western end of the Pyrenees live the Basque people, who have their own language and traditions. Northern Spain is "wet Spain": a green, lush countryside facing the Atlantic Ocean. It is also an industrial area. Bilbao is Spain's most important industrial town, and Gijón has a steelworks. La Coruña has been a naval port and ship-building town since before the days of the Spanish Armada (1588).

## Holiday Spain

Spain's south and east coasts face the Mediterranean Sea. This is "holiday Spain," with skyscraper hotels that accommodate people who come from other parts of Europe to enjoy the hot summers and the warm winters. The Balearic Islands in the Mediterranean and the volcanic Canary Islands in the Atlantic Ocean are also parts of Spain that are popular with tourists.

## Towns and villages

Spanish towns and villages are dominated by large churches. Most people are Roman Catholics, and festivals and processions take place on holy days and saints' days. The *plaza mayor* is the central square. The shops around it are often in a cool, covered arcade. Shops are shut from lunchtime to late afternoon for the *siesta* (time for sleep and rest). But in the cooler evenings, the main streets and plazas, with their open-air restaurants, come to life.

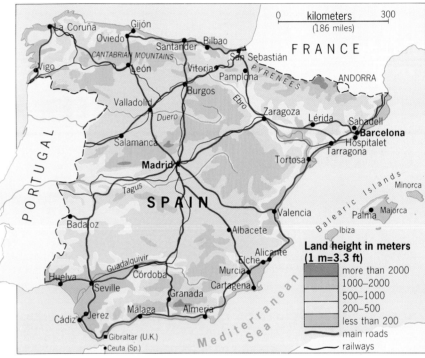

**Area**
504,780 sq km
(194,896 sq mi)
**Capital**
Madrid
**Population**
39,568,000
**Language**
Spanish, Catalan, Basque
**Religion**
Christian
**Government**
Parliamentary monarchy
**Currency**
1 peseta = 100 céntimos
**Major exports**
Agricultural products, textiles, machinery

Barcelona was the site of the Olympic Games in 1992.

◀ Evening time in Alicante, a town in southern Spain. The blinds on the windows are still down after the afternoon siesta (rest).

## SPANISH HISTORY

► A painting showing the Muslim governor of Seville holding a council.

A wedding led to the unification of Spain in 1479. The couple were cousins—Prince Ferdinand, heir to the throne of Castile, and Princess Isabella, heir to the throne of Aragon. When they succeeded to their thrones, the two kingdoms effectively became one. Isabella and Ferdinand were strict Roman Catholics. They introduced the Inquisition, a court that used torture and execution to compel all Spain's people to join their religion. At least 2,000 people were burned at the stake, and the Jews were driven out of Spain.

► Troops supporting General Franco examining villages and searching for arms during the Spanish Civil War (1936–1939). Over 750,000 people were killed in the war.

Spain has had an exciting and turbulent history. By the 5th century B.C., Phoenicians, Greeks and Celts had established small settlements, but the country was divided among many small, warlike tribes. It is a difficult country to fight over, because of its mountains and its dry central plateau. It was the highly efficient Roman army that finally conquered the whole peninsula and made it part of the Roman Empire.

Roman rule lasted for almost 600 years. Then a Germanic tribe, the Visigoths, swept in and took over. They set up a kingdom whose nobles warred among themselves. In 711 A.D. one of these nobles, Count Julian, called in Berber warriors from Morocco to help him rebel against his king, even though they were Muslims, not Christians.

Under their Arab leader, Tarik, the Berbers landed at a rocky point which ever after was called Tarik's Rock—in his language, Gebel Tarik (Gibraltar). In seven years the Berbers, aided by a host of fellow Muslims—Arabs, Moors and Syrians—had conquered all but the north of the country. For nearly 500 years most of Spain was an Islamic country, though Muslims were generally tolerant of Christians and Jews. Spain under the Moors became famous for its universities, its medicine, and its art and architecture. The Alhambra (castle and palace) at Granada is one of the most elegant and finely decorated buildings in Europe.

### The years of power

The Muslim rulers quarreled among themselves, and by the 11th century Spain was divided into over 20 small states. The Christian kingdoms of the north, led by Castile, took the opportunity, and bit by bit reconquered Spain for Christianity until only the kingdom of Granada in the south remained a Muslim state. The two Christian kingdoms of Castile and Aragon united in 1479, and almost all Spain was under one rule again. In 1492 two very important events occurred: the Muslims were driven out of Granada, and an expedition under Christopher Columbus landed in the Caribbean. Columbus was from Genoa in Italy, but it was Queen Isabella of Spain who provided the funds, and Spaniards who reaped the benefit.

In the following hundred years Spanish adventurers known as the *conquistadores*, conquered a vast empire in Central and South America, and untold gold and silver were looted and brought back to Europe. In the late 16th century, under King Philip II, Spain became one of the richest and most powerful countries in Europe.

Spain's "golden age" did not last. A series of disastrous wars and equally disastrous, feeble kings weakened the country. It declined rapidly in the 18th century, and eventually its American colonies rebelled and became independent.

### Civil War 1936–1939

In 1931 the king, Alfonso XIII, was driven into exile and a republic was set up. Five years later a military revolt against an elected left-wing government plunged the country into civil war. Spaniards suffered terribly during the three years of fighting between the Republicans and their allies on the one side and the fascist "Falange" on the other. In 1939 Spain fell under the rule of a fascist dictator, General Francisco Franco.

Franco held power until his death in 1975. Although he was friendly with the dictators of Germany and Italy, Adolf Hitler and Benito Mussolini, he kept Spain out of World War II. When he died, Alfonso's grandson, Juan Carlos, became king, and free elections were held. ◆

# Spanish-American War (1898)

The Spanish-American War occurred between the United States and Spain in 1898. Victory in the war established the U.S. as a major world power.

## Causes of the war

In the late 19th century, many Americans had come to believe that the U.S. should annex Cuba, a Spanish possession. Supporters of annexation argued that Cubans were being mistreated by their Spanish rulers, and that the U.S. had a duty to "liberate" Cuba from Spain. That view gained support when revolution broke out in Cuba in 1895. As the fighting continued without either the Cubans or Spanish claiming victory, Americans called for an invasion.

In late January 1898, President William McKinley sent a U.S. battleship, the *Maine*, to the harbor in Havana, the Cuban capital, to help protect Americans who were still in the country. On February 15, the *Maine* suddenly blew up, and some 260 people were killed. Americans blamed the Spanish for the explosion, and "Remember the Maine!" became a rallying cry for Cuban independence and U.S. military action.

The U.S. declared war on Spain on April 25, but the battles that followed were fought in Spanish possessions. On May 1, American naval ships under Admiral George Dewey sailed into Manila Bay in the Philippines and destroyed the Spanish fleet. Other engagements followed in the Philippines as well as in Cuba and Puerto Rico.

## Results of the war

After nearly eight months, the Spanish surrendered, and a peace treaty was signed on December 10, 1898. Under its terms, Cuba became independent and the U.S. acquired Guam, Puerto Rico and the Philippines. ◆

Among the leading supporters of an American invasion of Cuba in the 1890s were two influential newspaper publishers, William Randolph Hearst and Joseph Pulitzer. In their papers they published sensational, often exaggerated accounts of atrocities against the Cubans, stirring up anti-Spanish feeling throughout the U.S.

The Spanish-American War made Theodore Roosevelt a national hero and propelled him to office as Vice President in 1900. (He succeeded to the Presidency when President William McKinley was assassinated in 1901.) As head of a U.S. military unit called the Rough Riders, Roosevelt became famous for leading a charge up San Juan Hill in Cuba.

One important consequence of the Spanish-American War was the building of a canal through the Isthmus of Panama, a narrow neck of land connecting North and South America. The necessity for such a canal was emphasized during the war, when battleships traveling between the Atlantic and Pacific oceans had to go all the way around South America. The Panama Canal, which opened in 1914, created a shortcut between the oceans.

▼ See also
Cuba
Guam
Panama
Philippines
Puerto Rico
United States of America

BIOGRAPHY
Hearst, William Randolph
Roosevelt, Theodore

# Species

A species is a "kind" of living thing. Although every individual in a species is different from all the others, just as you are different from your friends, the members of a species are genetically so alike that they are able to breed together. They cannot, however, breed successfully in the wild with members of other species, which are genetically different. In a few cases people have brought closely related animals together and they have mated in captivity. For instance, a donkey and a horse may mate, but the foal will be a mule. It may grow up to be strong, but it will be sterile and unable to mate in its turn, so each species is kept intact. Some scientists are beginning to change this with genetic engineering, but they have not made a new species so far.

## Species names

Species are the lowest level in the system of biological classification created by the Swedish scientist Carolus Linnaeus in the 18th century. The names of species, as is the case for all levels of classification in his system, are in Latin. He worked out a method of giving two-part names to every different species.

The first part, which is called the *generic* name, is shared by other closely related species. It is always written with a capital letter. The second name (the *specific* name) is written with a small letter. It often describes the animal, and may be used with a different generic name for many species. For instance, the name *sylvestris*, meaning "of woodland," is given to many species, including cow parsley (*Anthriscus sylvestris*) and the wild cat (*Felis sylvestris*). However, the two parts of the name together refer only to one species. For example, *Equus caballus* is the horse, while *Equus asinus* is the donkey and *Equus burchelli* is the common zebra. ◆

**Number of animal species known**
About 1.5 million
**Number of animal species thought to be undiscovered**
Over 8 million, mostly very small creatures. Some people think that there may be as many as 30 million species in all.
**Number of plant species**
About 380,000

▼ See also
Animals
Classification of living
  things
Genetic engineering
Genetics
Plants

BIOGRAPHY
Linnaeus, Carolus

# Spices

Spices are used in cooking to add flavor and color to our food. Spices come from a variety of different parts of different plants. They are usually dried to preserve them and should be kept in airtight containers away from light. They may be used whole or ground. The way in which they are used affects their flavor.

## LOOKING BACK

Spices were known and used by the ancient Chinese, the Egyptians, Greeks and Romans. Everywhere spices were very valuable. They grew in a small number of places such as the Moluccas of Indonesia, known as the Spice Islands, and everyone wanted them. They were used to preserve food, to cover up the taste of food that was going bad, and as medicines.

An important spice trade grew up between East and West. For a long time this was controlled by Venetians and merchants in the Middle East. Then, in the 16th century, Portuguese sailors discovered the Moluccas and took over the islands and the spice trade. A hundred years later the Dutch East India Company moved in. Their monopoly lasted until the islanders rebelled and the company went bankrupt. Indonesia is still the world's largest producer of cloves and nutmeg. ◆

Garam masala is the Indian name for a mixture of spices used to add spiciness to an Indian dish toward the end of the cooking time. Here is a simple mixture: 2 teaspoons ground cardamom, 1 teaspoon each of ground cinnamon, ground cloves, ground black pepper and ground cumin.

The word "curry" in Tamil (a language of southern India) means "sauce." Indians, Bangladeshis and Pakistanis use different combinations of spices to make curry for each dish.

Whole cumin seeds fried in oil taste different from ground cumin seeds which have been toasted under the grill.

Spices were almost unknown in Europe until the Crusaders first tasted them in the Holy Land. When spices did reach the West they were so expensive that they were kept under lock and key in special spice boxes.

## Some Favorite Spices

**Pepper** is sometimes called "The King of the Spices." It is used all over the world. Peppercorns are the berries of the pepper vine. Black pepper is dried unripe fruit, and white pepper comes from fruit picked when almost ripe, with the dark outer skin removed.

**Ginger** is the rhizome (underground stem) of another tropical plant. It is used fresh, dried and ground, or preserved in sugar or syrup. Fresh ginger needs peeling and grating before use. Ginger is used in a variety of dishes.

**Cloves** are dried buds of a tropical evergreen tree. They are highly flavored and only a small quantity needs to be used. They are used to flavor meat such as ham, and sweet dishes such as apple pie. Cloves have also been used as medicines to treat indigestion and toothache.

**Chilli** is the general name given to a variety of hot South American peppers. They may be green or red and are usually long and tapering and full of seeds. Chillis have a very sharp and fiery flavor. Dried red chillis are ground to make chilli powder.

**Nutmeg** and **mace** are two flavorings that come from the fruit of an evergreen tree which originally grew in the Moluccas or Spice Islands. Fresh nutmeg is enclosed in a hard brown shell that is itself enclosed in a crimson mesh called mace. Both are used in many different dishes.

**Cinnamon** is the dried and rolled inner bark from the shoots of a small tropical tree. It can be used in this "stick" form, but more often it is ground. It is mostly used to flavor cakes, cookies and other sweet foods.

▼ See also
Cooking
Food
Herbs

# Spiders

Spiders, like insects, have jointed legs and bodies that are made in sections or segments. But, unlike an insect, a spider's body consists of two, not three parts, and it has eight, not six legs. Also spiders cannot fly, although baby spiders and adults of small species may "parachute" on long silk threads. Female spiders are often much larger than males, who have to resort to tricks to avoid being eaten as they court their hungry mates. The large webs that often decorate hedgerows are usually made by female spiders.

## Silk

All spiders can make silk. It is formed as a liquid in the creature's body and is squeezed through organs called spinnerets at the back of the abdomen. As it makes contact with the air, the silk hardens instantly. Spiders make several kinds of silk. Some is used to protect eggs and another kind to wrap up prey. Some use it to make webs to catch their prey. Some kinds of silk are very strong—stronger than a steel thread of the same diameter. Other kinds are very elastic and can stretch to nearly twice their original length. The strands of silk that we see are often made of several finer threads, each as little as 0.00003 mm (0.0000011 in) in diameter.

## Spiders as hunters

All spiders are carnivores. They feed mainly on the flesh of insects or other tiny creatures, although the largest species may catch animals

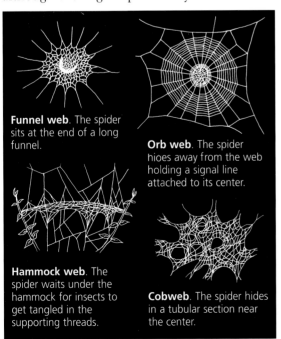

**Funnel web**. The spider sits at the end of a long funnel.

**Orb web**. The spider hioes away from the web holding a signal line attached to its center.

**Hammock web**. The spider waits under the hammock for insects to get tangled in the supporting threads.

**Cobweb**. The spider hides in a tubular section near the center.

as big as small birds and mice. When a spider has caught its prey, it uses pointed fangs to inject venom (poison). This paralyzes the prey and also contains digestive juices that break down the prey's flesh, making it a liquid, which the spider then sucks up.

Like most flesh-eaters, spiders can run fast, at least for a short distance. Wolf spiders use their speed and strength to outrun and overcome their prey. A few kinds, such as the jumping spiders, have large eyes and can see and judge distances well. But unlike most hunters, most spiders are very short-sighted. Perhaps because of this they use their silk to make traps to catch their prey.

## Spider traps

Most people have seen the circular orb webs that hang from branches and twigs. Some of the lines are sticky, and a fly or other small creature that blunders into them is caught. The spider, which detects the vibration in the web, has oily feet, so she can run over the glue and is not trapped herself. She injects her victim with venom and wraps it in silk. She may eat it at once, or keep it hanging near the edge of the web until she is hungry.

Other sorts of traps made by different kinds of spiders include hammock webs and funnel webs. Trap-door spiders catch their prey by quickly opening a silk trap door over a burrow and grabbing it. Some spiders spin a small web and drop it onto their prey. The bolas spiders, which are well camouflaged, hang beneath a twig, and at dusk spin a line about 5 cm (2 in) long, at the end of which is a bead of very sticky gum. The spider seems to sense the approach of a moth, and swings the line toward the insect. Large moths may escape, but small ones are drawn in, bitten and wrapped in silk. ◆

**Distribution**
Almost throughout the world. Often in houses. Some live in fresh water
**Largest spider**
More than 10 cm (4 in) long (the leg span may be twice this length)
**Smallest spider**
Less than 1 mm (0.04 in) long
**Lifespan**
Some large spiders have survived for 15 years in captivity. Most probably live for much less than this.
**Biggest webs**
Some webs spun by orb-weaver spiders have measured 5.7 m (18.7 ft) around the edge
**Phylum** Arthropoda
**Class** Arachnida
**Order** Araneae
**Number of species**
About 35,000

◄ Spiders use their poison to kill strong and active prey. This garden spider has caught a wasp, has injected it with venom, and is now wrapping it in silk.

**W**hen spitting spiders are very close to their insect prey, they squirt a jet of gum from each fang, which glues it to the ground. The spider then bites its captive and takes it away to eat.

**See also**
Invertebrates
Scorpions
Venom

# Spinning

Spinning is a way of twisting fibers together to make thread or yarn. Wool, cotton and other fibers can be spun. Spinning disentangles and straightens the fibers, drawing them out until they are the required thickness, and then twists them together.

## Spinning devices

The simplest device for spinning is a *drop spindle*. This is a stick with a small disk at one end, called a whorl, that keeps the stick turning during the spinning process. The thread is tied to the spindle and twists as the spindle turns. The spinner adds more fibers to the thread from a bundle held in the hand or on another stick called a *distaff*. From time to time the spinner winds the thread she has made onto the spindle.

In Europe people made thread with a drop spindle until the spinning wheel was introduced during the Middle Ages. A spinning wheel combined a wheel with a small pulley. The wheel was turned by hand or by a pedal. A string ran over the wheel and the pulley to turn the spindle, which in turn twisted the fiber. Spinning wheels worked much faster than drop spindles, but the spinner could still only spin one length of thread at a time.

A machine for spinning a number of threads at once was invented in England in 1764 by James Hargreaves, who named it the "Spinning Jenny." From that beginning came other mechanical devices powered by water to drive the wheels of spinning machines in cotton mills, and low-cost mechanized systems for spinning spread to the U.S. and other countries. Similar systems remain in use today, although usually driven by electricity, not water. ◆

The spinning of fibers into thread or yarn is an ancient craft. Cotton was spun in India as early as 3000 B.C., and the spinning wheel was later developed there. It spread to Europe during the Middle Ages. Today both drop spindles and spinning wheels are still used in some parts of the world.

The development and use of spinning machines in the U.S. in the late 18th century created a demand for more cotton. This in turn led not only to the growing of more cotton on southern plantations but also to the invention by Eli Whitney of the cotton gin. The gin separated seeds from cotton fibers and replaced the slower process of removing them by hand.

There is a picture of a drop spindle in the article on Rugs and carpets in this volume.

---

# Spirituals

Spirituals are religious songs that became associated with blacks in the U.S., beginning in the early 19th century. They are considered a traditional type of American music and are still referred to as "Negro spirituals." (The word "Negro" was once used to mean an African American.)

Spirituals were influenced by both traditional African folk melodies and hymns sung by whites at religious meetings in the South. They were usually based on Bible stories from the Old Testament. They were sung with great emotion and feeling by slaves not only in their worship services but also as they worked in the fields.

Spirituals were first performed on the stage in the 1870s by a singing group from Fisk University, an African-American institution in Tennessee. The Fisk Jubilee Singers toured the U.S. and Europe, and their performances made spirituals widely known. Later black concert singers such as Marian Anderson and Paul Robeson made them even more popular. Today spirituals are frequently performed by singing groups and soloists. ◆

**Some Famous Spirituals**

"Deep River"
"Go Down, Moses"
"Little David"
"Roll, Jordan, Roll"
"Steal Away"
"Swing Low, Sweet Chariot"
"Were You There?"

▶ During their concert tour of England in 1873, the Fisk Jubilee Singers were painted by Edmund Havel, court painter to Queen Victoria. The Jubilee Singers performed for the queen and her family during their tour.

# Sponges

▶ An azure vase sponge from Roatan, Honduras.

Although some sponges can creep a little and others react slightly to light or to touch, they are not able to see, hear or move. Until the 19th century, most people thought that sponges were plants; in fact they are animals.

Since ancient times, sponge skeletons have been used by people for scrubbing and bathing. Today, most scrub sponges are man-made, but natural sponges are still highly valued for cosmetic uses.

Sponges may be many different shapes, sizes and colors. Their bodies are covered with a tough skin that is pitted with tiny holes and some larger openings. Inside they have a skeleton made of microscopically small hard parts called *spicules*. These form a network that supports passages and chambers leading from the small surface holes. The chambers are lined with cells called *collar cells*, each of which has a whip-like structure. Beating together, they cause water to flow through the passages. The water contains oxygen and tiny fragments of food. Food is caught by the collar cells and passed to amoeba-like wandering cells, which carry it to the parts of the body where it is needed. Waste products pass out of the large holes on the surface as the water is pumped out. ◆

**Distribution** All in water, most in the sea, some in the very deep sea
**Largest sponges** About 2 m (6.6 ft) high, such as the loggerhead sponge, *Spheciospongia vesparia*
**Smallest sponges** Several species about 1 mm (0.039 in) high
**Amount of water filtered by sponges** A sponge 4 cubic cm (0.244 cu in) in volume can filter about 0.5 liters (0.53 qts) per hour. A sponge 10 liters (10.6 qts) in volume can filter 360 l (380 qts) per hour.
**Phylum** Porifera
**Number of classes** 3 (glass sponges, calcareous sponges and horny sponges)
**Number of species** About 10,000

▼ **See also**
Animals
Invertebrates

# Spores

In some organisms, a male cell joins with a female cell to produce a new individual. In animals, a sperm cell from a male may fuse with the egg (ovum) of a female; this will produce an embryo that will develop into a new young animal. In a flowering plant, the pollen from one flower may fertilize another flower to develop seeds that will grow into another plant. This is sexual reproduction.

Other organisms do not have male and female cells that join to make another organism. They are asexual and may have spores to reproduce themselves.

Spores are minute single cells able to grow into a *clone* (a new individual identical to the parent). Algae, mosses, ferns, fungi and bacteria all reproduce from spores. Spores usually have a thick, protective outer coat that helps them survive difficult conditions. Some bacterial spores are still able to grow after being boiled for half an hour. Most spores are produced in large quantities to ensure that some will find the right conditions for growth. A giant puffball may contain as many as 7 trillion spores.

Because spores are so small, it is easier to find the *sporangia* that produce them. Look at the underside of fern leaves in late summer, when collections of sporangia form brown velvety patches. The thousands of tiny black dots on moldy bread are also sporangia. The air is full of millions of different spores ready for growth. ◆

▼ **See also**
Algae
Bacteria
Clones
Ferns
Fungi
Mosses
Mushrooms and toadstools
Reproduction
Sex and sexuality
Yeasts

▼ The brown patches on the underside of this fern leaf are the sporangia that produce the spores. The plant is a long beech fern growing in Michigan.

# Sports

▼ **See also**
Fitness
Games
Olympic Games

▼ These different sports are divided up according to the type of activity involved. All the sports listed have articles in the encyclopedia.

Everyone needs to exercise regularly to stay healthy, and one of the most enjoyable ways to do so is to take part in organized sports. Throughout history, people have done this, from the ancient Greek Olympic Games to the wide range of sporting activities available to us today.

Millions of people around the world enjoy watching sports. They delight in the skills and artistry of the participants, and the drama of the contest. But perhaps the chief reason people watch sports is to follow a particular personality or a team, their country or their favorite club.

Modern sports have developed into a major industry, thanks largely to the power of television. Worldwide audiences for soccer's World Cup and the Olympic Games are measured in billions. As a result, companies are eager to advertise their products at sporting events.

Some people feel that money now has too great an influence over sports. They do not want to see sporting authorities giving up their power to outside influences such as television. It is also important that a fair share of the money earned in professional sports be made available to young people for facilities and coaching. ◆

**Team games**
Baseball
Basketball
Football
Hockey, field
Hockey, ice
Lacrosse
Polo
Soccer
Softball
Volleyball

**Table sports and board games**
Billiards
Cards and card games
Chess

**Winter sports**
Ice skating
Skiing
Winter sports

**Racket sports**
Badminton
Squash
Table tennis
Tennis

**Water sports**
Canoeing
Fishing
Rowing
Surfing
Water sports
Yachts

**Target sports**
Archery
Bowling
Darts
Golf

**Animal sports**
Bullfighting
Horses (covers horse racing)
Polo
Show-jumping

**Miscellaneous**
Gymnastics
Marathons
Mountain climbing
Orienteering
Track and field

**Aerial sports**
Gliders
Hang gliders (includes parascending)
Skydiving

**Combat sports**
Boxing
Fencing
Judo
Karate
Martial arts
Wrestling

**Wheeled sports**
Auto racing
Cycling
Motorcycles
Roller skating

# Springs

You can use springs to store energy for a short or a long time. This energy can be allowed to escape quickly or slowly from the spring. As it does so, it can move something or drive a piece of machinery around. Clocks and watches were once driven by coiled-up springs. And springs like this are used in the "clockwork" motors in some toys. A spring is usually made of a special type of steel so that it will return to its original shape, however much it has been squeezed, bent or stretched. The steel in the spring must also not crack or break after it has been bent a large number of times. The metal spring may be a thin flat strip, a wire or a rod. It can have many different shapes, such as those in the drawings.

▼ **Some different kinds of springs.**

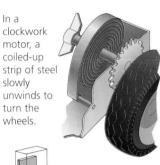

In a clockwork motor, a coiled-up strip of steel slowly unwinds to turn the wheels.

Helical (coil) springs are used in so-called innerspring mattresses to make them comfortable to lie on.

The spring in a bell push is a strip of flexible metal.

Leaf springs are used in some trucks. The "leaves" are flexible strips of steel clamped together.

Some road vehicles have air springs. These are rubber and fabric containers filled with air. When the spring is pushed down, the air pushes back out. This helps the vehicle to stay level even on a bumpy road.

Rubber and rubber-like plastics called *elastomers* can act as springs, too. They are often used to cut down vibration. Engine mountings are usually made of rubber or elastomer, and some bicycles have suspension systems that include elastomer springing. ◆

▼ **See also**
Automobiles
Clocks and watches
Locks and keys

# Squash

(1 m=3.3 ft)

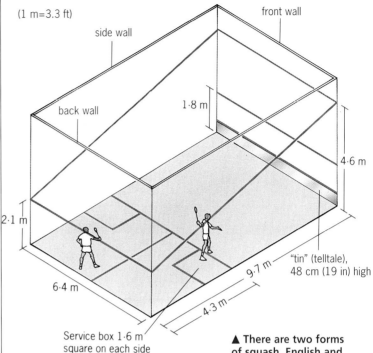

side wall
front wall
back wall
1·8 m
4·6 m
2·1 m
9·7 m
"tin" (telltale), 48 cm (19 in) high
6·4 m
4·3 m

Service box 1·6 m square on each side of the court. The server must have at least one foot inside the service box.

Squash is a variation of an older game called "racquets." It is played in an enclosed court, usually by two players, with a soft ball and a strung racket. Squash is a very energetic game, requiring quick bursts of speed and energy to get to the falling ball or to intercept a hard shot. Players score points by hitting shots that their opponents are unable to return. Players must hit the ball before it bounces twice, and must return it so that it hits the front wall. When the ball is in play, it can bounce from all four walls.

Because of the four-walled court, the game is not easy to watch and has never been an important spectator sport. Transparent courts are specially built for big tournaments, however, and the game is sometimes shown on television.

Squash is one of a group of games that developed in English boys' schools in the 19th century. ◆

▲ There are two forms of squash, English and American. This is an English squash court. In the U.S., squash is played on a narrower court with a much harder ball.

Racquetball is an indoor court game similar to squash. It is played with a short-handled, paddle-shaped racket. Racquetball was invented in the U.S. by Joseph Sobek in 1950

▲ Squash rackets are made of wood, fiberglass or carbon graphite, and the balls are made of rubber.

# Squid

Squid are relatives of the snail, but they have no shells. Instead they have a stiff, horny support inside their bag-like bodies. This is called the pen. Squid also have ink sacs, and they are sometimes called the "pen-and-ink animals." The head, with its large eyes and big brain, is attached at the front of the body bag. Eight long arms surround the mouth, and there are also two even longer tentacles.

Squid live mostly in the open ocean. They propel themselves with jets of water. Some move so quickly that they can become airborne and skim over the waves for a distance of 20 m (66 ft) or more. Squid feed mainly on fish, which they catch with their long tentacles. Like the arms, these carry suckers, which often have claws to help hold the slippery prey. Squid are themselves the food for many kinds of animals. Giant squid living in the deep sea are an important part of the food of sperm whales.

In the darkness of the deep sea, squid often use brightly colored light organs to signal to each other and dazzle attackers. Usually there is at least one light organ near their eyes, so that the squid will not be blinded by the light which may be produced by a hunting fish. ◆

▼ **See also**
Invertebrates
Mollusks
Oceans and seas
Octopuses

▼ The parts of a squid.

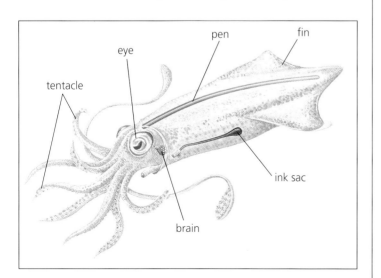

# Squirrels

Unlike most small mammals, squirrels are active during the daytime. Their eyesight is better than that of other rodents, and they are able to judge distances very well as they climb trees and leap from branch to branch.

## Tree squirrels

Tree squirrels are well adapted for tree-climbing because they have very sharp claws that enable them to cling onto tree trunks and branches. They always climb down trees head first using the claws of the hind feet as anchors.

Tree squirrels feed on nuts and fruits and sometimes gnaw at trees to get at the sap. Like many rodents, squirrels store surplus food, usually by burying it. They may forget where they make their larders, but they have a good sense of smell and are able to find nuts even if they are buried under 10 cm (4 in) of soil. Tree squirrels make secure nests in hollow trees and also dens among the branches, called dreys.

Brown and gray squirrels are fairly common in the U.S., and so are red squirrels. Black squirrels are rarer.

## Flying squirrels

Flying squirrels are small relatives of the tree squirrels, which have membranes between their legs. They are able to glide rather than fly, but they can steer to avoid branches. The northern flying squirrel stretches all four limbs when flying from tree to tree.

## Ground squirrels

Some of the relatives of common squirrels live on the ground and many of them burrow. They are called ground squirrels and include prairie dogs, chipmunks, gophers and marmots. ◆

▼ **See also**
Rodents

▼ Tree squirrels climb down trees head first.

# Sri Lanka

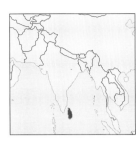

Sri Lanka is a tropical island country off the southeast tip of India. Most of the island is lowland, with a mountainous area in the central south.

One of the peaks, called Adam's Peak, has a small hollow at the summit that is said to be a footprint. The mountain is visited by pilgrims from Sri Lanka's three main religions: Buddhists, Hindus and Muslims.

Sri Lanka exports tea, rubber, coconuts, and gemstones such as sapphires, rubies, topaz and garnets. Most people eat rice, but the country does not grow enough of its own. The streets of Colombo are busy and colorful, but there are many poor people. Some children even have to live in the streets begging, polishing shoes or selling cigarettes and plastic combs for money to survive.

**Area**
65,610 sq km
(25,332 sq mi)
**Capital**
Colombo
**Population**
17,800,000
**Language**
Sinhalese, Tamil, English
**Religion**
Buddhist, Hindu, Muslim, Christian
**Government**
Parliamentary republic
**Currency**
1 Sri Lankan rupee = 100 cents
**Major exports**
Tea, rubber, coconuts, gemstones

**▼ See also**
Asia
Buddhism
Commonwealth of
  Nations
Gems
Hinduism
Islam
Tea

## LOOKING BACK

People have lived on Sri Lanka for 5,000 years. Traders have visited the island for centuries. It was called Taprobane by the Romans, Serendip by Arab merchants, Ceilão by the Portuguese, and Ceylon by the British, who captured it from the Dutch in 1796. The island became independent from the British in 1948, and the name was later changed to Sri Lanka, which means "Resplendent Land." Tension between Tamil Indians who settled in the north and native Sinhalese has led to violent conflict. ◆

▼ A crowded Colombo street scene with jewelry shops advertising in English as well as in Sinhalese.

# Stained glass

Stained-glass artists work with glass, lead and light. The artist plans the window carefully, drawing a full-scale design, called a "cartoon," which shows the positions of the lead lines and the colors of the glass pieces.

In the Middle Ages, artists used glass made in their own workshops. Today artists choose from glass that has already been colored (by adding various metal oxides to the molten glass mixture), blown and flattened into sheets.

Following the cartoon, the artist cuts the glass. Some pieces have designs painted on them, and these pieces are fired to fix the paint.

Once the glass is ready, the artist starts to lay out the network of leads. Following the outline of the cartoon, he bends the leads and slides the glass pieces into place. Then the leads are soldered together and any gaps are filled with cement. If the panel is a large one, the leads are strengthened with tie bars. Then the panel is ready to be permanently fixed into its window frame. ◆

▲ In the Middle Ages, windows acted as picture books for a congregation, many of whom could not read. This panel comes from a window in England's Canterbury Cathedral. It illustrates the biblical parable of the sower who sowed seeds on different kinds of soil.

▼ The network of leads that form the window.

**▼ See also**
Cathedrals
Churches
Glass
Middle Ages

# Stalactites and stalagmites

▲ Some of the stalactites in this cave in Romania have joined with the stalagmites to form strange-shaped crystalline pillars.

### Stalactite and Stalagmite Records
*Longest unsupported stalactites*
About 10 m (33 ft) long, in Gruta do Janelão, Brazil
*Tallest stalagmite*
In Krásnohorská cave, Slovakia: about 32 m (105 ft) tall
*Tallest cave column*
The Dragon Pillar, Guizhou, China: 39 m (128 ft) tall

**A** good way of remembering which is which is to learn these sentences: Stala**ct**ites **c**ling to the **c**eiling. Stala**g**mites **g**row from the **g**round.

▼ **See also**
Caves

Stalactites and stalagmites are found in many limestone caves. Stalactites hang down from the ceiling as thin stone columns. Stalagmites rise from the floor as pillars of stone. They join together to form a column of rock stretching from ceiling to floor.

Limestone, the rock that forms stalactites and stalagmites is sometimes called "dripstone." Limestone is made mainly of a chemical called calcium carbonate. When rain-water seeps through cracks in limestone, it dissolves some of the calcium carbonate. So the water dripping from a cave roof contains a lot of this chemical.

Every time a drip forms, some of the water is evaporated and a tiny deposit of calcium carbonate is left on the cave roof. These grow very, very slowly to form stalactites. The drips that reach the cave floor deposit calcium carbonate there, which gradually piles up to form stalagmites. If the cave stays undisturbed for thousands of years, huge and spectacular formations can grow. ◆

# Stamps

Postage stamps are used to show that the cost of sending a piece of mail has been paid. Modern stamps have an adhesive backing and are perforated so that they can be easily separated without tearing. Individual countries have their own national stamps. The designs on postage stamps can be used for a variety of purposes—for example, to honor the country's leader or national heroes, to commemorate or celebrate a special event, or to show aspects of the history or geography of the country. They also show how much each costs.

When mail goes through the postal system, the adhesive stamps are canceled with an inking stamp so that they cannot be re-used. These canceling stamps will show the date on which they were used, and they may also contain a slogan or message.

Companies that send a lot of mail often use franking machines instead of stamps. They pay a sum of money to the post office and the machine will frank envelopes or labels until that amount of money is used up. People can also buy envelopes and other stationery in which the price of postage is included.

▼ **See also**
Postal services

▶ This stamp collection is based on the theme of famous people.

▼ Stamps that have been incorrectly printed are highly sought after by collectors. One of the most famous is known as the "inverted Jenny," issued by the U.S. Post Office in 1918. It shows an upside-down Flying Jenny biplane, used to carry mail. The plate block of four of the "inverted Jenny" stamps, shown here, sold for $1.1 million at a New York auction in 1989.

▼ Stamps are often issued to commemorate historic events; such stamps are known as "commemoratives." This commemorative (many times enlarged to show detail) was issued by the U.S. Post Office in 1892 to honor the 400th anniversary of Columbus's arrival in America.

## Philately

Many people enjoy *philately*, the study and collecting of stamps. Most philatelists collect stamps according to a chosen theme, perhaps old stamps, stamps of a particular country, or stamps that depict a particular item, such as trains or birds. The value of stamps varies a great deal, depending on their condition and their rarity. ◆

# Starfish

Starfish are not fish, but they live in the sea and are star-shaped, with arms that branch out from the central disk of their body. Most starfish have five arms, but some have many more. Often their outer skin is rough or spiny, and inside they have a skeleton of jointed rods, which strengthens and supports them.

▼ Starfish cannot see but they are able to detect changes in light and dark. This starfish is testing the amount of light using light-sensitive cells on the tips of its arms.

In grooves on the underside of a starfish's arms you can see a large number of pale, waving tube feet. These are like balloons pumped full of sea water. Each tube foot has a sucker on the end, so that it can hold onto food, or the seabed as the starfish moves about.

You can see a starfish's mouth in the middle of the underside of its body. Most starfish are flesh eaters. Some take very small prey, but others feed on larger animals, such as mussels. They do this by pulling the two parts of the mussel shell open, using their strong tube feet.

If a starfish is attacked, it can recover from serious injuries, and can regrow whole arms, provided that part of the central disk of the body survives. Because of this you can often find a starfish with one or more arms much smaller than the others. ◆

**Distribution**
Only in the sea, but at all depths and on all sorts of seabed
**Largest starfish**
About 1 m (3.3 ft) in diameter
**Smallest starfish**
About 5 mm (0.2 in) in diameter
**Number of young**
Varies, but some starfish spawn up to 1 million eggs in a season.
**Lifespan**
Variable, but most live for several years.
**Phylum**
Echinodermata
**Class**
Asteroidea
**Number of species**
About 1,600

▼ **See also**
Invertebrates

# Stars

The brightest star in the sky is Sirius, sometimes called the "Dog Star." The nearest star (apart from the Sun) is Proxima Centauri, which is 4.3 light-years away. It belongs to a triple star, Alpha Centauri. The other two stars are only slightly farther away.

American astronomer Annie Jump Cannon (1863-1941) classified more than half a million stars between 1911 and 1938 while working as an assistant at the Harvard College Observatory in Massachusetts. Her work is considered one of the greatest achievements in 20th-century astronomy because it has helped other astronomers learn how stars have evolved over millions of years. In the course of her work, Cannon discovered hundreds of previously unknown stars.

◄ The light from red and blue stars, reflecting off the gas clouds around them, make this part of the sky unusually colorful. The brightest star at bottom left is Antares. Just to the right of it is a globular star cluster called M4. Above Antares you can see dark dust clouds blotting out the light from stars behind.

There are about 5,780 stars that can be seen by eye without a telescope. About 2,500 are visible from one place on the Earth at any one time (on a clear dark night).

On a clear, dark night you can see hundreds of twinkling stars in the sky. These stars are huge glowing balls of gas like our Sun, but they are fainter because they are so much farther away. The light from even the nearest stars takes years to reach us. We look up at the stars through air that is constantly blowing about, so their light is unsteady and they seem to twinkle.

Hydrogen gas particles crash into each other in the center of stars and give off nuclear energy. Scientists call this nuclear fusion. This is what makes stars shine.

Our Sun is one ordinary star among millions. They are all speeding through space but look still to us because they are so far away. The patterns they make in the sky stay the same. You might sometimes see what people call "shooting stars" flash across the sky. They are not really stars at all but meteors, which are chunks of rock and bits of dust falling into our atmosphere.

## How stars are made

Stars are being created all the time. They start off as clumps of gas and dust in space. Once the material begins to collect, the force of gravity makes it pull together even more strongly. In the middle it gets warmer and denser until the gas is so hot and compressed that nuclear fusion can start. When this happens, a new star is born.

Astronomers look for new stars in the gas clouds of space. Often, lots of stars form close to each other in a giant cloud and make a cluster. The smallest stars contain about one-tenth the amount of material in the Sun. The biggest may be 50 times more massive than the Sun.

## Star colors

If you look carefully at the bright stars, you might notice that some of them look quite red while others are brilliant white or bluish; our Sun is a yellow star. The colors show up even better on photographs.

The stars shine with different colors because some are hotter than others. The Sun's surface is about 6,000 °C (10,832°F). The red stars are cooler and the blue-white ones hotter, at about 10,000 °C (18,032°F) or more. The colors are the same as you see when a piece of metal is heated up in a furnace. It first glows red-hot, then brighter and yellower until it is white-hot.

## Giants and dwarfs

Although the stars are so far away that they look only like points of light, even in the world's biggest telescopes, astronomers have determined that stars cover a huge range of sizes. They often call the large ones "giants" and the small ones "dwarfs."

The Sun is a smallish star, though some are even smaller. The unusual kind of star called a *white dwarf* has a diameter less than one-hundredth that of the Sun. In contrast, there are some truly immense stars, called *red giants*, that have puffed themselves out till they are several hundred times the Sun's size. The bright red star called Betelgeuse in the constellation of Orion is about 500 times bigger than the Sun. If Betelgeuse were at the middle of the Solar System, it would swallow up the Earth and reach nearly as far as Jupiter.

## Star clusters

Stars often form together in families, called clusters. One of the easiest to see is called the Pleiades or Seven Sisters and is in the constellation of Taurus, the Bull. There are six bright stars, and many more come into view in a telescope. Photographs of the Pleiades show up the shining gas between the stars. There are many other beautiful clusters similar to the Pleiades, each with a few hundred stars in it.

There is also another kind of star cluster where many thousands of stars are packed together into a tight ball. This is called a globular cluster because of its globe-like shape.

## Double stars

The Sun is a single star on its own, but that is quite unusual among the stars. Most are in pairs. The force of gravity keeps them together, and they orbit around each other like the planets going around the Sun. The brightest star in the sky, Sirius, is a double. The nearest stars to the Solar System, Proxima Centauri and its two partners, make a triple star called Alpha Centauri. There is a famous "double double" of four stars in Lyra.

Sometimes the two stars in a pair pass in front of one other. This blocks out some of the starlight and makes the pair look fainter for a short time. The best-known double like this is called Algol, "the winking demon."

Both stars and planets look like tiny dots in the sky. However, stars give off their own light, while planets, which are much smaller and closer, are only seen because they reflect the Sun's light.

▼ The life cycle of two stars. Above is a massive star. It will explode as a supernova and end up either as a neutron star or as a black hole. Below is a less massive star, like our Sun. Material blown off stars as they evolve is recycled into nebulas, which become future stars. The blue arrows show this process.

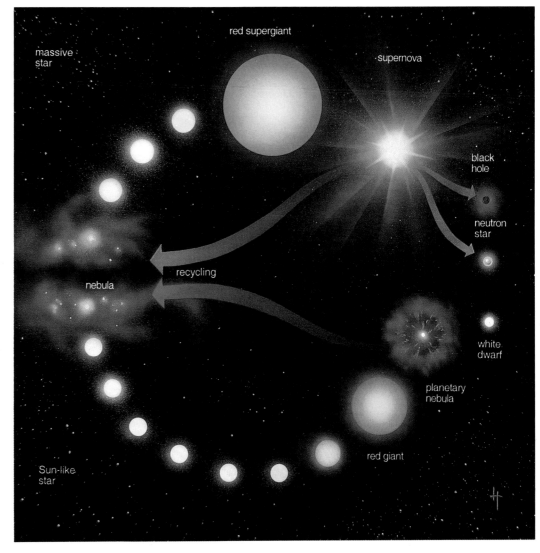

massive star

red supergiant

supernova

black hole

neutron star

recycling

nebula

white dwarf

planetary nebula

red giant

Sun-like star

▲ The Helix Nebula. The star at the middle of the pink ring has blown off a shell of glowing gas into space.

## Variable stars

You might imagine that the stars are all shining steadily, but many of them go up and down in brightness. They are called variable stars. Some change in a regular way but others suddenly get brighter or fainter unexpectedly. They can vary because the star pulses in and out or because it lets off a bright flare. Some variable stars are doubles with material flowing between the two.

Some stars vary dramatically, like Mira (its name means "wonderful"), which can sometimes be seen without a telescope, then fades out of view. Others, such as the Pole Star, change so slightly that it is hardly noticeable to ordinary observers.

## How stars change

Stars do not live forever. They make nuclear energy from the hydrogen gas in their cores where it is very hot, but a time comes when all the fuel is used up. When this happens, the star changes and eventually it dies. Old stars swell up into red giants. They can blow off some of their gas into space, like a big smoke ring. Astronomers can see stars like this at the centers of shells of glowing gas.

The Sun is already about 5 billion years old and is thought to be about halfway through its life. In the far future, the Sun will become a red giant and swallow up the planets near it.

After that, it will shrink until all its material is squashed into a ball about the size of the Earth. It will then be a white dwarf and gradually fade away. Stars more massive than the Sun end with a tremendous explosion, called a *supernova*.

## Supernovas

When a supernova goes off, it shines as brightly as millions of Suns put together for a few days. The inside of the exploded star that is left becomes a beeping radio star, called a *pulsar*.

Nearby supernovas in our own Galaxy are rare. Only three supernovas have ever been recorded: by Chinese astronomers in 1054, by Tycho Brahe in 1572 and by Kepler in 1604. Astronomers can spot them quite often in distant galaxies because they are so bright.

In 1987, a supernova exploded in a galaxy very near to our own called the Large Magellanic Cloud, which can be seen from countries in the Southern Hemisphere. It was very bright, so astronomers could study this important event carefully.

## Star names

Many of the bright stars have their own names. Most of them have been handed down to us from Arab astronomers of centuries ago. Arabic names often start with the two letters *Al*, such as Altair, Aldebaran and Algol. Others come from Greek or Latin, such as Castor and Pollux, the "heavenly twins" in the constellation Gemini.

Stars are also called after the constellation they are in, with a Greek letter in front. Alpha Centauri, the nearest star, is one example.

Fainter stars do not have names. Astronomers know them just as numbers in catalogues. ◆

### Stargazing

You can start on any clear, dark evening, as long as you have a safe place near home. Try to keep away from street and house lights; then your eyes get adapted to the dark and you see more stars. See what patterns you can imagine in the stars. Notice bright ones and faint ones. See if you can find some red stars. You will find a star chart in the article on Constellations.

# "Star-Spangled Banner, The"

"The Star-Spangled Banner" is the national anthem of the United States. The words were written in September 1814 by Francis Scott Key, a Maryland lawyer and amateur poet. He wrote the poem after watching the successful defense of Fort McHenry, near Baltimore, by U.S. troops against British bombardment during the War of 1812 (1812–1815).

Key had his poem printed on sheets of paper called handbills. These were distributed in the streets of Baltimore a few days later, with the suggestion that the words be sung as a new patriotic song, to the tune of a popular English drinking song called "To Anacreon in Heaven." Later that fall the song was officially published with the title "The Star-Spangled Banner."

The song quickly spread throughout the U.S., and it was often sung on patriotic occasions. Finally, in 1931, Congress approved "The Star-Spangled Banner" as the official U.S. national anthem. ◆

**See also**

Maryland
National anthems
War of 1812

**BIOGRAPHY**
Key, Francis Scott

◀ The original "star-spangled banner," which flew over Fort McHenry in 1814 and inspired Francis Scott Key's poem, is displayed at the National Museum of American History, part of the Smithsonian Institution in Washington, D.C.

### "The Star-Spangled Banner"

"The Star-Spangled Banner" has four verses, but usually only the first verse is sung:

*Oh! say, can you see, by the dawn's early light,*
*What so proudly we hailed at the twilight's last gleaming?*
*Whose broad stripes and bright stars, through the perilous fight,*
*O'er the ramparts we watched were so gallantly streaming?*
*And the rocket's red glare, the bombs bursting in air,*
*Gave proof through the night that our flag was still there.*
*Oh! say, does that Star-Spangled Banner yet wave*
*O'er the land of the free and the home of the brave? . . .*

—Francis Scott Key, 1814

# Starvation

Food is the most basic human need, and yet at least 500 million people (one-tenth of the world's population) suffer from hunger. Most of them live in the developing countries of the Third World, and many of them are children and young people. Every year about 15 million children die of hunger and related causes, so underfed that they cannot resist disease.

Starvation occurs when a person has nothing to eat. During the first few days a starving person suffers from severe hunger pains. Gradually these pass, and the person gets progressively weaker as the body uses up its store of fat and energy. Body weight drops, the limbs decrease in size, and ultimately the person dies.

Starvation and poverty are closely linked. During the 1970s and 1980s the number of starving people in the world doubled, a situation made worse by widespread drought in Africa. Aid in the form of loans to developing countries is often seen as a solution, and many international organizations work hard to try to relieve hunger. But many people believe that mass starvation can only end if land is used more carefully to grow food and if the resources and wealth of the world are distributed more fairly. ◆

**See also**

Developing countries
Drought
Famine
Floods
Malnutrition
Poverty
Third World
Vegetarians

# State and local government

**▼ See also**
United States of America

Some smaller towns and villages in the U.S. hire an administrator called a city manager to run the various departments of local government.

Other countries also have regional and local governments.

In addition to the national (federal) government in the U.S., there are state and local governments. The structure of these governments is often similar to that of the federal government. Just as the U.S. government includes an elected head, called the President, and an elected lawmaking body, called Congress, every state has an elected head, called the *governor*, and a lawmaking body that usually includes a senate, along with a house or assembly. Nearly every state also has a state supreme court; in some states justices are elected, while in other states they are appointed by the governor.

The state lawmaking body makes laws for the state, and the state supreme court makes sure that the laws do not violate the state constitution. The governor's job is to make sure that state laws are enforced and that the various departments of state government are run effectively.

Local governments are governments of cities and towns within a state. Cities are usually headed by elected mayors, who govern with the help of an elected lawmaking body called a city council. ◆

# Statistics

**▼ See also**
Averages
Computers
Graphs
Probability

Statistics are sets of numbers, often called data, that record information about things in an organized way. Every day, people collect more and more data about the world and record them as statistics. Records are kept of the weather, price rises, examination results, population changes and so on. The word "statistics" is also used for the branch of mathematics that deals with this data.

Statisticians are mathematicians who invent methods to organize statistics into tables, to display them in charts and graphs, and to interpret the data with mathematical formulae, so that it is easier to draw conclusions and make predictions. For example, statisticians who study medical statistics have discovered that most people who develop lung cancer smoke cigarettes. Statisticians can compare a smoker's chance of dying from lung cancer with the chance of dying from other causes.

## Organizing statistics

The statistics table below records the scores of children taking the same examination in two different schools. The data are recorded as a frequency table that gives the number of children achieving scores in set bands. To make these numbers easier to interpret they can be plotted as a bar chart, or *histogram*. The histogram of the scores from the two schools shows that on average the children in school A did better than those at school B, but that there is a much wider range of scores at school B. Statisticians call the range of the numbers in a set of data its *distribution*. They make calculations, often with the aid of computers, to find numerical values for quantities such as the average and the distribution of a set of data.

## Handling and interpreting statistics

Statistics must always be handled with caution; otherwise false conclusions may be drawn. For example, it would be wrong to use the average examination scores for schools A and B to conclude that children who attend school B always do less well than those who attend school A. In fact, the statistics show it was a child at school B who achieved the highest examination score. ◆

| Examination score | Number of children | |
|---|---|---|
| | School A | School B |
| 0–9 | 0 | 0 |
| 10–19 | 0 | 2 |
| 20–29 | 1 | 5 |
| 30–39 | 3 | 16 |
| 40–49 | 6 | 32 |
| 50–59 | 19 | 22 |
| 60–69 | 40 | 16 |
| 70–79 | 14 | 7 |
| 80–89 | 3 | 3 |
| 90–100 | 0 | 1 |

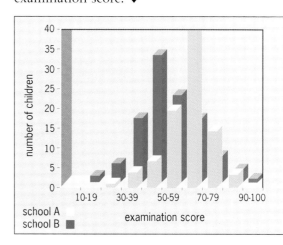

school A □
school B ■
examination score

# Steam engines

Steam engines were the first fuel-burning engines to be invented. During the 18th and 19th centuries, they were the main source of power for industry. With coal as their fuel, they drove machinery in factories and later powered ships and trains. Today, there are very few steam engines left. Other types of engine have taken over.

## How they work

Most steam engines use the pressure of steam to push a piston up and down a cylinder. The steam is made by boiling water over a fire of burning coal or oil. Steam from the boiler is let into the top of the cylinder by a valve. The steam expands and pushes the piston down. When the piston reaches the bottom, the valve changes position. Now, the valve lets the first lot of steam escape and feeds fresh steam into the *bottom* of the cylinder. This pushes the piston back up. When the piston reaches the top, the valve changes position again, the piston is pushed down, and so on. The up-and-down movement of the piston is turned into round-and-round movement by a crank. The crank moves a heavy flywheel that keeps the engine turning smoothly. The flywheel can drive other wheels or machinery.

Steam engines work best with high-pressure steam. To withstand the pressure, the boiler, pipes and cylinders have to be very strong. In some engines, there is a condenser to collect and cool the escaping steam. The steam condenses (turns into water), goes back into the boiler and is used again. With a condenser, a steam engine can work for longer without running out of water.

## LOOKING BACK

The first practical steam engine was built by Thomas Newcomen in England in 1712. It produced up-and-down motion and was used to pump water from mines. In Newcomen's engine, steam trapped in a cylinder was cooled by a spray of water. This made the steam condense and created a vacuum in the cylinder. The natural pressure of the atmosphere pushed the piston into the vacuum. Newcomen's engines were sometimes called atmospheric engines because of the way they worked.

James Watt made the big breakthrough in steam-engine design. He built an engine that used steam pressure to push the piston. It also had a separate condenser for cooling the steam. Within five years, Watt had developed engines that could produce rotation and drive machinery. His engines provided much of the power for England's mills and factories during the Industrial Revolution.

During the 19th century, the design of steam engines improved and they became widely used. They powered the locomotives of the new railway system. They hauled coal from mines and worked the huge hammers that shaped metal. They drove the traction engines used for threshing and ploughing. And they moved ships across the sea.

By 1900, internal combustion engines and electric motors were starting to replace steam engines. They gave more power for their size and did not need huge supplies of coal and water. Today, most factory machinery is driven by electricity, and trains are diesel or electric. However, in most electric power stations, the generators are turned by huge steam turbines. ◆

The first steam-powered machine was made by the Greek scientist Hero about 100 A.D. It was a tiny ball-shaped boiler with nozzles sticking out of its sides. Jets of steam from the nozzles made it spin around when the water boiled.

**History of the Steam Engine**
**1712** Thomas Newcomen builds an atmospheric engine. It is the first practical steam engine.
**1765** James Watt repairs Newcomen's engine and improves it.
**1782** Watt invents his sun-and-planet gear, a type of crank that turns up-and-down movement of a piston into rotation.
**1804** Richard Trevithick builds the first steam locomotive.
**1807** U.S. inventor Robert Fulton launches the *Clermont*, the first successful American steamboat.

▶ In a steam engine, steam pressure is used to move a piston up and down inside a cylinder. The up-and-down movement is changed into round-and-round movement by a crank.

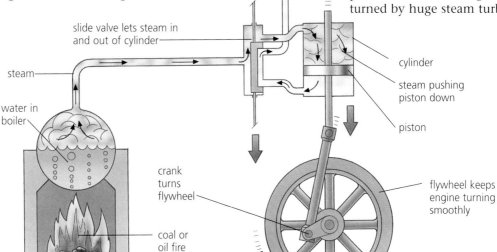

# Stick insects

▲ The perfectly camouflaged stick insect will not be seen by birds or other small predators.

**Distribution**
Almost all warm countries, especially in Southeast Asia
**Size**
Up to 25 cm (9.75 in) long, the longest of all insects but very narrow
**Food**
Plant food; each species normally eats only one kind of plant
**Phylum**
Arthropoda
**Class**
Insecta
**Order**
Phasmida
**Number of species**
About 2,000

▼ See also
Camouflage
Insects

The body of a stick insect is long and twig-like. Stick insects are usually colored green or brown and are often covered with bumps or spines.

This makes them match the stems of their food plants so that it is almost impossible to see them. They normally sit quite still during the daytime and feed and move about at night.

Among many kinds of stick insect, males are very rare, and the females lay hard-shelled, seed-like eggs without mating. This method of reproduction is called *parthenogenesis*. The eggs may take over a year to hatch, and when they do so, more females than males are born.

Some kinds of stick insects are kept as pets. Their cages need to be kept in a warm spot, but out of direct sunlight. They must have fresh leaves to eat. When changing the food plants, be careful not to throw away the insects. They are so well camouflaged it is easy not to see them. ◆

# Stock market

The term "stock market" refers to the buying and selling of shares, or *stocks*, in companies. This happens at places called *stock exchanges* in major cities throughout the world.

## Stock exchanges

A company that wants its shares listed on a stock exchange must prove to the exchange that it has enough capital (money) and is in good financial shape. The New York Stock Exchange (NYSE), founded in 1792, is the nation's oldest and largest, and lists only the biggest companies. More than 2,000 companies are currently listed on the New York Stock Exchange.

## Bull and bear markets

The stock market generally reflects the state of a nation's economy. When the economy is strong, stock prices rise: this is called a "bull market." If the economy is weak, stock prices decline: this is called a "bear market." The financial collapse of the stock market on Wall Street in 1929 led to the Great Depression of the 1930s in the U.S. and eventually throughout the world. ◆

▼ See also
Depression, Great
Economics

The people who specialize in buying and selling stocks are called *stockbrokers*. They charge a fee called a *commission* for their services.

The American Stock Exchange is another large stock exchange in New York City. Other major stock exchanges in the U.S. are located in Chicago, Los Angeles and San Francisco. The Stock Exchange in London and the Bourse in Paris are among the leading stock exchanges abroad.

Stock exchanges are located in the financial districts of large cities around the world. In New York City, the financial district is called Wall Street. In London, it is known as the City. In Tokyo, the financial district is called the Marunouchi.

▼ The New York Stock Exchange, on Wall Street in New York City, is one of the largest and oldest stock exchanges in the world.